ACHIEVING QUALITY IN FINANCIAL SERVICE ORGANIZATIONS

Achieving Quality in Financial Service Organizations

HOW TO IDENTIFY AND SATISFY CUSTOMER EXPECTATIONS

Robert E. Grasing and Michael H. Hessick

Q

QUORUM BOOKS

New York • Westport, Connecticut • London

Library of Congress Cataloging-in-Publication Data

Grasing, Robert E.
    Achieving quality in financial service organizations : how to
  identify and satisfy customer expectations /
Robert E. Grasing and Michael H. Hessick.
        p.   cm.
    Includes index.
    ISBN 0–89930–230–0 (lib. bdg. : alk. paper)
    1. Financial institutions—United States.   2. Consumer
satisfaction—United States.   I. Hessick, Michael H.   II. Title.
HG181.H44   1988
332.1′2′0688—dc19   87–24937

British Library Cataloguing in Publication Data is available.

Copyright © 1988 by Robert E. Nolan Company, Inc.

Library of Congress Catalog Card Number: 87–24937
ISBN: 0–89930–230–0

First published in 1988 by Quorum Books

Greenwood Press, Inc.
88 Post Road West, Westport, Connecticut 06881

Printed in the United States of America

The paper used in this book complies with the
Permanent Paper Standard issued by the National
Information Standards Organization (Z39.48–1984).

10   9   8   7   6   5   4   3   2   1

Contents

Figures and Tables   vii

Preface   ix

1. Why Quality Has Become the Latest Focus   1

2. Quality Efforts Today   13

3. Understanding and Achieving Quality   63

4. Simplicity: The Improvement Process   93

5. Accuracy   121

6. Timeliness   143

7. Consistency   169

8. Attitudes   191

9. Success   211

10. Quality Expectations: How to Get Started   237

Bibliography   245

Index   247

Figures and Tables

Figures

2.1   Ad from The New England   14

2.2   Ad from Metropolitan Life   15

2.3   Ad from American Express   16

2.4   Ad from First Chicago Bank   18

3.1   Sample Quality Survey   85

3.2   Quality Graph from First Chicago Bank   89

4.1   Organization Pyramid   95

4.2   Decision Matrix   106

4.3   Management Profile Summary   116

5.1   Error Free Performance (UNUM Life)   123

5.2   Transactional Service Equation   127

5.3   Error Control Chart   135

5.4   Recommended Inspection Procedures   137

6.1   Customer Time Line   154

7.1   Sample Quality Output Matrix   183

9.1   Historical Organization Shape   224

9.2   Present-Day Organization Shape   225
9.3   Productivity Equation   227

Tables

4.1   Summary of Organization Levels and Improvement Tech-
      niques   119
5.1   Control Sampling Chart   138

Preface

One might question why we chose to write a book on quality considering the thousands of people who have spoken on the subject and the millions of words that have been written about it through countless articles and books.

The reason why is twofold. First, most of the discussion to date on the subject has been heavily oriented toward the manufacturing environment. Although many of the problems that exist there can be compared to problems that exist in the financial services community, there are major differences in the industries. Financial services companies do not have true production lines. The products produced are often in the form of service rather than durable goods, and although "professional" workers in both industries may perform somewhat similar functions there are few similarities between the work performed by clerical and blue-collar employees. Financial services companies have different cultures and they have their own set of unique quality needs.

Our second reason for writing the book is that we were tired of reading about "quick fix" schemes to improve quality that did little more than emulate the Japanese-style approaches or that, even worse, did not present the reader with a clear picture of how to achieve quality. It is one thing to describe the attributes of quality; it is quite another thing to achieve them.

This book would not have been possible without the support of the many financial services companies that helped us shape our ideas, and test and prove them in the real world. We want to thank the companies that participated in our quality survey and especially the senior executives who agreed to be personally interviewed and who so graciously allowed us to reproduce those interviews in this book.

1   *Why Quality Has Become the Latest Focus*

Read the headlines. "Are Banks Obsolete?"(*Business Week*, April 6, 1987); "Met Closes in on Home Mortgages" (*National Underwriter*, September 27, 1986); "Financial Services Tantalize Bankers" (*National Underwriter*, September 27, 1986); "New Collars; New Values" (*Newsweek*, April 4, 1987); "A Rationalization for Failure" (*Chicago Tribune*, August 27, 1986); "Corporate Banking Astir" (*ABA Banking Journal*, March 1984); "Can America Compete?" (*Business Week*, April 20, 1987); "Productivity: Why It's the No. 1 Underachiever" (*Business Week*, April 20, 1987). Different headlines, but they all tell a similar story. The financial services industry is in a state of flux. It used to be simple. Banks competed with other banks. Insurance companies competed with other insurance companies. The term "financial services" was a generic one that we used primarily to categorize companies that were not really the same, but that didn't fit into a "neat" grouping such as "manufacturing" or "agricultural." While financial services companies shared some common characteristics (they all provided some type of financial-oriented service), they mostly remained as separate and distinct industries. Insurance companies sold insurance. Banks provided traditional banking services.

Then a number of things occurred that changed all the rules of the game. Foreign competition in almost all industries increased. Manufacturing declined, and many companies diversified into what was then considered to be the more stable financial services industry. Large manufacturers like Armco Steel bought companies like Northwestern National Insurance Company and a host of subsidiaries like Pacific Mutual Insurance, North Pacific Insurance, Continental Western Insurance, and several others. Their goal was to diversify away from the primary business that faced declining sales and increased production costs.

About the same time came increased deregulation. Old line, solid companies were bought and sold at an amazing rate. Mergers and acquisitions became the name of the game. Deregulation continued, and companies began offering services and products that were new not only to them but new to their entire industry. Banks began selling insurance and stocks and bonds through subsidiary companies. Each industry attempted to grow at the expense of other, less progressive industries.

Then came the rapid development of "new" products. Small companies gained major shares of the market virtually overnight. All this opportunity had its price. Many companies got in too deep and became victims them-selves of the merger mania. It was unusual for a week to pass without our hearing about a new deal.

The dust has now begun to settle. We have not yet seen the end of this cycle, but patterns appear to be developing. The "survivors" have developed a wide variety of strategies to succeed, but more and more of them focus on fulfilling the true essence of their businesses—providing quality to their customers. Those companies that are able to succeed in meeting the cus-tomers' needs will survive and prosper. Those that do not, will not.

Some people would argue that this has always been the case. Since the day the first business was established, companies have had to provide value in order to succeed. But things have changed. Customers' perceptions of value are different today than they were a few years ago. The economic environment has become much more competitive for financial services companies, and the customers themselves have changed dramatically. Let's examine some of these changes in more detail.

AMERICA'S LOSS OF ITS COMPETITIVE EDGE

It comes as no surprise to any of us that America has lost its competitive edge. It used to be that products made in the United States were coveted. Their quality was the best in the world, and their value to the customer was unquestioned. The label "Made in Japan" was the kiss of death for products. That designation conjured up images of poor quality and cheap materials.

What happened? How did we lose our position as the world's industrial leader? Why do we now cherish foreign products? The answer brings us back to the issues of quality and value. Specifically, the loss of them in products and services produced in the United States. What caused the prob-lem? Productivity—or lack of it. The simple truth is that we have not kept up with the rest of the world's productivity growth. During the 1950s and 1960s real gross national product climbed by 4 percent or more in eleven years. It averaged 3.8 percent in the 1960s. With this growth came the impossible. Companies handed out raises with near reckless abandon, and still increased profits. Workers' income climbed by more than 4 percent a year and the economy boomed. Productivity gains kept us going.

But we became complacent. Sometime in the early 1970s the downward spiral began. Perhaps it was the Vietnam War, the aging of our factories, the rapid rise in OPEC oil prices, or other inflation. The cause is difficult to pin down. But the result is not; we began to slide. Average wage increases remained high, over 7 percent, but the gains were hollow. Inflation ran rampant. From 1948 to 1965 productivity grew at a rate exceeding 3 percent. During the period spanning 1965 to 1973 it dropped to just over 2 percent. From 1973 to 1979 it fell further—to less than 1 percent. The most recent period, from 1979 to 1986, has seen it climb moderately back to 1 percent. It appears to have settled there for a while, but the future is very uncertain. In 1986 the manufacturing industry on the whole was able to keep unit labor costs flat, but other industries were less successful. Once more, prior to 1986 wages continued to increase during a period of declining productivity. Thus, increased costs were simply built into the products through higher prices. While all this was occurring, other countries were more successful. During the period of 1981 to 1985 for example, Korea's productivity grew at a rate that was six times that of the United States. Japan's rate was almost three times as great, and Britain's, Norway's, Germany's, and Sweden's rates were more than double. It is not surprising that the United States lost its edge.[1]

Business Week magazine claims that economists have come up with a plausible explanation for why the productivity drain occurred. They claim that the slowdown began with the arrival of baby boomers on the job market. Many of them were unskilled and lacked experience. At the same time, energy prices rose to levels never before imagined, and government regulations increased dramatically. Inflation was high as well. To combat all these negative factors, managers sought investments in projects that conserved energy, not capital or labor. Capital spending was cut to compensate for lower inflation-adjusted rates of return. This resulted in the average age of manufacturing plants increasing from 13.8 years in 1980 to 15 years in 1986.

Many of us working in financial services companies might read these facts and shake our heads in astonishment, having thought all along that manufacturing firms have been the culprits and that financial services firms have been better managed. Unfortunately, the facts simply do not support this conclusion. In fact, were it not for the poor performance in service companies, United States productivity rates overall would have grown by a respectable rate of 2.2 percent since 1979.

Stephen S. Roach, an economist at Morgan Stanley and Company, claims that more than $160 billion has been invested in high-tech equipment, including computers and communications gear, without realizing broad-based savings or increased productivity. "Data processing divisions went on buying binges believing that productivity paybacks would be automatic," says Roach.[2] Unfortunately, this has not been the case. The increased technology may even have contributed to productivity declines by virtue of the fact that they gave managers the ability to generate more management information, which managers did, without using it to improve their operations.

Our own experience confirms this belief. For example, during a recent discussion with a major Blue Cross/Blue Shield organization located in the Midwest, an executive told us that he was installing a very expensive new claims processing system. We asked him what his projections for staff reductions were as a result of the new system, and he corrected us by explaining that more people were going to be needed. We asked why his company would do that, and he replied, "To obtain more management information." Many of us have become enamored with the power of today's generation of computers. Unfortunately, we have not yet learned to use them very effectively in helping us to address our productivity problems.

The fact that the service industry is the culprit should be alarming, because the service sector is growing in relation to manufacturing. In fact, in 1956 the number of white-collar workers first exceeded blue-collar workers. In 1969 the difference exceeded 30 percent. By 1980 the United States had 60 percent more white-collar workers than blue-collar workers. During the period from 1968 to 1980 the number of professional and technical workers grew to an amazing rate of 67 percent.[3] The service sector today contributes some 14 percent of the United States' gross national product. By comparison, manufacturing industries account for just 10 percent.[4] During this same basic period of time, from 1970 to the present, but most dramatically during the past five or so years, the nature of financial services companies has evolved into something much like the name implies. As we discussed earlier, ten years ago banks, insurance companies, brokerage firms, and others were all grouped into a category of businesses called financial services, but the grouping was in name only. Banks offered only banking services, insurance companies offered only insurance services, and so forth. That changed. Retail companies like Sears, Roebuck and Company expanded into insurance with Allstate Insurance Company; J. C. Penney bought a casualty insurance company in Westerville, Ohio, and a life insurance company in Dallas, Texas. American Express purchased Fireman's Fund Insurance Company. Banks and thrifts bought brokerage firms and entered into partnership with insurers.

Name changes emphasize this point. Companies offering a broad-based family of financial service products no longer want to be thought of in the same fashion as they once were. The Bankers Life Insurance Company of Des Moines, Iowa, has renamed itself the Principal Group. New England Life in Boston, Massachusetts became simply, "The New England." Banks are no longer called "First National Bank," but "First National Corporation" instead. The name changes have occurred within every financial services sector.

Changes in the Customer

During this same period of turmoil and declining productivity, America's "baby boomers" came of age. Born in the post–World War II era from 1945 to 1965, they became a dominant factor in shaping all our lives. By the year 2000 they will represent the United States' biggest growth segment.[5] In fact, people twenty-five to forty years of age number almost 70 million. Contrary to some economist's theory that the "boomers" are unskilled and lack job experience, typically they have college degrees, professional careers, and a desire to live the good life, not only at retirement at age 65, but today, while they are young and healthy.

Statistics show that this is possible. Households making more than $50,000 per year are expected to rise from 10 percent in 1985 to 18 percent by 1995. Much of this is due to working women. In the past twenty years the proportion of women who work has doubled. The proportion of families with at least two wage earners passed the 50 percent mark. During this same period, the labor force became better educated. The median amount of schooling of the labor force as a whole increased to more than one year of college.[6] Currently, 50 percent of high school graduates go on to college, although only 70 percent of students complete high school, in contrast to 98 percent in Japan.[7] One in four women has reached a higher educational level than her husband. And, while women are having smaller families today, there are more women in child-bearing years. This is triggering a temporary new baby boom, and births hit 3.7 million in 1985. As the old baby boomers move through their lives, the general population of the United States will naturally grow older. Currently, the median age is thirty-one and a half years. Within the next 40 or so years it could rise to over forty years. By then, 21 percent of the United States' population will be sixty-five years of age or older.[8]

Have things begun to settle down? Have the changes in the customer been pretty well defined? Do we know what has happened to them, and what lies ahead? Hardly. *Business Week* magazine recently ran a special report, entitled "Warning: The Standard of Living Is Slipping." It said,

What's happening is painfully simple: The U.S. standard of living, long the envy of the world, has hit the wall. In fact, there is overwhelming evidence it's already slipping for many people and may drop even more unless the United States can reverse its productivity decline of the last fifteen years or so.[9]

The article also quoted former Labor Department Under-Secretary Malcolm R. Lovell, Jr., as saying, "The standard of living hasn't been going anywhere for a decade." During the past fifteen years, wages for nonsupervisory workers (about four-fifths of the work force), adjusted for inflation, have fallen each year.

Those people employed in service industries have certainly fared better than their counterparts in manufacturing, because competition for goods produced by low wage foreign producers has been intense, and many manufacturing employees have been forced to accept pay cuts to save their jobs. Unions have been of little help either. In years past, unions have played a major role in getting manufacturers to increase wages. But, as the companies have suffered, so too have the unions. In fact, unions currently represent fewer than 18 percent of all workers. This is half of what it was in 1955. The rate of new sign-ups for unions is also down. In 1980, only 0.2 percent of eligible workers were joining unions. This rate is one-fifth of what it was in 1955.[10]

But, the service jobs primarily help the well-educated top tier of the work force. And, unlike in the past where managers were almost assured of lifetime employment, corporate restructuring has affected white-collar workers as companies have whittled away at their expenses and become "lean and mean."

Richard S. Belous, an economist with the Conference Board, predicts that if we don't start growing again, the falling standard of living could cause even greater changes. The once accessible opportunity for advancement could be cut off and employees could grow dissatisfied, even more so than today. This might open the door to a resurgence of unionism in white-collar industries that have traditionally supported unions very weakly.

How serious is the problem of the declining standard of living? After adjusting for inflation, the median household income in 1973 was almost 8 percent higher than it was in 1985. And this has occurred during a period when the number of people employed has risen from 40 percent of the population in 1970 to 46 percent today. During this same period the overall labor force has grown by almost 28 percent, and now numbers more than 115 million. Two-thirds of the 33 million new workers are women, who now constitute 44 percent of all employees. If you consider that hourly wages adjusted for inflation have fallen by 8.7 percent since 1973, it becomes obvious that it has been these added workers who have helped keep the average family income as high as it is.

Business Week magazine highlighted an example of what would have happened if, during this same general period, men had remained the sole breadwinners. A thirty-year-old male earned, in 1986 dollars, an average of $25,253 in 1973. Ten years later, the same thirty-year-old man earned only $18,763 after adjustment for inflation. This is not a pretty picture. In fact, the average income of two-parent families fell by 3.1 percent between 1973 and 1984. Some experts have predicted that the drop would have been three times as great had women not decided to go to work.

Many women would argue that the reason they went to work was to satisfy their needs for self-fulfillment. They simply were not happy living the life of "just" wives and mothers. They needed the challenge of corporate

America to help them realize their true potential as human beings. While this may well be true, it is a moot point. The plain fact remains that even with two workers in the same family, their income has not increased. One would think that a second income should make the family better off. It should give them the opportunity to lead a better life. But, the sad reality of the situation is that today, two workers in the same family are needed just to sustain what is considered by most people to be a middle-class standard of living.

Yet, we are an innovative civilization. Rather than roll over and play dead because it is harder to realize the American dream, we have discovered a way around the problem. Debt! Young couples today, who know nothing about the Great Depression, think nothing of amassing debts that would have scared their parents to death. Mortgages on homes have become an accepted way of life, and consumer installment debt has climbed to 16 percent of personal income since 1973, when it was only 13 percent. This increased debt has had an effect on the lives of young people, though. For the most part, many of them are putting off important things like marriage and having children until later in life. Instead of getting married at twenty-two years of age as their fathers did 30 years ago, men on the average today are waiting until they are twenty-six. Women have shown similar patterns. Instead of tying the knot at age twenty, like their mothers did, they are waiting until they are twenty-three.

These delayed marriages have had a secondary effect on the couples as well. Because they are getting started later in life with marriage, they are also getting started later in life with having babies. There was a time when the popular belief was that women should have their children before they reached the ripe old age of thirty. It is not uncommon at all today for women to *begin* their families at age thirty. And many couples who start "late" still elect to have more than one or two children.

However, for whatever reason, young couples today have also decided to have fewer children than their parents did. It is not uncommon to see childless couples and, in fact, the birth rate has dropped from 24 children per 1,000 women in 1960 to 15 per 1,000 today.

Another change in the typical American lifestyle has been in housing. Families are living in smaller houses than their parents did, and many of them have forgotten about the dream of a single-family home surrounded by a white picket fence, with a station wagon in the driveway next to the basketball hoop, and a dog. Less than half of new housing units today are single-family homes. In the 1970s the number was over 60 percent. This same trend trickles down to related areas as well. For example, the typical family aged between twenty-five and thirty-four spent 14 percent less on furniture in 1981 than a similar family did in 1973. Fifteen percent less was spent on personal care, and 38 percent less on charity.

Of course, the hardest hit have been single people and families without

8   ACHIEVING QUALITY IN FINANCIAL SERVICE ORGANIZATIONS

two wage earners. Single women currently head 16 percent of all households. In 1973 the number was only 12 percent. Their median income is
just $13,660 per year, and many of these households are well below the
poverty level.[11] All of this "doom and gloom" simply means that customers
for today's financial services company are different than they were just a
few years ago. The chances are that they are more willing to spend money
than their parents were, but they spend it on different things. They are
generally better educated, more sophisticated about investment options and
how they work, less loyal to any one financial services company, more
mobile, more demanding, and generally harder to please.

Changes in the Market

By far, the biggest change in the financial services market has been the
advent of increased competition. It has come in the form of interstate
banking, rapid product development, foreign competition, and a "blurring"
of the lines of distinction between companies within the financial services
industry (banks, insurance companies, brokerage firms, etc.).

Let's assume that you are half of a young working couple who have
managed to save enough money to consider the purchase of your first home.
You go to the local Century 21 office and ask for a broker to help you find
a house that satisfies your needs and is affordable. The agent is thrilled at
his good fortune. It is not often that someone just walks into the office and
asks for help finding a house. He mentally begins to size you up. How much
can you afford? How much will the commission be? After several days of
driving through neighborhoods, you decide to make an offer on a house.
You do, and it is accepted by the seller.

Now the fun ends. You must find a bank to finance the loan you need.
You form a mental picture of having to walk, hat in hand, into the cold
marble structure located downtown, a fifty-minute drive through traffic.
Once you enter the bank, you'll be asked to wait for a loan officer to help
you. That person will probably treat you with a condescending attitude and
make you feel like a couple of crooks who are out to defraud the bank.

You meekly ask the real estate agent for a recommendation as to which
bank has money to lend at the best possible rate. To your amazement, the
agent says that he can arrange the financing through his company. It seems
that Century 21 is owned by Metropolitan Insurance. "How does that help
us?" you ask. "We're not ready to buy homeowners insurance, we are just
looking for a loan." The agent replies that Metropolitan now offers home
loans. In fact, Metropolitan is projecting $6 billion in mortgage originations
in 1989, after all its computers are in place in Century 21 sales offices.[12]

The agent says that if that doesn't work out, you should try Sears. "I'm
not ready for a home repair job yet, I'm still looking for a mortgage," you
reply. You guessed it, Sears offers mortgages, too. In fact, they are already

one of the top ten largest mortgage servicing companies in the United States today. My, how the game has changed! The old adage, "You can't tell who the players are without a scorecard," has never been more true than it is today in the financial services industry.

The strains put on financial services companies are enormous. "We're in a gut fight for survival," says Thomas S. Johnson, president of Chemical New York Corporation, about his company. *Business Week* did a feature story titled "Are Banks Obsolete?" The article stated, "Evidence is mounting, however, that the strains on the banking system are not temporary but endemic. Twenty percent of all banks insured by the Federal Deposit Insurance Corporation reported a loss in 1986."[13]

Not only is the competition coming from nontraditional American companies like the Met and Sears, but foreign competition is increasing as well. According to the New York Federal Reserve Bank, large United States corporate customers now borrow four dollars from foreign banks for every ten dollars they get from major U.S. banks. In addition, competition has increased within the banking industry itself. Interstate banking will force a wave of consolidation in the industry. It is just getting started, but it will have a major impact on the industry.

Thrift organizations face similar pressures. Joe Morris, chairman of the U.S. League of Savings Institutions (representing more than 3,400 savings and loans and savings banks), was interviewed by *Mortgage Banking* magazine. When asked about the future of the industry he replied, "We will see the continuation of the trend toward consolidation in the whole financial services area, including thrifts and commercial banks. The prediction of 2500 thrifts by 1990 is not unrealistic."[14]

HOW THIS HAS AFFECTED STRATEGIES

Michael E. Porter, noted author and Harvard Business School professor, categorizes three generic strategies for companies to use in competing:

1. Overall cost leadership
2. Differentiation
3. Focus[15]

The first strategy, cost leadership, requires aggressive construction of efficient-scale facilities, vigorous cost reduction efforts, tight expense control, and minimization of cost in areas like research and development, service, sales force, advertising, and so on. The achievement of overall cost leadership allows a company to earn above-average returns in an industry despite the presence of strong competition.

Unfortunately for financial services companies, achieving a low overall cost position often requires a high relative market share. Few financial services companies have been able to gain a high national market share. For example, the largest market share of wholesale lending for United States banks is a measly 4.5 percent.[16]

The second generic strategy for competing is that of differentiation. It strives to distinguish the product or service offered by the company and thus create something that is perceived by the industry as being unique. Differentiation reduces competitive pressures because of brand loyalty by customers, and this makes the customers less price sensitive. The result is that companies can charge higher prices and thus produce higher earning yields.

Unfortunately, as was the case with the low-cost strategy, differentiation has some drawbacks. Most notable of them is that it often precludes the company from gaining a high market share. While this is not a problem on a national scale, it is within smaller, more localized markets.

The third generic strategy for competing is that of focus. It involves filling a market niche. Accomplishing focus allows a company to compete in a narrow market area even though it could not do so on a larger scale. Focus necessarily involves a trade-off between profitability and sales volume.

Our experience indicates that most financial services companies today have chosen to compete on the basis of differentiation. They do not believe that the strategies of least cost or focus are viable.

We recently surveyed executives at the top one hundred commercial banks, property and casualty insurance companies, life insurance companies, and savings and loans; the top fifty mutual savings banks, and Blue Cross and Blue Shield plans; and the top ten mortgage service companies on the subject of quality. One question dealt with how they planned to compete in the next few years. They were given the following options: product design, distribution systems, quality/service, price, or other. Thirty-four percent chose quality/service. The next highest category (20 percent) was price.

The Quality Rub

Herein lies the problem. If the majority of financial services companies choose to differentiate on the basis of quality and service, will it be possible for any of them to succeed? If most companies are trying to be better than their competition because they offer better quality and service, will it be possible for the customer to distinguish between them?

The only way that this will be possible will be for some companies to be better at achieving quality than the others. Unless there is a marked difference between one company's quality and that of its competition, the customer will be unable to distinguish the advantage either offers. The result would be that the companies do not actually achieve differentiation at all.

Porter calls this being "stuck in the middle." A company that is stuck in the middle is in an extremely poor competitive position. It is almost guaranteed low profitability. It either loses its largest customers to low-cost competitors, or it is forced to bid away its profits to keep the business.

Once a company gets stuck, it usually takes time and a major amount of effort to get free. There seems to be a tendency for firms in this situation to flip back and forth over time among the three generic strategies. Since the three strategies are so different from one another in how they are achieved, this action almost always is doomed to failure. We all know what happens to financial services companies operating in this manner in today's competitive environment.

How To Survive the Quality Rub

The key to surviving the quality rub is to establish quality goals that are well above those of your competition, and then achieve them. This sounds simple enough. But if it were truly that easy we wouldn't see the large numbers of financial services companies disappearing that we do today. The remainder of this book is devoted to helping you to establish your quality goals and to achieving them.

CHAPTER SUMMARY

The following are the key points made in this chapter.

1. The entire economy of the United States is in a state of flux. Financial services companies are caught in the middle of the problems. They are failing at an alarming rate. Those that don't fail are rapidly swallowed up by bigger, healthier companies.

2. Productivity has been growing in the United States at a rate that is far below that of other industrialized nations throughout the world. America has lost its competitive edge. Major investments in high-tech equipment have failed to increase productivity.

3. The customers of financial services companies have changed dramatically. They are better educated, more informed about financial products, more demanding, in greater debt than their parents, and less loyal. Their standard of living has fallen and they expect financial services companies to deliver the best products possible at the lowest cost.

4. The market for financial services has changed as well. By far, the biggest change has been the increase in competition. It is coming from within the industries themselves, from foreign countries, and from nontraditional competitors.

5. There are three generic ways to compete:

   • Overall cost leadership

   • Differentiation

• Focus

Most financial services companies have chosen to compete through differentiation—specifically through providing high levels of quality and service.

6. The "rub of quality" is that if the majority of companies choose to differentiate on the basis of high quality, then the customer will have a difficult time "knowing it when he sees it." If most companies produce high quality, then it will cease to become a form of differentiation.

7. The only way to succeed with this strategy is to set quality goals that are well above the rest of the industry. Achieving them without pricing yourself out of the market will be a major challenge, and is the subject of the remainder of this book.

NOTES

1. Norman Jonas, "Can America Compete?" *Business Week*, April 20, 1987, pp. 48–52.

2. Ibid.

3. Lloyd W. Mosley, *Customer Service—The Road to Greater Profits* (New York: Chain Store Publishing Corp., 1972), p. 31.

4. Judith K. Paulus, "A Rationalization For Failure," *Chicago Tribune*, August 27, 1986, pp. 1–15.

5. Doug Carroll, "Imported Cars Have Foothold for Future," *USA Today*, March 25, 1987, p. B–1.

6. Rosabeth Moss Kanter, *The Change Masters: Innovation for Productivity in the American Corporation* (New York: Simon and Schuster, 1983), p. 43.

7. Jonas, "Can America Compete?" pp. 48–52.

8. William Dunn, "Marriage Buoys Stability, Income," *USA Today*, April 29, 1987, p. A–10.

9. Norman Jonas, "Warning: The Standard of Living Is Slipping," *Business Week*, April 20, 1987, pp. 48–52.

10. Clemens P. Work, Jack A. Seamonds, and Robert F. Black, "Making It Clear Who's Boss," *U.S. News & World Report*, September 8, 1986, p. 43.

11. Jonas, "Warning: The Standard of Living Is Slipping," pp. 48–52.

12. Stephen Piontek, "Met Closes in on Home Mortgages," *National Underwriter*, Life Insurance Ed., September 27, 1986, p. 1.

13. Sara Bartlett, "Are Banks Obsolete?" *Business Week*, April 6, 1987, pp. 74–82.

14. "An Interview with Joe C. Morris," *Mortgage Banking*, February 1987, p. 93.

15. Michael E. Porter, *Competitive Strategy: Techniques for Analyzing Industries and Competitors* (New York: Macmillan, The Free Press, 1980), pp. 35–40.

16. Sara Bartlett, "Are Banks Obsolete?" pp. 74–82.

2   *Quality Efforts*
Today

QUALITY AWARENESS: ADVERTISING

Quality is becoming more prevalent in the financial services industry today, but what are companies really doing to initiate the quality process and manage it? The evidence starts with advertising in many of the business periodicals.

Mellon Bank's full-page advertisement states in bold letters "Quality Banking," and reminds us that they take the time to know their customers and to study the industries they represent. The New England takes a page to show the environment and end products of craftsmen while they ask the question, "Does it seem that commitment to quality is becoming a thing of the past?" (Figure 2.1). Their own solution is simply stated, "Come to New England."

Metropolitan Life Insurance Company's full-page ad (Figure 2.2) explains how they encourage each and every employee to think big through their quality improvement process. They go on to explain how employees choose individuals' goals based on the customer needs—"Bigger goals than ever set before."

American Express pictures a customer in their full-page advertisement (Figure 2.3) and focuses on how the customer is "the driving force behind everything we do." The customer is described as wielding influence and authority. The customer is respected and consulted. There is no question, based on the ad, that American Express strives to meet customer's needs and has made this their overriding commitment.

A First Chicago (First National Bank of Chicago) two-page advertisement (Figure 2.4) states that "quality comes from care." They feature Bob Waterman, co-author of *In Search of Excellence*, as a spokesperson about quality. The ad goes on to reinforce that "a caring attitude must pervade an orga-

Figure 2.1
Ad from The New England

14

Figure 2.2
Ad from Metropolitan Life

HOW TO BE A HEAVIER HITTER.

At Met Life we do it by encouraging each and every employee to think big.

We call it the Quality Improvement Process.

This is how it basically works: Every employee helps choose his or her own goals, based on customer needs. Bigger goals than ever set before. Then the employee also helps develop plans to reach them.

We know it's important to our people to be the best they can possibly be.

It's important to our customers, also. Met Life's Quality Improvement Process is designed to bring them extraordinary service.

GET MET. IT PAYS.

Figure 2.3
Ad from American Express

Reprinted with permission.

nization and be applied to everything it does." They speak openly about the direct link between quality and productivity.

Other companies build the quality theme into all their advertising. One example is Chemical Bank. Under their corporate name in every ad is the statement, "The bottom line is excellence."

What this advertising tells us is that these companies definitely believe that readers (potential customers and investors) are concerned with quality.

QUALITY SURVEY: MACRO RESEARCH

To help us determine where image was being reinforced by substance we polled the financial services community with a simple nine-point questionnaire.

Our objective was to compare these companies with our clients' approach to quality. In many cases the results substantiated our believe that most organizations have defined quality as a strategic objective (88 percent specifically address quality in their corporate plan), yet they are still groping with what quality really is (only 55 percent have defined quality for their organization).

Many companies intuitively believe that poor quality costs them money, but only 20 percent have measured what that cost is to their organization.

Another enlightening fact is that more than 50 percent of the companies responding were working at improvement through quality teams (55 percent), idea incentive programs (67 percent), functional workshops (50 percent), or systems analysis (69 percent). In some sectors, such as thrifts, there were no reported improvements achieved. This indicates that measurement may be a problem in certain financial services sectors.

Overall improvement appeared to be good, yet short of full potential. Service levels (timeliness) were up by 25 percent. Accuracy was up by 30 percent, and to date, the respondents reduced operating expenses an average of 9 percent. Our experience is that companies can, on average, reduce expenses by between 25 and 40 percent through a comprehensive quality process. The actual savings depends on four vital factors:

1. The condition of the company at the start
2. The culture of the organization
3. The levels of analysis utilized
4. The involvement of every employee

INTERVIEWS WITH DEDICATED EXECUTIVES

The surveys told us something about macro quality issues, but not enough about the companies' real commitment, how they got organized, and where they feel they are on the success line. We therefore interviewed several company presidents and senior quality officers who kindly volunteered their time and thoughts to discuss more detailed issues.

We think the following excerpts from those interviews will give you a sense of how difficult it can be to be effective with a large-scale quality

Figure 2.4
Ad from First Chicago Bank

FIRST FORUM

BOB WATERMAN
ON WHY QUALITY IS CARING.

When two people have equal technical skills, the one who cares will do the job better. Whether the job is repairing autos, designing computers or offering bank services, quality comes from care.

Today, quality and productivity are the service industry's most important issues. As jobs once moved from farms to factories, they are now shifting from factories to service companies. And within the service sector, quality means service.

Some say quality is free. But my experience is that it's better than free because quality makes money and generates productivity.

Improving quality and white-collar productivity cannot be achieved by edict or a time and motion study. Both require a total approach that starts with the customer. For quality truly exists only in the eye of the customer. The place to start looking for quality is in the customer mirror.

A caring attitude must pervade an organization and be applied to everything it does.

Every service function is a process. Each process has customers. Even internal groups have internal customers. And each process must be measured in terms relevant to its customer. At a hospital, how many botched x-rays per 100 patients? At a bank, how often is the wrong account debited or credited?

Next, make a heroic assumption. Assume that no matter how well a process is being done, it can be done better by a factor of 3, 5 or even 10.

The people doing the job know it best and will have the best ideas on how to improve it. Put them in the driver's seat. Educate them on quality and service. Let them look into the customer mirror, evaluate their own process, make the measurements, then set their own goals and find the best ways to make improvements. Meanwhile, management must cheer them on.

Then, to put genuine quality into your efforts to improve quality and service, hoist a safety net under everyone and reward those who are getting results. Companies who are absolutely dependent on quality and productivity treat their employees with the same quality they extend to every other part of their business.

At First Chicago, we recognize that errors cost customers time and money. So we created a Performance Measurement Program in 1981 to provide every customer with more than just our verbal promise to deliver superior quality service.

Customers tell us that timeliness, accuracy and customer service responsiveness are their highest priorities. Nearly 700 charts measure these critical customer-sensitive issues. As a result, we've achieved significant performance improvement in each of our product lines.

Many customers also accept our standing invitation to attend weekly performance measurement meetings. In session are those in the driver's seat: the individuals responsible for every process that yields quality service in each relationship.

Scott Bates, senior vice president of First Chicago's Cash Management Sales Department, wants to share our total approach to quality service with you.

Call Scott at 312-732-2193. He cares.

⊛ FIRST CHICAGO
The First National Bank of Chicago

Mr. Waterman, co-author of In Search of Excellence, is writing a major new book to be published by Bantam Books in 1987.
© 1986, The First National Bank of Chicago.

18

Figure 2.4 (continued)

process, and will indicate why commitment and success are highly correlated.

On Formulating the Quality Steering Committee

We have every possible extreme involved and represented.
—Charles Soule, Executive Vice-President,
Paul Revere Life Insurance Company.

SOULE: Along about 1981 for a number of reasons, myself and some of my staff really began to actively talk about quality. At that point we actually put a proposal together for the company to begin to put together a quality process of some kind. We didn't get anywhere.... Then in '83 Aubrey Reid [President and Chief Executive Officer] called me down and said, "I just got a call from Bob Bauman and he's asking that all of the AVCO divisions start up and create their own quality programs, so here's your chance." He said one other interesting thing, he said, "I don't want to make a big deal out of this. We're going to do it because they say we've got to do it. We don't have the kind of problems that others do, but we've got to do something." The reason why AVCO was so interested was because of some problems they were having with the new tank engine. I really believed that it was an opportunity for us to be able to compete in the marketplace. It was becoming more and more difficult to compete in other ways; rates, products, underwriting...were becoming more and more difficult to differentiate. So, I looked upon service and quality as a way of perhaps differentiating. And, in fact, if we did it right and were successful it would be a more difficult thing for our competition to match.

NOLAN: So many companies have talked to us about quality and said, "It's easy for those companies that are not good quality organizations to make improvements. When we see all those stories about organizations getting cost reductions and improvement in service and quality we just kind of laugh at it saying, 'Yeah, what were they before? They are probably now what we are.'" Were you aware that the perception of Paul Revere in the marketplace was high before you started?

SOULE: We heard exactly the comments you just made repeated over and over again here. "Why are we doing this? We're already a quality company." In many cases when we would introduce it and discuss it in different departments in the company, they took offense at it. They would say, "Are you saying that we're not a good quality operation? We are. We know we are." We would respond, "Well, of course you are, but you can always improve." Then we would get into this discussion about competitive advantages. I think by the time we got the program and the training put together, we began to focus in a little different way on things, like *listening to the customer*, and don't point a finger at someone else being a problem with poor quality. Make sure your own house is in order first. I think very quickly, as the teams got started and the need was to get off this finger-pointing and really focus in on yourself, all of a sudden they realized there were a lot of things they could do. I think there's another thing too that's a distinction of what you just said. It was interesting to go to the AVCO quality quorums and see the different perspectives from a manufacturing company. Early on we were not talking the same language at all. We had the advantage of not having had quality *control* functions, people, departments in our company. With manufacturing firms when you talk quality they immediately thought quality control, elimination of scrap.

What do I really want to do, and, what's the bottom line? Well, of course, it's improving quality in fact and in perception. What I really want to do, though, is to give every employee in this company a sense of ownership and an understanding of how they can contribute, and do contribute, to the quality of the product we are giving in the marketplace. It's through that sense of ownership that they do that and through their own sense of importance. That I, in fact, can bring something to this product, to this table, that nobody else can. There are still all kinds of opportunities to do more there today. We've made some headway. If you listen to clerical employees, they feel their job is more important now. They feel more a part of the whole. They will say, "For the first time someone is listening to my ideas, it's the first time I've sat around the table and talked about what I might do to help my section, or my department, or the company. Incidentally, it's nice to have people listen to my ideas." That's what I think is so different between what we're doing here and what Japan is doing. Japan's quality system works entirely differently. It's more top down. We purposely made ours nonvoluntary because we said, "If it's a culture change we're going to go for—this goal of getting more ownership—we've really got to have everyone involved. But, if we're going to require that they be involved, we can't ask them to do it on their own time; we have to do it on company time. And, we have to have something in it for them."

NOLAN: How much of the success of your process do you think can be attributed to that front-end getting to know what quality is all about and research?

SOULE: A tremendous amount, and I myself don't know if anyone else involved recognized how important that was when we were going through it. There were pressures, incidentally, to get it up quick. AVCO said, "What's going on, you've been at this three months now and nothing is happening." I think there were two, maybe three, significant things that happened during that six or seven months start-up time. One was what I refer to as "messing around" with this word quality. We went through a lot of sessions messing around; as you get into it you realize just how many different definitions there are, just how many different opportunities there are to take this and run off in different directions. On the Steering Committee we had every possible extreme involved and represented, and fairly vocal. We had to go through a series of meetings to bring those extremes together and find a common ground. One of the things that was happening (really the reason why you folks got involved) was that this quality need surfaced, and at the same time in our plan for that year was the question of improving our effectiveness through value analysis. We were ready to do something there when this quality thing popped. Many of our early conversations on the Steering Committee were, "We've got these two things, how are we going to do them?" One group said, "Look we do value analysis first and get that out of the way, because we've got to bring those bottom line savings down quick, and then we address quality." The other extreme said, "Hey look, if you believe in quality that's the absolute wrong way to do it. Quality will bring you this, it might take a little longer, but you give a different message to your people." So, there was this tug and we wrestled with that. Finally the term "Quality Has Value" came to me. I was trying to pull the two groups together. The thought that quality in the quality teams was doing things right, and value analysis was doing right things kind of popped together, and Quality Has Value tied those two words together, but also the fact that quality has to have value. When we worked that through and began to put it together things jelled very quickly. It was just one of those dumb luck things. So, that messing around with quality was important. The second was the training. We also had some dumb luck there. We knew as we put the program together we had decided to have everyone be involved and to have these teams and they were going to be structured this way. Then we had to address how to train the team leaders. We had some ideas of things we wanted to do, group dynamics and that kind of thing. We talked with Al Materas in Human Resources, and Al said, "Look what just came across my desk—it's a good program for our level of people." Finally, we got to the step of working with you folks (thank heaven you fit into the program). You adjusted your normal approach a little bit to fit ours, and we worked through the questions that came up of how will the value analysis workshops and quality teams work simultaneously, will they cross over each other or is there going to be friction? We worked through those programs pretty well. What then I think was a help to us was to have you take the time to come up here almost weekly and attend our Steering Committee meetings. You got a feel for just where we were heading.

NOLAN: When you traveled to Japan did you get a feeling that you were heading in the right direction?

SOULE: I think for AVCO two things came out of that. First of all, we did come back with some ideas. The first thing you come back with is that nothing can be taken from Japan and transported here, it just can't happen. It's an entirely different culture and environment. But there are some little things you pick up, it's probably the little things that make it go, not the hype you hear. The second thing for me was a reaffirmation of what we would do. I had a chance to visit manufacturing firms. But also, I visited some service industries and they were in the dark ages, not just in quality but in service. If I came away from Japan with one new thought to myself, it's that the advantage they have is that they are an island nation, small in area, their people live on 10 percent of the land, and they all are focused on the same goal. They know in order to survive, and to survive with a decent standard of living, that they have to compete in the world marketplace. The worker understands it, the banks understand it, the government does, and corporations do. They don't work against each other. And, they find ways of working together to make that happen. We in this country have such diverse differences; geographically, culturally, socially, and economically, that we just don't have that same common understanding, that drive. They don't verbalize that. That's why, incidentally, the service industries are not as far along, because they're not exporting. But, those that are exporting know good and well what they have to do in the marketplace to survive. That's what motivates them, the worker understands.

NOLAN: In evolving your quality process, where do you place your emphasis on improvement between the three aspects of the control system, the improvement process, and the planning aspect?

SOULE: There's no question in my mind that our employees, because of quality, know more and think more about who that customer is. And that they can make an impact on that customer. There is much more they can do, and we've got to help them find those ways and make it easier for them to do it. As new employees come aboard we've got to continue to reinforce that. Although we've made some gains, there's tremendous opportunities that are still there. The trick is going to be how do you keep moving in that direction, how much do you use incentives? How much do you use financial incentives? Do we develop a profit sharing, and what are the pluses and minuses of that? We wrestle and continue to wrestle some with this bottom-up top-down thing. Ideally you would like to plant the seed and let it germinate, and let your employees on their own develop the optimum response to customer's needs. It's going to take a little more time to do it that way, but it's better than management saying, "This is the direction you have to go." We can influence their activities, their quality team projects in the direction we feel is the right one. If we do that we kind of then take away the ownership. That's a delicate line to balance. There's a need for a little bit of both, and there's a need for more in one quality team than another. There's a need at times to inject a little bit of top-down to get things going and then back off. You've just got to be careful not to go too far in either direction. And really, the value analysis and the quality teams had that balance from the start. That continually has to be fine tuned, and the whole process itself has to be fine tuned. The one area that we still have not totally solved is how we measure it in a way that gives us something we can turn around and use as an incentive. Going back to Japan, I can remember a couple of instances when they demonstrated quality by stacking the scrap for a month in one location where everyone tripped over it. Scrap is a little more difficult for us to verify and make visible. We can't talk in quite the same tangibles. There are two opportunities for doing that, neither one is as objective as you would like it to be. One is to somehow count quality. There is a mechanism for doing that, but the further you go in that direction the more it's top-down, the more the employee says, "They talk about quality and they talk about putting the responsibility on me, but here they are checking on me." The other possibility is through measurement. Surveying your customers. Regardless of how good your quality really is, how many errors there are, what does your customer think about your quality? Isn't that really what it's all about? The bottom-line objective is to have a process that's going to make your customer feel better about you so he or she will buy more or behave differently. Really, the important thing isn't what's in fact, it's what their perception is, so let's measure their perception.

It always amazes me when I see other evidence of this issue of perception versus in fact. Over the years, in dealing with our customers, how they think about the quality of our service, accuracy, or time service, has some wide boundaries based upon what I in fact know is going on in here. Within some fairly broad boundaries their opinion has nothing to do with the service we deliver. If you know that and if you're smart enough to be able to develop a sensitivity to the hot point you can do something about it. If you have good telephone communications and other good ways of communicating, that can get you over a lot of those bumps when service is not as good as it ought to be. So that just underlines the importance of perception.

NOLAN: In many organizations they say that what doesn't work is the brass bands and arm bands approach with all the bells and whistles. But it seems like you have gone to that brass bands and arm bands approach, and it seems to be working here. Maybe you can comment on whether that was the culture before and if you see a change in culture because of your annual meeting on quality and celebration. Does that change the culture?

SOULE: The brass band and arm bands is another one of those issues that we really wrestled through in the Quality Steering Committee. I can remember discussions—pins? That's really horrible. And then the whole discussion of how do you reward people, do you give a financial reward, do you give gift certificates? And you have one group saying, "You gotta do that, because, if you have a program where the company's benefiting, you have to share some of that with the employees." The other group said, "Hey, we're paying them for that already, that's part of their job." One thing we're finding, it's becoming clearer to me at least, is that the needs of the company vary considerably from one group to another as far as the things you can do, or should do, to motivate them, to bring them in as part of the program or make the program speak to them. The brass bands and arm bands speak to our nonexempt people, they've got to feel an involvement in a different way. It's got to be a more tangible, more visible way. Conversely, professional people, underwriters, actuaries, and our management group, tend to be a little bit turned off by too much of that. I don't want to make a black and white statement, there is a definite division, but it's not all black and white. The exempt group needs to be motivated in a different way. They can be turned on by the importance of this in helping to reach your departmental or corporate goals, and helping us develop a company that's more competitive in providing more career opportunities. It's much easier to talk to them about things you can do to attract the customer, because they're interfacing daily with the customer, they know who the customer is. They require different treatment and we continue to have a few problems, because we tried to put together a program that encompasses both groups the same way. We went through different kinds of thought processes about the way to measure performance of a quality team by the number of ideas and dollars. We didn't want to emphasize dollars, but we went through the logic of using either that or [the] number of ideas. That combination was a tremendous motivator and continues to be for our clerical employees. The professional midmanager groups had difficulty with that. Midmanagement teams or professional teams would get together and wrestle with it, wondering if, "Is that really something I ought to take credit for as a part of this process, or is it part of my regular job? How can I take credit for it if it's part of my regular job?" Our answer to that has been, "Don't get hung up on it, it's the process, the quality process, that allows you to do something sooner than you would have done it or better than you would have done it. Take credit for it." That's what it's all about, I don't care whether the savings are a hundred dollars or fifty cents or nothing, if it allows you to do something that's valuable and do it more quickly then it's worth doing. The second year we started with different guidelines. We said, "We're not going to reward you based upon the number of ideas and dollars or savings. We want you to set some goals. And then we will measure you on those goals' quality, and reward you based on that." We had all kinds of trouble with the clerical group and goal setting. It was just amazingly difficult for them to relate to that, so we finally said, "Fine, if you want to establish your goals in terms of number of ideas and dollars, that's fine." On the other hand, the exempt group was saying, "Ah, goals—now I've got something I can sink my teeth into. I don't have to count ideas, I can work on some big project that's important for the whole year long and I'll just set up measures." That kind of a thing needs a different approach for the two groups.

NOLAN: Is there another company or financial services organization that you or your management team looks to and says, "Gee, that's a quality organization. That's a company that really stands out and we'd like to be thought of in that way at some point in time."?

SOULE: In the insurance industry one would be Northwestern Mutual, and I'd say head and shoulders above anybody I know. It's a culture, it's not an issue. I don't know whether or not their outputs have less errors, but their people and their customers claim they do a better quality job than anybody else does. The other service company, and it's part service and part not service, is IBM.

NOLAN: We've heard from some companies that there aren't enough good quality financial services organizations. We wonder what the reason for that is?

SOULE: I think it's a lack of competition. I see a distinction in Japan. A clear distinction between service companies and manufacturing companies. I think their quality process surfaced and developed and was nurtured because they needed something to compete with. Think of what happened in Japan. We used to make jokes about Japanese equipment and products, we thought it was junk. It even went back to the war. There is an interesting story about MacArthur bringing in Deming with his concepts, and they look at MacArthur as a god, a demagogue—his office was turned into a museum. We heard the president of Toyota when I was over there say, "This guy was brought in by MacArthur, and we thought that MacArthur was bringing over to us a philosophy, an approach, that was an integral part of American business. It wasn't until fifteen years later that we realized that this guy was peddling something that was foreign in New York." And it's only been in the last few years that anyone here knows about Edward Deming.

NOLAN: What would you say to a senior manager of a smaller company when he says, "We're not big enough, we don't have the resources, Crosby says quality is free, but it's really not, because it takes time away from production and we're just not ready to focus on quality yet?"

SOULE: I think if you're in the process of introducing a quality program and that question doesn't come up, then something is wrong. That's a basic question, one we wrestled through. I can remember our bean counter saying, "Hey, this is what you want to do, you want to take 1,400 people, pull them out of their work place for an hour or three-quarters of an hour a week, let's see that's this many hours and this many dollars, that's a million and a half bucks. We need to hire X number of people just to keep productivity the same." We went through that. The answer is, if the process works then you're going to see more savings than the cost is going to be. Now, sure the savings, the time you invest today isn't going to return in a month or six months, but it's going to come. Let's you and I be honest with ourselves. Everyone of us wastes a half an hour a week, anybody can afford half an hour a week. As a matter of fact, I remember this discussion. Anybody that's been involved in a production atmosphere of any kind, white-collar or blue-collar, knows that when I need to get increased production because I'm in the middle of a contest, I can, I think, increase production more than fifty percent. I can push for a day or two days, I really can. Half an hour, duck soup, particularly if people come away feeling good about it. So once we got into that, and there was a lot of suspicion. Not only in the Steering Committee, but when we introduced it to the company, same kind of reaction. We never lost it, we didn't have to hire one person. It's a smoke screen, but you've got to address it.

NOLAN: When you bring up ownership, some organizations are using ownership literally. That's when part of their award is stock—a share of stock, two shares of stock, depending upon what the improvement has been. The feedback is that employees really feel good about that. Now they are truly owners in the company and it's not just in a pension plan, it's in stock.

SOULE: There's a whole other issue of this ownership. I think ownership is a key part of this and anybody can respond to that. If I have a company of 50 employees, and I can really get each employee to understand what they are doing and why they are doing it, how they impact the end result, and recognize them for it either tangibly or just verbally, I've improved efficiency, I've improved the cost of my operation. I know that's true, anyone can respond to that. There's another piece though, that I think is in the background that's created the environment for these programs in this country. The employee's attitude, perception, demands, and expectation of his or her boss or employer is tremendously different today than it was thirty years ago, twenty, ten or five years ago. They want more information, they want to feel a part of what's going on, and they will respond to that in a way that would not have been possible thirty years ago. In order to get the optimum that they offer us, we've got to respond. The quality process is perhaps the best example I can think of here of true participative management. They are participating.

Breakfast of Champions

> Once every two months we have a group that we recognize as being a Carteret Champion, and they get a framed award plus five shares of stock.
>
> —Robert J. Mueller, President, Carteret Savings Bank

NOLAN: Is quality a strategic issue with Carteret?

MUELLER: Very much so. We're going through a transition, and have been going through a transition over the last three or four years. Just to recap some of it very briefly, we were a New Jersey–based thrift up until 1979 or 1980 and then the interest rates proved to be impossible for us—we were paying more for deposits than we were getting from the lending side— that couldn't exist too long. A bill was passed in 1982, which in fact deregulated the savings and loan business. We decided that we had to raise capital, and of course, capital is the name of the game in our business—it is in commercial banking, and it is in savings and loan banking. What it really comes down to is the ability to access capital. So we decided to expand our geographical horizons. While we were in the process of taking advantage of the deregulation—commercial lending and the service corporation, building some houses—we did get access to the capital market and became a public company. We're still working on the profitability factor—we've got a balance sheet that, albeit improving, is not where it needs to be. So, as a result of that we're at a stage where we need to give ourselves more time to prove our ability to make money and develop and fine tune our skills in some of the most important areas, whether it be developing other services to sell in the retail branches or whether it be in mortgage banking, or any other areas that we have. We're basically dealing with the same market, the same green dollar bills, the same types of services that our competition is. It comes back to one thing, and that's service and quality—we have to deliver that product to the customer in a manner that that customer wants it delivered. A little over a year ago we decided to try and give our people, our employees, that message. We went into this Excellence Program that you may be aware of. And we've had about 350 or 400 people going down to the supervisory level go through this program for three days. It's a seminar situation. We have Tom Peters' videotape— he does a fantastic job—talking about the material that basically went into his book. It really created a much better atmosphere internally.

NOLAN: Is there a company, either in your industry or in related financial services industries, that you look to and say, "That's the company—that's what we want to be like"?

MUELLER: The problem is that it's very difficult to compare us to a financial services company, because they all have different backgrounds. Some started off with a lot more than others. When you look at the savings and loan business, you look at a Great Western in California, which I think is a very well managed thrift. They're in California, which is a tremendous advantage, or has been over the last fifteen or twenty years—could we ever get there? I don't know, but I think that I would lean more toward the Great Western than I would the commercial bank or the company out there that just views itself as a supplier of financial services. I think Great Western is more of the kind of company that I see ourselves being. Home Federal in San Diego is another one—well managed, good sophisticated people running the different areas—they're opportunists and yet they understand the benefits of their region. To me, the benefits of being in New Jersey are not the same benefits of being in California.

NOLAN: Have you done any education of the new employees, other than the sessions that you've had down to the supervisory level?

MUELLER: We've continued the Excellence Program down through the supervisory level. We've cut the three-day program down to one day and, obviously for one day you're only going to get a third of the benefit that you get out of three days, because people don't get quite as familiar with the other people in the room and they don't communicate as well in one day. We still think it's a good idea, and it's working pretty well. The other thing we've done is expand our employee orientation for new employees, and we do some different things. For example, either Bob Pierson [Vice-Chairman] or myself will visit with every group of new employees. We also have a film that we show—we use it at shareholder meetings—it gives people an overview of what the company does, so at least when they walk out of the room after having seen this tape on the company, and having seen us, they have an impression, and hopefully, it's a positive impression.

NOLAN: How do you keep in touch with your progress on quality improvement?

MUELLER: I go over to the mortgage company periodically and sit on the telephones with our customer service people. Three-quarters of the phone calls are inquiries and 25 percent of them are complaints. The reason I do that is not because I want to look over their shoulder, in fact they think it's a real treat when I come over, they like that. I'm really getting two things. One, I get an education, because if a customer calls in with a question and we've got the screen there, I see exactly what we have in terms of internal capabilities for reporting information. If they're having a problem coming up with the information to tell the customer, then that's one way in which I can really appreciate it, because you're sitting there on the phone with that person on the other end wanting to know why we analyzed their escrow and told them their payment was going to go up. So you've got to be able to tell them right then and there. The other reason I like to do it is because, the only time sitting in this office that I talk to a customer is when they're really mad. They've gotten so annoyed about something that they try to call me up or write to me. They're really boiling by the time I get to them. You've got to deal with those situations, and I do—I always write back, and I always follow up to make sure that we responded to them, that we did everything we could to make them happy, but nine times out of ten it's not much fun. So I go over there to listen to normal people who have inquiries and questions. It's an uplift to me to know that three-quarters of the people who call in, all they really have is a question.

NOLAN: Have you appointed a manager in charge of quality for the entire organization, not only the services, but all of it?

MUELLER: We haven't done that, but that's an interesting concept. We haven't quite gotten to that. But I can see, as we start to do more and more of these things, we're going to say, "We're not well organized enough." We need somebody who can get that done, so I would agree with that, I think that's a good step.

Quality is the one thing that we can do right now, irrespective of this transition I was describing before. We're in a very competitive environment. Anywhere we go, even if we go to good markets like Florida that's very fast-growing, it's very competitive. But when you really start to tear down the competition and look at who you're competing against, all the companies are different. We do measure ourselves, by the way, in a number of areas, but not on a coordinated basis. We know how much computer downtime we have, for example. We know our response time on mortgage applications, and in consumer credit we know how fast we turn things around, so we're measuring a lot of what we're doing but not on a coordinated basis.

NOLAN: Did you give your quality process an identity?

MUELLER: Our program was initially called Towards Excellence. It was something everybody could understand.

NOLAN: Have you done anything with recognition for employees with good quality ideas?

MUELLER: We have the suggestion program that came out of this excellence thing—it was something the employees wanted. We have, in different parts of the organization, cash award-type recognition. It's not a highly regimented, highly formal thing—we use it with different programs that we have for giving people recognition. The chairman [Bob O'Brien] engages in what we call the Breakfast of Champions. Once every two months we'll have a group that we recognize as being a Carteret Champion, and they get a framed award plus five shares of stock. Or a pen and pencil set, something for their desk. We thought a lot about what to give them, and we decided on the stock. The first breakfast we had was just within the last couple of months. It took longer than it probably should have to try and figure out what is a champion. Is it just going to be anybody that the supervisor says is a champion? Or is it going to be more of a detailed review of what they've really done? We try to make sure that they've really done something. We also really like to recognize people who have been here a while, somebody who's been here a couple of years. We have the breakfast right here in the board room.

NOLAN: Do you feel that there is a turnaround, that attitudes are upbeat?

MUELLER: I think the attitudes are on an upbeat. One of the things I like about the excellence program is that we developed a way to expand it by cutting down the program and making it available to more people. I think the next step is how do we keep this going. You need something like this going on all the time if you're going to try and keep in touch with your employees.

NOLAN: How do your middle managers feel about your push for quality?

MUELLER: I think they like it. What they don't like is for us to say something and then just walk away. But, if we say something and then we prove to them over a period of time that we really mean it, they see that as direction and they like direction. The excellence program has been going on for eighteen months at the most—we're just beginning. The question is how can we keep it going.

Quality Is More a Journey than a Destination

> Our Chief Executive Officer...coined this phrase which has been quoted a few times, "quality is more a journey than a destination."
> —John Falzon, Senior Vice-President,
> Metropolitan Life Insurance Company

NOLAN: What is it that led to Metropolitan's decision that quality is an important strategic issue?

FALZON: The initiative is from the Chief Executive Officer, he has pushed the issue of quality ever since he was President and Chief Operating Officer and then of course with more influence as the Chief Executive Officer. He's convinced that quality is the differentiating factor in a competitive environment, that when you get it all down and separate out what distinguishes companies from one another, that quality will be the most enduring of the attributes the company can bring to the marketplace. So he has pushed quality and he's asked me to take on the role as the quality officer for the company. He asked me to do that job in 1984. We used to talk about it quite a bit, and he coined this phrase which has been quoted a few times, "Quality is more a journey than a destination." I've come to see the wisdom of that statement, because over the time that I've had this position and since we've embarked on a journey toward quality I've seen that it never remains exactly the same, there are opportunities for improvement, and the things that we did a year ago are being modified today, hopefully in an enhanced fashion and in an evolutionary way that enables us to provide an even higher level of quality than what we had before. When we got it started we went out and we convened a meeting of the heads of the departments, the major departments of the company, and we asked them to tell us if you're going to have a quality program at Metropolitan what do you need to be successful. They came back and told us about all their views, and in a sense gave me a blueprint for how a quality program ought to evolve, so that when we developed the specifications for it, if I were consistent with their direction they would buy into it. What they told me in effect was that it had to have a very strong customer orientation, that it had to involve all the employees of the company, and we had to do things for business reasons, they shouldn't be for academic purposes only. We developed a program, essentially, around those foundation elements and created a quality network that was overlaid on top of the formal organization. The essential parts of the network were to establish a person in every organization who would be a quality officer. And, by the way, there were some other things besides those foundation elements that the department heads' committee told me—what they said, in effect, was that it had to be a line-driven operation. It should be a driving force and the staff organization should remain lean and not contribute to corporate overheads, and that if we were going to have a system it had to be the same system that was going to be applied throughout every department of the company, whether people washed dishes, or whether they paid claims, or whether they did underwriting or investment analysis; it had to be the same across the company. When we went back to them we talked about establishing a network. The cornerstone or keystone of the network would be a person called a quality officer, and that quality officer would form a committee of individuals. They would run what we termed an identification meeting where they internalized and said, "What is it that we produce as a product or service, major products and services, and who do we send them to, who are our customers?" Then we said once we identified those things that somebody in the organization should come forward and take ownership of each product or service, and that person would become the product champion. With the product champions and the quality officer you had a quality improvement counsel for the organization, and the product champion would form a quality improvement team. It would be made up of all the management people who were in charge of the units that contributed to the development of that product or service. Then, finally, the network was rounded out by natural work teams, which really were all the first-line managers who were participating in quality improvement teams, and the people who reported to them. Now everybody in the organization was involved from the bottom all the way to the top, and we told them what they had to do was really challenge themselves. In each of their organizations they had to challenge themselves—first of all by setting up measuring devices, ways in which they could measure the performance of delivery of their products and services. Secondly, they would have to challenge themselves to do a better job. The mere fact they're meeting their standards, whatever they set up in the measurements, they should try to tighten it up a little bit and do better than they've done before, for no other reason than to meet their own expectations. Thirdly, they would go out and talk to their customers and conduct some sort of customer dialogue, so you've got feedback from the customer that tells you precisely what the customer thought about the way you were delivering things. And finally, to seek out and eliminate wherever possible what we term extra processing. Extra processing essentially was all of the cost associated with doing things more than one time. Now in clerical operations you say, "Well that's going to be a little more difficult to identify, because it's not the same as a factory where you have recycling of a production line, or you have a scrap heap where you pour damaged articles coming out of inspection." We found a lot of illustrations that highlight the fact that extra processing is rampant within a service type clerical environment. Just anecdotally, I identified for people how you can see it in the claim operations. I went up visiting a claim operation that I was associated with before I took this job, and at the mail desk claims are coming in and they had one file for clean claims, then they had a pile of correspondence, and then they had a pile of claims coming back from the Post Office and returned checks. I was saying to the people up there that every pile except the first one was evidence of this extra processing. They were defensive and said, "It's not our fault." I said, "It's not a question of fault, it's just a question of identifying where extra work is coming from and treating the cause rather than the symptom." That was a simple illustration of a great deal of extra work. Claims were coming back because they were incorrectly addressed, because the claims to the doctors did not include the diagnosis, writing to somebody because they forgot to fill in boxes 2, 4, and 6. All of this said that people weren't being instructed properly so that they could do what they were supposed to do correctly the first time, and what we were doing was coping with the disturbance. You would think that's easy. I thought I would challenge myself to identify where would that kind of extra processing exist in a more professional type environment, so I took the problem up with the attorney who is in charge of our litigation unit, and we started to talk about the processes that they were engaged in and it wasn't long before we discovered plenty of opportunities. When we really started to discuss the essence of extra processing, doing things because we didn't do it right the first time, we got down to the point that perhaps the whole litigation unit wouldn't exist if somebody did things right the first time.

NOLAN: So you looked at it from a broader view?

FALZON: Very broad. That was the communications to people, so what we did there was to structure a training program around all of those things. How to form a network of people, how to identify extra processing, how to conduct group problem-solving sessions (we had a special instruction on problem solving team building), how to use certain tools that were effective in the work place for identifying the kind of cases you look up, Pareto Principle, fishbone diagramming. And, we wrote about a four-and-a-half-day training program for trainers, and then the trainers took the information back in a recorded form and delivered it to all the people in their organization who were occupying first-line supervisory positions and above. Our first flush at this thing was to get to about 3000 people. In terms of time frame, we took the job in June of 1984, we conducted the training program in August and September of 1985. It took us a year to know what we wanted to do and to construct a training program so we could effectively deliver it. Then the departments conducted their training during the fall of 1985. Along with that we had a certain amount of hype in that we asked people to run identification meetings to say what the products and services were. We asked them to run an announcement meeting to say, "Look, we're going to be going off to school in a little while and when we come back this is what's going to happen to you." We had a very big event in the spring of 1986, we called it launch day. Everybody starting out had the training, it had been given out to everybody in the organization down to the first level of supervision. We provided people with what we call the Natural Work Team Leaders Guide and an Employee Handbook that fit together. It was the same as in the training program, but now was going to be used by the first-level manager and the people reporting to that first-level manager to repeat the whole thing about "who is our customer, what are our products and services, how do we improve upon it, how do we engage in problem solving, should we talk to our customers, and how do we conduct that dialog." Things got started after the first quarter of 1986. There are only three people on this staff, plus some people I borrowed to construct and deliver the training program. But there were two big holes. One was that we told them to go talk to the customer, but we didn't tell them how to do it. The second was that we hadn't performed a natural integration between the quality improvement process as we described it, which was targeted in at the department level, at the operation level of the company, and the strategic planning of the company. So there were two holes. I guess it was around the spring of 1986 that I came across some research that had been completed by a group of professors down at Texas A&M. It was the best thing I've seen as it applied to companies like ours, because it was original research into what is quality in a service-type environment, and how do you measure it? It was really right on target as to what we were talking about. It identified certain characteristics of a service environment that distinguish it from a product. It's intangible, you can't feel it, taste it, touch it, and because you can't then you can't pretest it before you deliver it to be sure of quality. Very interesting.

NOLAN: You talked about the measurement. That's one of the things that most of the companies that we are dealing with are so concerned with, to make sure that the measurement is consistent. There are two different forms of measurement. One is measuring what the customer's perception is and expectations are.

FALZON: That's what their research showed in the final analysis, that the quality in the service sector has to be measured by the gap that may exist between the expectation level of the customer on the one side and the perceived level of service delivery on the other side.

NOLAN: We've been measuring the expectations and the perceptions and then working at narrowing that gap.

FALZON: Well, the measurement they came up with originally had ten characteristics that you want to measure things by. They found a high correlation between quite a few of them and were able to shrink them down to five elements they measure: reliability, how well you deliver in terms of the way you promised to deliver—dependably and accurately; responsiveness—that's how promptly you're doing things. Another one they call tangibility—what are the physical surroundings within which the service is delivered. They claim in a service you can't separate the process from the outcome. Process and outcome occur simultaneously, so the people delivering the service play very important roles. There are two other elements that they measure. One they call assurance, which is the knowledge and the capability of the individual who's delivering the service and that person's capability of projecting a feeling of trust and confidence. The last is the ability to respond to an unusual situation and provide personalized service. Their study concluded that you can't separate process from outcome, and nonroutine situations are as important as routine situations. When they put all the facts together they were able to construct an instrument to measure quality in a service sector. Traditionally, we said establish a measuring device; people did measure by ability. They measured time service, error rate, and productivity. Take a claim transaction, we measure them upside-down and backwards. After a lot of years of looking at it and pouring over it, but we never measured what the customer said, so you don't know and you could be falling apart on process or falling apart on nonroutine situations, because you have a tendency to measure the outcomes and you measure the routine situations more than anything else because it lends itself easily to measurement. So, we pulled one of those professors in and we constructed a training program. We cycled all our quality officers and trainers back through the training program to teach them how they could, for their own kind of products and services, construct a measurement system and then use it to go out to the customers to measure themselves from one period to the next. The interesting part of this study said that you have a gap, but the gap exists on the provider's side. The initial reaction is always beat the people over the head who deliver the service. The fact of the matter is they found that on the provider's side there were four distinct areas that contribute to the gap that exists on the customer's side. And every one of those four you could point to something that managers do wrong if the gap exists. There are ways of finding out which one of those gaps is really the culprit, and to which extent. There's a third phase of the study going on that we are participating with five other companies—two communications companies, two banks, and two insurance companies, and we're one of the insurance companies. We are participating on the third phase that looks at those four factors and determines which of those four factors has the biggest impact by and large, and then what are the things that managers do that contribute to each of those gaps, and which of those things are more important? These influencers on the gaps are called independent strategic variables that they had gone into formal literature that had been produced on these subjects. We have a Managing for Excellence course that we created, and there's 43 items that we teach managers that are important in management organizations and people. There's a high correlation between those independent strategic variables and the 43 items, so we're making a nice big move, if we can get back to our own people and talk about interpretive aspects of conducting a survey and getting them back to things we've been talking about in the management courses, we've making a nice connection between the whole process here. That was our answer on how to talk to your customers. The other piece was connecting up the strategy planning part of the company. In the latter part of last year, we involved ourselves with Russell Acoff from the University of Pennsylvania, I don't know if you've ever heard of him, but he's a guru in the strategic planning area, he gives a lot of talks, he's well known and he has a process of planning called interactive planning. We found that his interactive planning process and our quality improvement process are very closely tied together. We introduced interactive planning, starting with the president and the people who report to the president, and it's working its way right down through the organization. As the percolation occurs it will come down and accomplish the things we did in the quality improvement process. That's where we are today. Where we're going to go tomorrow now is to create another training program to teach people how to use the interactive planning process, and show them how it's evolutionary to the things that they were doing last year and how this is a step-by-step thing—emphasizing, once again, that it's a journey not a destination, and as you move along you get better at the job.

NOLAN: You had talked earlier about the first pass reaching three thousand people.

FALZON: We duplicated it for the field organization and we went down to another couple of thousand there.

NOLAN: So you probably reached about five or six thousand?

FALZON: Yes. Ultimately it should have gotten to the people in the workstation. By the way, we conducted an employee survey. We went to the workers and what we got back was substantial improvement over what had been going on before. We estimate that it's effective in about two thirds of the situations, and not effective in one third.

NOLAN: It sounds like you're doing a lot with education and you're conscious about participation. How about the element of recognition for people?

FALZON: Let me tell you what the president did. In our first year of operation, 1986, he wrote a letter to all the employees and said that in this first year of the quality improvement effort he wanted any employee of the company to write him a letter identifying another individual in the company who has done something that reflects on Metropolitan as being the quality company, and that that individual has done something special and it reflects his or her obsession with quality. The memo reads:

To: All Metropolitan Employees
From: President

As I think everyone knows, this year we're launching a quality improvement process for our company to stimulate and reward our joint commitment to make Met Life the quality company. I am pleased to announce a special quality awards program: during 1986 we will give up to 1000 special awards at $1000 each to anyone who renders some special service and takes some special actions to show that Met Life is the quality company. Met Life for these purposes includes our Property and Liability Company. Thus, as much as one million dollars will be awarded. There is no form, no procedures, no complications, just send me a note telling me who you recommend for the award and why. We will make a decision after considering what the person did to show an internal or external customer that we are the quality company. Any Met Life employee can recommend any other Met Life employee. Preferably don't tell the person you're recommending, since not every recommendation will result in an award. We're looking for originality, improvement, spirit, commitment—an obsession with quality.

Then he continued it this year, but we tightened it up.

NOLAN: Was there a criterion, or was there a committee that would review the letters and determine who would receive the award? I'm sure you got a lot of letters.

FALZON: We finished the first thousand and the letters we got coming in we paid more than we turned down. We changed the program a little bit this year to show what they did to service the customer specifically. We're looking for documentation on the customer to show that they did more than their job and they really took that extra step. This year what we're doing is putting a thousand dollars, grossed up for tax deduction, into one of our own products—the mutual fund. We have a lot of other awards like Team Awards, Creative Quality Improvement Teams, Natural Work Teams, and if they can demonstrate that they made a change in their environment that really improved the situation and they document it. Again no forms, they just write it up, give it to their quality officer, the quality officer and department head agree, they just sign it off and send it to us and we put a dollar value on it and send it back to them.

NOLAN: Do you see any of your other peers in the industry that are as far along in your mind as you are?

FALZON: No. Most of the progress is made in the manufacturing sector. But even in the manufacturing sector they have a little bit of difficulty with their nonmanufacturing activities. We're working with some people at the American Society for Quality Control, and there are a lot of people there who look to us to tell them what happens in the service environment.

NOLAN: I think the key is spirit and commitment from senior management, and applying leadership to the process and evolving it like you're saying.

FALZON: We are creating a whole communications package that's going out and we have a video which features the president and me being interviewed by Pat Collins and what we're talking about is past, present, and future. The past is about halfway where we'd like to be, and we introduced this whole business about going out and talking to customers and that's the past and the present. The future is the integration of the planning process.

NOLAN: Do many of your people see their other internal arms of the organization as their customers?

FALZON: Yes. That's the whole message. Even in our training program we created what we call the customer loop to show that if you were working next to me, and you need what I send you to do your job, then you become my customer.

NOLAN: Do you think that was eye-opening?

FALZON: Yes. We had one heck of a time in the field organization. See what happens in a relationship, I believe, is that if you service me 90 percent of the time, I presume that I'm your customer, but if I service you 10 percent of the time, I don't think during that 10 percent that you're my customer. We've established a relationship that prevails at all times, and that's not so.

NOLAN: The training that you talked about, is that all done internally?

FALZON: We contracted an outside outfit and we created a video case study. We brainstormed ourselves around what do we want to communicate about this whole issue of quality. We came up with 35 to 40 messages on how to do it better in a case study. Every time I see this case study I see something I didn't see before on the issue of quality. What we did was create a case study about a TV news team. All the people on the team were individually highly competent people. In fact, certain people have said they have won individual awards for excellence. However, the TV news team is losing viewer share. That's the setting, and they recognize it, so there's different characters in there—you may see yourself in there. They come to recognize that they have to work together as a team if they're going to be successful. Then they started using this problem-solving, team-building technique that we introduced, and then there's a little bit of a success story, but not concluding the story because it's a journey not a destination. They start to achieve some measure of success with the promise that there's going to be more, then the story ends there. It's broken down into five segments. You show it, talk about it, then have the group practice some of the things that they just did. It was a very great focus for the training program, and it added a lot of interest—people enjoyed it.

NOLAN: How often are you going to go back to that customer base?

FALZON: As far as I'm concerned, if you're not talking to your customer you can presume your relationship is deteriorating. I would say they shouldn't let a year go by. If somebody can do it every six months, I'd tell them they would probably be better off. One of the things they found out in this study, they presume that the good companies were those companies who consistently exceeded their customers' expectations, and so did I. They found out on average that even the best companies did it only sporadically, that by and large the best companies had the smaller gaps. The mere fact that you do a good job drives up the customers' expectations. What you have to avoid is your competitors driving up the expectation levels, and leaving you with a bigger gap. You can unwittingly and unrealistically drive the expectation levels up by your advertising, by word of mouth, or what our sales people have to say. On the other hand, you may not have done a good job of telling the customer how good you are, so his perception is lower because you haven't really told him all the good things you can do for him. You can affect that gap just by communications and not change anything you do.

NOLAN: How did you feel about it when you first got started? Did you feel it was going to be difficult?

FALZON: Yes, I knew it was going to be difficult. I went around and talked to a lot of other companies before I got started, just to find out what was going on. I talked to IBM, AT&T—all of the people who we are customers of, because I've got an entree to those people. IBM was very helpful, and AT&T, but I think it's only recently that they've got themselves moving. The most interesting company was Xerox. They had a fellow there named Fred Henderson. They were a company that went from 100 percent market share down to less than 25 percent market share. Fred Henderson said they had a cultural environment in the company, it was essentially one of internal competition, they had nobody else to compete with so they were fighting each other. He said one of the biggest things he had to do was to get them to stop fighting—to recognize the enemy was outside. He was after a very broad cultural change to happen to the company, and he was working it on a cascading basis where each group of people would identify what it is that they did personally. Like a boss sitting there saying, "I'm responsible for the bottom line of such and such product." He'd say, "No, what do you do every day?" They wanted to know what that employee did every day, so their orientation was things that you do, and who do you impact. The boss said, "Well I dictate." Do you ever ask your secretary, could you do it a different way to help her do the job better? It's an orientation about your actions during the day, and there being a better way to do it. I thought the way they went about things was very interesting. The foundation for their program is that competitive edge market. They encourage you to go out and, whatever you do, find out the company that does it best in the United States.

NOLAN: Do you have Value Statements or Mission Statements?

FALZON: Yes. In the interaction planning process. What it says is that you have the opportunity to create an ideal organization on the presumption that your organization was destroyed last night. This is called the idealization made up of two parts—one part is end planning and the other part is what they call a situation analysis. End planning is number one, create a mission statement, it has to have these characteristics. Then, create the specifications which are what products you should be in (presuming you were destroyed last night), what you think you should be doing, and what markets you should be servicing, what rules of the road and human resource skills and what you ought to pay your people, and how you want to run your organization. The third piece of it is the design—how to put the organization together, and what will be the relationships of the people who are in the boxes. Now you have what they call an idealization, which includes a value statement. Meanwhile you've created a situation analysis which is today's environment and all the conflicts of today's environment, and all the obstructions that have prevented you from reaching today's objectives. You match your ideal. If your ideal satisfies all the problems you've identified over here, then your job is then to go from where you are to this ideal. That sets up all the projects that you drop into the next phase of planning, which is how to get the job done. The quality process that we have designed said find out all your problems, then immediately work on your problems to restore order. It didn't include idealization. We call it interactive planning.

Managing Quality Is Like Gardening

> All you have to do is turn your head for even a moment and the weeds are back.
>
> —Paul Johnson, President, Connecticut Savings Bank

NOLAN: What led to your decision to make quality one of the key strategic elements for Connecticut Savings Bank?

JOHNSON: It was the only strategy that we were left with by the marketplace in terms of our size, our basic market position, and what we could do. And if you look at the alternatives of an organization like ours and tick them off in terms of what strategies you could have—you can be the low cost producer, you can be the technical innovator—you can create a whole series of strategies that relate to various market niches. For CSB, we knew that we couldn't be technically ahead of everyone else, we knew we couldn't have more locations—we couldn't be more convenient, we knew that no one has a product line that is exclusive to everybody else's product line— the industry is interchangeable within a very, very short period of time. If someone comes out with a new product, you can copy that product in a very short time. There was only one thing that we thought that we had that we could make a measurable, discernible difference over the long run, and that was the quality of our products and the quality of our people. And so, the stressing of that also fit in with the natural inclinations of management from the point of view that we've been a very, very people-oriented business, not only from the point of view of the people who work here. There was a synergy with that basic idea. But, the truth of the matter is that we were left with few other options.

NOLAN: Is there any company, and we won't limit the industry to savings banks or banks, we can say the financial services industry, that you would see as someone leading the charge—someone to pattern your company after?

JOHNSON: The difficulty with the industry is that it does not have players that I think stand out on a national basis. Everyone is trying to do the same thing, and none of us is doing it very well. And, to a degree the market really creates the eventual cycle of failure. If our concept of quality—quality service, quality products—is good and correct then we gain customers. And, as we gain customers we begin to overload our system. And, as we overload our system, we begin to run into quality service problems. So, if you're a brand new bank and you have one customer, you can give that customer spectacular quality. But, as a small community bank we have 165,000 customers. If we have 195,000 customers, it overloads the whole system. So the reason that I don't think that there are national leaders from a quality point of view is that the system itself really begins to destroy it. Only if you're an airline—everyone looks to Delta as a quality leader in terms of what they do. You can only put a finite number of people on a plane. You can only put a finite number of people through a turnstile at an airport. We have to find ways of off-loading our people and giving them quality service through those products that are not necessarily part of our present mix and those products that do not necessarily happen within our facility all the time. I can't say that nationally anyone that I can think of stands out for quality service the way certain organizations in certain industries would stand out for quality service.

I don't think that quality is the only way to survive. If you're the low-cost producer, people will put up with a reasonable amount of drudgery in order to buy your product at the lower price, or in banking at the higher price, depending on which product you're selling. It's difficult to become the low-price producer in this industry, because there's no technological magic in it, and the products are interchangeable.

NOLAN: Is there a corporate mission statement that all the employees see that relates to quality, or that brings quality into the focus, and supporting value statements about it, supporting philosophies about your mission statement?

JOHNSON: There's a mission statement. How deep in the organization it gets, you never know. Quality is not spoken of in the word "quality" in the mission statement. It is referred to more in terms of attitudes and in terms of service levels and what we're trying to bring as far as our customer is concerned. So, we may talk about that we want our customers to be served the way that you would like to be served if you were in a similar position.

I think that there is a very clear understanding among most of the people in the organization about what we stand for and what's important to us. And, you would probably hear the word "people" used more frequently than any other word in terms of our feeling about how you treat people. How they are treated both as customers of the organization and as employees of the organization. So that quality doesn't kind of hang out there as a single sign. It is blended in, it's like a salad dressing on top of a salad. But all the pieces are there—the quality permeates the whole thing—intricately part of the taste, but it's not one of the pieces that gets the most focus. If I look at the mission statement, it would be nice to say, "Our most valued asset is our consumer's trust," which is true. The difficulty is that for a very hard-driving organization, there are multiple consumers.

NOLAN: Should a focus on the people, the customers, be part of the orientation of new employees?

JOHNSON: It already is there. It's not as clearly defined and delineated as it should be, but it's getting better all the time.

NOLAN: If you had to look at the components of planning, improvement, or control of quality, what do you think that you have to improve most in the next year?

JOHNSON: Well, something that you haven't mentioned. And that is that, I don't think that quality stands out there alone at the end of the branch without friends on the tree. It's tied together in a total program, and part of the program that we're working the hardest on now is to find and set up compensation plans that reemphasize the concept of quality. And very carefully, surgically underline quality as an objective of an operating department, and then tie dollars to the accomplishment of that goal. And that is a very, very difficult thing to do from an operating point of view. In reviewing a plan on Friday, the second measurement was number of customer complaints. A pure mathematical measurement of the number of times that customers either write or call in order to complain about a particular problem. You can't just talk about it, it has to become part of the system—people have to believe it. And, with a fairly heavy turnover in individuals, it's hard to make sure that your beliefs are well in place. It's like a minister or a priest with a new congregation every three months, and you don't know whether their foundation is the same as the foundation of your prior flock. So you have to start all over again talking about the fundamentals, and when you talk about the fundamentals you're boring some individuals as you're bringing the others up to speed.

NOLAN: You bring up a good point about the customer complaints. A recent poll, actually a survey done throughout the country on customer complaints, found that only 4 percent of the people that are dissatisfied with customer service actually complain about it, and the 96 percent are the ones who are moving their business. The silent majority.

JOHNSON: We usually figure one to a hundred—if I get one complaint letter, a hundred people are unhappy about it. That's fairly close. There's a tremendous number of people who will never pick up the phone, and when they do they're tremendously frustrated. And when they finally work their way through the system and get to me, they're really frustrated. They'll take it out on the teller, or the branch manager, or a clerk in the department, or someone else before they finally get so frustrated—and it has to be a very aggressive person that finally picks up the telephone book, looks for my number, calls me personally and says, "I've got a problem with your bank." The nice part about this is, I'm here, I answer my phone, they're surprised when they get hold of me as easily as they get hold of me. And, what they usually need at that time is someone to listen to their problems and to be understanding about their problems, and very frequently they're right. And if they're right we try to correct it in order to make a change.

NOLAN: Where do you think that you will have to focus on improvement to reduce the overall complaints? Are the problems system-driven, or human driven?

JOHNSON: Our problems rest more probably with the human-driven component, which in some ways is more difficult to solve, but it's more of a challenge.

NOLAN: Since you started the quality process in operations and now it's moved into the branches, is there a visible change in employee's attitudes?

JOHNSON: I don't know. I think that the whole program is the best program that I've been involved in in 25 years in banking. We wouldn't be doing it if we didn't think it was sensational. It also fit absolutely perfectly philosophically with what I wanted to do on a long-term basis. And, I am absolutely committed to making the program work. We'll do anything to make the program work, because you can't spend that amount of money, go through it, and then put it on a shelf.

NOLAN: If you had to look at the areas of timeliness, accuracy, courtesy, attitudes, or knowledge, do you have a feel for one of those as being an area for improvement for you?

JOHNSON: There's no place that is super good or super bad, and there is no category that is worse or better than the others. We get spurts of brilliance, but that's probably true of any organization, whether it's well motivated or not, that all of a sudden someone will do something spectacular. I'd like to think that our attitudes are bringing it on with greater frequency, with greater intensity, with better understanding of what we're doing, but golly, an organization is very much like a summer garden—the weeds are cropping up all the time and you go through and you weed it and it looks perfect, and all you have to do is turn your head for even a moment, and the weeds are back. And, if you leave that garden for the whole summer, you will not recognize it as a garden when you come back. And all that analogy is designed to do is to say that the concept of management is one that requires constant attention all the time, with a high degree of vigilance.

Leaders change direction, and you can see examples of that all the time in the restructuring of American corporations where there will be a particular sense of leadership that's coming from one person. And I would ask, would Chrysler be different without Lee Iaccoca? Would American Motors have been different without George Romney being there for a period of time? Leadership, and I happen to believe in the cult of leadership, to me is the single most important ingredient in the course of an organization's period of time under that leader. Harry Gray drove United Technology to be the company that it was. It's a very different company today than it was under Harry Gray. You take any forceful American leader either in a major corporation or in smaller companies and you change that mix, you change the corporation overnight. You don't embed in the concrete of the walls the goals and objectives of the prior leader. You plaster it on the wall like wallpaper, and it comes off when the guy or the woman leaves. And it has to be reapplied, and the wonderful part about it is it can be reapplied. There is enough flexibility in the mind of the corporation to allow it to change. And I think that's one of the things that's great about it.

NOLAN: How do you feel about organizations that use an outside psychologist to develop testing for incoming people, to see if the people that they're getting are going to fit with the company, and whether they should be in customer positions or not?

JOHNSON: I think it can be helpful. I've worked for an organization that did that to a degree. I think it's helpful as long as it isn't taken to extremes.

NOLAN: Instead of starting from a corporate level and driving quality that way, you started out as a pilot basis. Was that done because you wanted to see that it would work first and fit with the culture; or was it done because there wasn't full agreement among the senior management staff on whether it should be accomplished companywide or not?

JOHNSON: I wanted to check out the consultant's capability. It was neither cultural nor an issue of agreement. You don't construct the entire village until you've had an opportunity to build one of the houses. It was a discreet test in an area that made sense.

System Versus Service

You ask what kind of system do we need, but we can't answer that question. We've got to tell you what kind of service we need.
    —A. R. (Jim) McMurrich, Vice-President, Sun Financial Group

NOLAN: Does Sun Life of Canada look to a leader in the industry and say, "Now there's a company that really has it together, and that's what we would want to pattern ourselves after?"

McMURRICH: Well, I think the companies that I know of as leaders, although I don't know as much about them as I would like to, are Fidelity,

American Express, and USAA. I've read more about Fidelity and American Express in general than I have about USAA.

NOLAN: Did you talk to people in other organizations about how they addressed improving service, or did you really come to a meeting of the minds with your senior managers and say "Here's what we think we should be doing next, based on reading and knowledge of what's going on in the market?"

McMURRICH: Well, I think it was a bit of both and quite a lot of talking with the Temple, Barker, and Sloan [TBS] people.

NOLAN: Have you defined service as an organization?

McMURRICH: We have not, and I think we'll get that as a by-product of our current work with TBS. We've had enough waves of one kind or another around here in terms of planning waves, or expense-cutting waves, or this wave or that wave, and I'm very skeptical of kind of throwing some words up on the wall and saying, "This is the new regime," without having something that's tangible and real that we are working with that reflects it.

NOLAN: Has someone been assigned responsibility for directing the new emphasis on service?

McMURRICH: What we've done is to put together for the purposes of the project a team of associates of three full-time people. We have a new person we just hired who has a customer service background, with the telephone company, no insurance background at all, to basically run one of the regional operations where the telephone company is doing the full range of services that they offer on a residential and business basis. And he is in charge of the service of the project. We have another guy who's been with us a year and a half, he's doing a good job for us. He's handling the management controls side of things. And we have someone who had been the manager of our monthly billing area who knows the nuts and bolts of that operation upside down and inside out. These three people are on the project full time. On the service dimension, the control dimension, and overall knowledge dimension. They'll be working with two people from TBS to put together the plans for the service control job design.

NOLAN: Do you coordinate that with Canada, or are you looked at as an autonomous group?

McMURRICH: We coordinate with Canada to the extent that we're dealing with systems matters. But, it's an interesting commentary on the emerging role of service as an entity in the insurance business that there is no formal service reporting tie to our corporate head office in Toronto. We have direct ties on all the various functional aspects—the actuarial, product development, systems, investments, agency, and all that kind of stuff, but when you mention the word "service,' you get told to, "Go do it yourself." It's a whole new concept for the organization. In order to develop a lot of the background that we need to make the kinds of systems commitments that we're going to have to make and that the organization is positioning itself to make, we had to basically develop a concept of service, which we did through a paper we wrote about a year ago and say, "You ask us what kind of system do we need, but we can't answer that question, we've got to tell you what kind of service we need." And, here's the kind of environment in which we see it developing and the kinds of interaction we see people having with customers. In the future we're going to have to put together a blueprint that satisfies the definition that you're looking for, although it's not something that we threw up on the wall.

NOLAN: How did you go about putting that paper together?

McMURRICH: The initiative came from one of the guys in Toronto who's now the president of the company. He said, "What do we need to replace our computer systems? Would you please put together an international group of people to look at this?" I said, "I'd be glad to, but can we step back and look at service instead of systems?" He said, "Fine." So I got three groups of people put together. One to be a blue sky group, which we called the service re-quirements group, to set up what are the service issues we're going to have to come to grips with. The second group we called the service delivery group. The big question there is how are we going to do it? What is the or-ganization roughly going to look like? It's far down the line, but we envisage an organization that is much more people-driven than systems-driven. Which is what we think our organization is now. So we thought that through, and then we wanted to have an organization where basically 90 percent of the basic service requests could be handled by what we consider to be our pri-mary front-line position. It could be done by telephone or by written corre-spondence. We also thought we had to have a split in our service that we called scheduled service, such as billing or annual reports, where we could have a different mix between the people side of it and the flexibility side of it, and the cost equation. We envisage there being the front-line service troops, and the customer-initiated service and scheduled service organiza-tion as being the two ways in which we deliver service. Then we needed to have an education and training component to help us keep the people up to their fighting strength and fighting trim, and we needed to have a technology group to keep both of the service things properly supported, and we needed to have what we call the "service management" component to really provide the customer thinking and the line of services that would attract the com-petition's and measure how we're doing with service and be sure the cus-tomer is satisfied. The whole customer marketing, customer service side of things was the missing component from the current thinking on service, and really what was necessary to drive service into a front-line, competitive unit. We had to think it, we had to plan it, we had to make sure we're up there in the ring with the leaders, and if we're going to do that it's not by accident. If we focus primarily on equipping the front-line people and delivering service, equipping the scheduled service operation to address planning what should go where, that was it. So many other pieces of the general equation fell into place behind that—bringing your people right to the forefront of your business. Well, that does a tremendous amount for you in terms of involving them and driving their training straight through the business needs, instead of just kind of scratching your head and saying, "What do these people need to know?" Knowledge needs are driven by your business needs.

There were four of us who developed the strategy, and they're all still here. There are two from Canada and two from here. We're a long way from delivering that particular framework, and by the time we get there the framework may change. But, it gives us a target to go for. In particular, I think it gives us a much better feel for the people side of things, but it's a long process for us to get that under way.

NOLAN: You've taken a step that many organizations don't take; I fear that they lose that planning step, to understand what it really is. They decide that they're just going to go do it, and many of the companies that we've talked to have in fact put in quality circles, and put in suggestion programs for improving quality and service, and haven't thought it through—haven't strategized "what are we trying to accomplish with this, how do we involve the customer?"

McMURRICH: We still have to deliver on that. I think we're really in a position now where in the next six weeks I want to see up on the wall, "These are the services that our customers want us to deliver in the billing area. These are the processes by which we are going to deliver that service, and these are the elements by which we are going to know that that service has been delivered." And we're going to make sure that the customer knows that the service has been delivered and is happy, and here are the means by which we are going to control that process, and the service side of it, and the production side of it.

NOLAN: Do you eventually, or do you already have some form of control mechanism in place on those timeliness and accuracy issues?

McMURRICH: We have in one area, in basically our postservice sales area. I would say we don't really have any de facto service measurements at all, they're all productivity measurements. All the measurements are work counts, and work-on-hand, ins-outs. We don't measure service at all, not even a turnover measurement coming out of there. But in our New Business department we started about a year ago to develop what we consider to be service measurements: measuring the length of time that an application takes, from the time it gets here until the time it gets acknowledged back to the field, and measuring the time it takes from the time we have all the underwriting departments in-house until the time the decision is made, and measuring the time it takes from the time the decision is made until we have the policy in the mail. It took six months to get people to produce those statistics. I was practically dancing on table tops, and eventually I realized that the reason I had to do that was because people just didn't consider it to be important. They had their work count things; you know, they put out six hundred policies last week and the week before they only put out five hundred, so things are looking up. We're getting more of a focus on error prevention, I think. People are realizing that that's one of the reasons that they've got so much on their desk tops.

NOLAN: Who do your service people see as the customer?

McMURRICH: They see primarily policyholders as customers. The TBS people have told us that people in our administrative areas see the agents as being basically no different from anybody else from another department who's screaming out to get something done. Policyholders they look at as being legitimate customers, but we apparently haven't done a good enough job of selling the agents as customers. Probably not a good enough job in breaking down our internal departmental barriers, either.

NOLAN: When you start the improvement process that is a big breakthrough—for people to identify their customer.

McMURRICH: I think that that's one of the key things that we want to address in the training—to fill in all the gaps between the two extremes that we've got. I think we're going to build in better knowledge of where the department fits in relation to the whole. But if you have a thought-through program that gives people a feel for what the business is intending to do and where their role fits into it, and how the agent fits into it, how the policyholder fits into it, then they'll act that way. They'll act as if they know it. And here again, you get right back to the human resources side— can we truly depend on graduates of the local high schools to act that way, or should we be looking for different kinds of people? Where do we recruit our people from? Do we recruit them from places we should be recruiting them from? Maybe not.

NOLAN: What we've seen with some organizations is a reluctance to think of timeliness from the customer's standpoint. Timeliness is viewed as an internal component rather than an external component. Are the measurements typically when we receive them and when they leave the door?

McMURRICH: Oh, most definitely. Not just internal, but departmental. Sometimes it's internal desk top to desk top. If we get something in our reinstatement department that needs to go over to our math department for some calculations; as soon as the math department gets it written out and it goes to the out box, then it's not mine anymore—it's theirs. They're the ones who are taking six weeks to do it, not me—that kind of thing.

NOLAN: How do you feel about recognition and reward for people once you get your service strategy in place and you're starting to look at the human element?

McMURRICH: I'm not all that happy with the traditional job grading and compensation practices for that. I've been doing some reading lately on skill-based pay and the concepts of paying people for what they know and what they're capable of doing, as opposed to paying people for the job they osten-

sibly do. I find that the whole idea of committing jobs to paper in bureaucratic detail is unnecessary. To run some of these job point systems just
doesn't wash with the way you want people to do jobs. Nor does it wash with
the flexibility that you want to have in terms of advancing people. Why not
start it, perform job descriptions or perform them at a point in time and then
they move on and the job stays in the same place. How do you reward someone in a context like that? I think you've got to be prepared to reward people
as they develop, as they move to another rung on the job ladder, or you'll be
spending half your life writing job descriptions. And that's what happens.

NOLAN: You've been stressing the human relations or human resource
aspects of service improvement and quality. Is there today a strong em-
ployee-orientation process that will give people the feeling of what the
company stands for and what is expected of them before they get into
departments?

McMURRICH: That is something that we recognize and it's a problem
that we've got to address. It's done sporadically. Some departments do it
well, a couple of people in my administrative organization started to have
new employee functions, where we bring them in and tell them about the
area and have different managers put on talks, and those have been very
successful and very much appreciated by the employees. Generally, the
training responsibility has been handled at a departmental level, which we
firmly believe is at this point the wrong level to handle it at. We've got to
be looking at training as a top-level issue that I think we've got to have. It's
like having your eyes opened rather wide—where have we been?

Agents' Feelings about Consistency of Processing Time

> Don't make it ten days this week and forty days next week. They have
> trouble getting attuned to that.
> —Paul Snyder, Senior Vice-President—Finance and Administration, Re-
> liance Insurance Company

NOLAN: How did you decide that quality was going to be a strategic
issue?

SNYDER: We made a decision in 1983 that we were going to move the
processing for all of our policies out of the branch environment and create
service centers. So, in our profit center and also in the other Reliance
subsidiaries, service centers were created. Our profit center encompasses
the 27 Eastern states. We set up four service centers—in Dallas, Texas;
Durham, North Carolina; Columbia, Maryland; and King of Prussia, Pennsylvania. We had hoped that we would get plenty of willing people from
our branch offices who would transfer into the service centers, so that we
really would not lose that much in terms of experience. It didn't work out
that way. We found that people from Canandaigua, New York, and

Albany, New York, and Boston weren't willing to move to King of Prussia. So we ended up having to hire people in the King of Prussia area, in the Durham area, totally inexperienced in insurance. We got some people from other companies, but we ended up having to do a lot of training. That, in addition to the fact that the people who were running this profit center at the time, thought that they could run a service center that has somewhere between 200 and 250 people in the same way, with the same control systems, with the same work flows that they used in a branch, which would have been maybe one-fifth of the size. In a branch environment, if somebody lost a file, they'd yell across the room and Susie over there would have the file and they'd get together. In a service center, where we've got somewhere between eight and ten thousand files out on the floor at any point in time, you obviously need different systems to control the process. We didn't have that. So we created somewhat of a mess for ourselves, and it took a couple of years to work through it. In October or November of 1985 we were starting to see ourselves emerging from the initial crisis, but we recognized that we were still not doing things as well as we should be doing them. We were clearing the backlog, but we still weren't getting policies out on time the way we should. When we did get them out a lot of times the price would be wrong, the insured's name would be spelled wrong—things like that. The other problem that we had, and it's a real problem in the insurance industry obviously, is that our statistical coding was not accurate. So, my boss said to me, "I'd really like us to develop a culture sort of like Frito-Lay, where no bag sits on a rack for more than twenty-four hours. Where people really start to take a much stronger interest in their job and doing it right the first time. And also, that they are almost evangelical in their desire to please the customer—that would be part of the change in culture as well." He asked me to change the culture as quickly as I could. I spent several weeks at the end of 1985 reading up on who the quality gurus were—reading about Deming, and I happened to come across the Crosby book, and I think I felt that the Crosby concepts really fell in with our organization and, to some extent meshed with my boss's orientation. Deming is so much aimed at quality control and collecting statistics, it doesn't really give you the impression that people get much fun out of what they're doing. It's a very scientific, mechanized approach. My boss believes in people having fun, you know, you get people caught up in things, recognizing of course that the quality concept should be implemented as a process and not as a program that's a short-term thing. So, I saw some of that in the Crosby fourteen steps—the idea of having a zero defects day, and close down the plant for half a day and have people come in and make speeches. You know, you have posters on the wall and the recognition step is something that I knew he would be totally in concert with. So I talked to the Crosby people and I decided that that was the direction that we should go in. We embarked on the process, I guess in our field management meeting in January 1986. Ray Hafner and I put on a presentation where we showed Crosby's film, "The Quality Man," and we talked about the fourteen steps. We really kicked it off at that time. It moved slowly in 1986, we really didn't get a whole lot done until we were able to get all of our senior officers down to the Quality College in September 1986. Ray went out to all of our field locations and started talking about the fourteen steps, almost in a "it's coming, it's coming" type of way. We're at the stage now where we have developed our own alternative to Crosby's education, focused just on our company and focused on insurance, with specific case studies that relate to us. We've put together what I think is a pretty good course. We just piloted it this week and we got some pretty good feedback on it. It involves case studies; problem situations where people have to get together and figure out how they would solve them. We've actually done some videos of a problem situation and after people view the skit they go back to a workshop and figure out how to solve the problems, or what's wrong with this insurance company. We've also, as a result of our going down to the Quality College, got a boost toward setting up a Steering Committee, so we have a Steering Committee which is made up of the president's staff. It's basically all the senior vice-presidents, and we get together every other Friday for breakfast for an hour and we talk about the quality process, what each other is doing, running the process overall.

NOLAN: How much of the company does that encompass?

SNYDER: That's a good question. There is some overlap, because we have different quality improvement teams that have different objectives. For instance, to get back to the service centers, we have a quality improvement team whose principal priorities would relate to the timely and accurate processing and generation of policies. And in a case like that, that's not just administrative people who have to sit on that quality improvement team, but it's also the underwriting people, because the underwriters were the people that were our suppliers. The underwriters in the branch are the ones that took the original application and wrote up the worksheet and sent it into the service center. So, we have a mix of some underwriters, some administrative people on that particular regional quality improvement team. We also have some branch managers, because then they can hear what the problems are, or at least they can play a role in discussing what they might be doing at the branch level that's resulting in a policy not coming out accurately. We continue to follow the Crosby concept in that the team would not actually resolve problems, they would talk about their priorities and decide when they've got problems who should go out and resolve them. So they would set up a corrective action team, a CAT, and it might involve somebody from the typing department or an underwriter from one of the branches, etc. They go out and work on the problem and come back and report to the quality improvement team. Now, an underwriter who might be assigned to that team might also be part of the underwriting discipline quality improvement team, which would go down from the home office to the field level and include people all the way up the ladder. Maybe one of their priorities is, "How do we get underwriting guidelines out effectively to the field?" All together I would say we have maybe 300 people on quality improvement teams of some sort. All the claim officers have quality improvement teams. As a percentage that would be about 15 percent on the quality improvement teams. The message is getting out. We have a quality newsletter called QED, we've done several quality videos that the president or other people have done which can be shown on a VCR out in the field. So we are communicating with people, but it's really going to be when this training takes hold, which will apply to every-body in the company, that people will totally understand what the quality process is. I would have liked it to have moved a little faster. But it took us a while to develop a good training program. We didn't want to jump into it too fast and do a slipshod job. We have to follow our own concepts there.

NOLAN: When you did research on this, did you talk to any of your peers in the industry? Is there any one company out there that you think has it all together in terms of quality and that you'd want to pattern yourself after?

SNYDER: No, there is not. I talked to people at Air Products. They weren't sure exactly what direction they wanted to go. I talked to people at Campbell Soup, they felt the same way. I went down and met with the people at Rohm and Haas. But it seemed as if most of the companies I talked to were so new into the concept, and I usually asked the question, "Have you really seen the fruits of the process yet?" And the answer was, "No we haven't—I can't quantify for you that it's working." So I didn't think anybody was really far enough along with measurable successes that they could say, "Yes, this is absolutely the right approach that we've taken." I felt that I was in a little bit of a quandary, but that everybody else wasn't quite sure either. And certainly in the insurance industry, we did talk to some people at Hartford. I did read some things about Paul Revere, and I had read something about New York Life, that they had done some things with quality. But I couldn't find very much on P&C companies doing anything.

NOLAN: If quality is so important, you recognize that it's an important issue, what does that say about the industry—that there aren't any leaders out there?

SNYDER: Well, it says first of all that our industry has not been listening to its customers. It also says that our industry is missing some big oppor-tunities, or individual companies are missing some big opportunities. We're not absolutely sure whether it will give us a competitive advantage, but I certainly believe that it will. My job here is to try to get us to the point, to prove to everybody that it will get us a competitive advantage. It's inter-esting. We've been going through a program where we bring agents in from each of our branches for a couple of days. And we give them a chance to meet home office people that they wouldn't normally meet—they might meet some people from the Claims Department and they talk about reserving processes, and they spend a couple of hours with the actuaries, and they spend time with people like me talking about the quality of this service center. I met with the agents from Louisville a couple of days ago, and I asked them whether they were happy with the service they were getting from the central service center. They said, "It's definitely improved over where it was two years ago." We're in the process of having a survey done by Yankelovich, which used to be one of our subsidiaries, on agent preferences and I've worked a couple of questions into that survey about service. Is it important to get a policy in 21 days? Is it important to get it in 30 days? You know, what are the hot buttons. I think one of the things that I've heard initially is that they're looking for consistency more than speed. In other words, if you're going to get it to them in 21 days, well that's fine, they can get used to that. But, don't make it ten days this week and 40 days next week, because they have trouble getting attuned to that. If it's the same time consistently, they can adjust to that. But, clearly I believe companies are missing opportunities from a customer service standpoint. We've still got a problem of being inefficient in our industry. When we went into this we got some estimates of how much rework we have in our service centers from service center managers. And they all thought that 25 to 30 percent was a reasonable number. Experts say 40 percent for service industries. So obviously we're missing some real opportunities there, by not getting people to do things right the first time internally.

NOLAN: Do you feel that there are missing pieces in the process at this point?

SNYDER: After I went through the training I thought to myself, "The piece that's missing here is the customer service piece." I think it's implied, that if you get to the point where you've got zero defects, your customer service is going to be superb, and nobody will ever call and say, "Where's my policy?" because you got it to them sooner than they were expecting it. But in the real world you're going to have some policies drop through the crack, and things are going to get lost, or you're going to get them wrong, and agents are going to call and say, "Where is it?" and you have to teach your people how to be responsive, how to deal with that situation when people call. You can make up for a lot if you're courteous and responsive when somebody calls, and you get back to them within 24 hours and you fix the problem, whatever it is. That's one piece that I thought was missing from Crosby. And that's what I absolutely wanted built into our in-house training program, and we've done that. When we hired new people in the service centers, we were trying to train them how to do the basic things, how to enter a premium, how to settle a claim, and we didn't have time to get into more subtle things like how to deal with customers. So I think it's just a question of telling people, "This is the way I want you to act." We're doing that now, and we're doing some things with phone etiquette—I think we can make progress pretty quickly.

NOLAN: It goes even further back—to the hiring.

SNYDER: Well, there's two pieces to it. That brings to mind another thing that the Quality Steering Committee decided we absolutely had to do, and that was to build into the performance evaluation process an evaluation of how someone has participated in the quality process. We have a standardized matrix that you fill out when you do a performance review—a different one for clerical versus managerial versus officer. We've actually filled in some specific questions on participation within the quality process, so that it becomes increasingly visible to people and they understand that their performance to some extent is going to be evaluated based on their participation in the quality process. And, our CEO asked each of the division managers to have a specific quality objective within their 1987 objectives.

NOLAN: Is that published down to a level where the employees will see it?

SNYDER: I don't know. I'm not sure it does get down to the lowest level. I think we expect that through the training and through all this orientation that Ray has done, he's convincing people that we are absolutely committed to it. But I think we expect each of the division managers to try to get the message across. I don't know if you saw the quality statement that we have out in the reception area. It's a little plaque. "We promise to do things right the first time and in compliance with standards, and if we find that there is no standard we will set a standard." And that's really the way I had our divisional managers set their goals for 1987—set their quality objective. I asked them that, number one, they should encourage everyone in their division to participate in the quality process—if there's a quality improvement team, you encourage people to participate in that. But then, I think they also have to look at all the functions that they're performing in their division, and each of those functions has to have a standard. If it's settling a claim, how quickly are we going to settle the claim? If we're getting a policy out, let's set a standard—do we want it out in 20 days? 21 days? And then, develop a means of monitoring whether we're complying with that standard or not complying with that standard. If you sit and think about it in different divisions, there's all kinds of different tasks that we do, and maybe nobody ever sat down and said, "Okay, let's establish a standard here. How quickly should we do it?" That's really the way we're approaching the objectives.

NOLAN: How much further do you need to expand measurement?

SNYDER: Well, certainly I want to get to the point where I can start surveying agents, going beyond what Yankelovich is doing, asking in more detail what they need and what they perceive. As I said with some of the agents, it's frustrating for me when I think, based on our internal documentation we're doing well, and they say that our service is only average.

It's actually quite discouraging. But I also went on to say to them that the problem we have is of perception, because I'm sure on nine out of ten policies we got them out to you on time, but in the back of your mind is that one that took 60 days. That's what I've got to fix.

NOLAN: What you're pointing to is the consistency issue. If you get the consistency and control then you're not going to have the problem. What we talk about is, it's no good to have a spurt—you get a spurt of great service, you set new expectations. And then what happens is if you fall off from that you look like you're going backwards.

SNYDER: I believe that we actually have to be even more proactive in reinforcing those perceptions. And the way I intend to do that is, when we get to the point where we're totally satisfied that we are being pretty consistent, then to some of our key agents we may be sending a notice from time to time saying, "Based on our internal statistics over the last quarter, we got policies out to you within X number of days. Would you please let us know if that's not correct, because we want to make sure that our internal statistics are right. And if you had a problem with any particular policy that maybe we're not aware of, please let us know." So I think it'll be bringing it to their attention, and they'll say, "That's pretty good turnaround time and I can't think of any case that would jeopardize the credibility of that data, so they must be doing a good job." That's the piece that we have to do, instead of just sitting and hoping that their perception is going to change, I think we have to prod it along.

NOLAN: How do you feel about reward and recognition for your people who have made improvements?

SNYDER: We have the first annual president's quality dinner scheduled for Friday night. We have asked each of our regional vice-presidents to name three people—we gave them some criteria that were agreed to by the Steering Committee that should be used to judge the participants, and customer service was clearly one of them, but also an inclination to do things right the first time, somebody who did have perfectionist tendencies and tried to approach things from a prevention standpoint. We asked them to nominate three people from each of the regions and we nominated three people out of the home office, so we've got fifteen people coming to Philadelphia for the quality dinner. These are not officers and managers; these are middle-level people and a lot of clerical people. They're coming in here Friday around noon and will spend a couple of hours in the afternoon with the president of the company in the Board Room talking about quality, then we'll have a big cocktail party for them at 4:00 upstairs with all the officers of the company. We're flying them in; they'll bring spouses with them, and we're having a dinner over at the Four Seasons—it's going to be a big deal. We think that people are pretty excited about this, the people who have been selected. We had some tough choices to make, there were some cases that were a little close in deciding who would come. From what I've heard so far, we've picked the right people and we're certainly going to give it a lot of press. We have some tremendous video people in the company, so we'll do a video magazine on the whole event. We'll get that out to the field, and we have this QED newsletter that we publish monthly, so we'll really give visibility to the whole concept. I think that's going to go a long way toward meeting the recognition step.

NOLAN: Is everyone on the senior management team sold on the whole thrust of the Quality Steering Committee and what you're trying to accomplish?

SNYDER: I think generally they're sold on it. I don't know if Ray showed you another tape that we had shown at our field management meeting in Scottsdale this past November. That would have been like ten months after we originally kicked off the process. What we did was, one morning at our quality breakfast we had each of the guys, via tape, talk about the experience down at the Quality College and talk about their perception of the whole quality process, because they felt that they had to sell it to the people in the field to some extent, and that's what this video was aimed at doing. I think some of them said they went into it thinking that it applied only to processing and not necessarily to some of the other disciplines in the company, but after going through Crosby they had come to realize that there really were some leverage opportunities in the other disciplines, in underwriting and claims. I think everybody believes that it's a worthwhile concept. Absolutely.

NOLAN: That helps. When everyone is at a point when they believe in it then you start to see the attitudes change below them, and you get people to feel that this is a quality organization.

SNYDER: Well, one of the things that we continue to test, and you do this when you go down to the Quality College, the first ten minutes that you're there they give you a little quiz in which you're asked to evaluate your company, and there are questions like, "How do you perceive management's commitment to quality in your company?" and "How do you perceive the commitment to quality of your peers or other employees in the organization?" And, we've started doing the same thing in the training that we're doing right now. And so far, we're getting pretty good feedback on management's commitment. Ray mentioned to me the other day that what surprised him was that people weren't sure of the commitment of the other employees. People were saying, "Well I believe that it's a good idea, but I'm not sure that the guys that I work with are really that committed to it." But it's something that we've got to keep reinforcing, keep reinforcing. I won't give up, and I don't think my boss will give up. As long as we keep building it into the objectives every year we're not going to let people forget.

NOLAN: You mentioned your quality newsletter earlier. How much resource does it take to produce it?

SNYDER: Well, one of the things that we decided we really needed was somebody working full time on the communication piece. We have a writer, our communications guy didn't have the resources to devote full time to it, but we've got a writer coming in a couple days a week, a professional writer. He writes our newsletter, wrote the scripts for some of the skits that we've done within the training program; anything else that needs communication in an effective manner to the field he writes for us.

NOLAN: Did this professional writer go through the Quality College as well to get a feel, or just talk to people?

SNYDER: I don't think we actually sent him through the college, but we really put him through a pretty good indoctrination. We've had him read all the books, and I think he's pretty well up to speed at this point.

NOLAN: Is new employee orientation part of one of these videos?

SNYDER: Well, I don't think we're actually using a video yet for the employee orientation on quality, but we do give them material and explain the process. And that's something we need to do a little more with.

NOLAN: Where do you want to spend the most energy improving the quality process in the next two years?

SNYDER: I think I want to continue working with the quality improvement teams and get them to keep their enthusiasm going and keep looking for problems to solve. Intuitively I believe that successes are coming about. And, people think that they have been able to play a role in changing the way they do things at their level of the organization.

NOLAN: How do you get the teams started—appoint them?

SNYDER: Well, generally, Ray has gone out and spent the first couple of sessions with them, defining priorities more than anything else. Now, in the individual divisions, the division manager basically establishes, or helps to establish what the priorities are. He'll say to his quality improvement team, "These are the things that to me are problem areas." And then maybe we'll have somebody come in with some data. We had lots of data that the VP of administration who reports to me had, on how long it was taking us to get a policy out the door, we measured it at every stage of the process so we knew that maybe it was taking ten days in typing and only two days in entry. Well, typing is obviously the problem. We had enough data so we could lay a lot of data in front of the quality improvement team and say, "Okay, here's our priority. Here's some data that we've got, now go for it. Give us some ideas. Where should we go? Do you want to appoint a CAT team? How do you want to approach this?"

NOLAN: Have you attended any of the major quality conferences, like IAQC or ASQC?

SNYDER: No.

NOLAN: I'm just curious about what other kinds of things influence you other than reading.

SNYDER: Talking to consultants. The Philadelphia Chamber of Commerce has sponsored several Deming talks over the last couple of years, and we've sent people out to those. Ray has gone. To be honest with you, we have so many ideas on things that we can be doing right now—we don't need to go out and get any more ideas. Now, we've got to execute them. Right now we've got to do the blocking and tackling type of things. And there's plenty to be done there. Just getting people to answer the telephone right, and get that customer service attitude—there's a way to go there.

I think we may be out in front of the rest of the P&C industry. I don't read very much about other P&C companies either going down to the Quality College or affiliating with consulting firms. I feel like we're out in front.

On Measuring the Customer's Perception

> We use a policyholder survey. We also have simply stated in our objectives as having a national survey like *Consumer Reports* be in the top 20 percent.
> —Eugene Meyung, President, GEICO Insurance Company

NOLAN: What led you to decide that quality was a key strategic element?

MEYUNG: It's pretty simple. There are several independents, *Consumer Reports*, for example, that do surveys on insurance company service. Many years ago, before GEICO got into financial trouble in 1975 and '76, GEICO scored very high in the *Consumer Reports*, right up at the top of the list. After GEICO got into financial trouble the first thing was to get the company back into operation. We've done that. We're probably in as solid financial shape as anybody in the country, we are regularly turning out 30 percent return on equity, which nobody else in the world is doing, but in the course of all the trauma and the things that we had to do, well, we fell from grace in the eyes of the people who were sending their questionnaires to *Consumer Reports*. Then there's another survey called "checkbook." We didn't fare very well there either. We made it the company objective as one of our operating principles. One goal in that objective was to get in the top 20 percent in any nationwide survey.

NOLAN: Then it stemmed from the feedback through those things?

MEYUNG: Yes. We had used the outside service, and the results we were getting back from them looked like we were doing pretty well. That was the thing that really triggered us. We don't want to be in the bottom fourth. We want to be certainly in the top 20 percent. We figure it's going to take us five years to get there.

NOLAN: When did you set this up as an objective?

MEYUNG: We did two things. We have an elaborate business plan in process. Planning centers—that would be level three plans—we go all the way down to level five. We have objectives in our business plan. We also have a set of operating principles which the objectives in our business plan parallel. Now, our operating principles were disciplined balance sheet, underwriting profit, low cost operator, and invest for total returns, which is different from most insurance companies—they invest for investment income. What we did was added to our four operating principles a fifth one—specifically related to service. We added that in at the bottom, then we moved it up to the top this past November. Tracking those operating principles are objectives in our business plan. We moved the service objective to the first one in our business plan.

NOLAN: When you did that, did you assign it a corporate responsibility?

MEYUNG: We operate through six profit centers. The profit centers have the objective in their business plan to have specific goals.

NOLAN: They are trying to tie it back to the principles that you have developed?

MEYUNG: They put the plan together and we have a very elaborate challenge session where we go through and challenge everything that they have in there. During our challenge sessions your wife's liable not to see you for two weeks. We have 26 planning centers, but we have six profit centers. Many of the planning center managers challenge other people. Everybody challenges everybody else. So if anybody has a chicken goal then we have a rubber chicken award to give them. We parade the chicken around when someone has a goal that everybody thinks is not up to standard. So what happens is we have uniformity in our service goals, because it's based on the policyholder survey to reach certain levels. We have two such surveys.

NOLAN: Do those surveys determine the expectations and the perception or one of those two?

MEYUNG: This is perception of service. We ask you, if you've had a claim, was it paid promptly, was it handled properly, were you treated fairly?

NOLAN: Have you formally defined what quality and what service is other than the time service?

MEYUNG: I think we've defined it. We have all kinds of time and process standards. We've tightened those up, we've made some very dramatic changes. If someone calls in today and changes a car on a policy we'll probably have the change in the mail in seven or eight days, because we internally turn those things around on the average of 48 hours, instead of a goal of ten days or something like that. That's just an example. Inspecting a car, and this varies from area to area, but in this area we have a standard that says we'll inspect your car within three and a half working days 80 or 85 percent of the time. So we have all kinds of time and process standards.

NOLAN: How far down into the organization does your objective to improve and to work at quality and service go?

MEYUNG: Right now we're in the process of trying to impact a cultural change on the organization. We think it's a five-year deal. We certainly are attempting in every way we can to get our people to focus on the customer.

We have a profit-sharing plan and an ESOP plan, and a typical employee who's been here five years and has gotten the last four awards has probably somewhere in the neighborhood of between 65 or 70 percent as a stock interest in the company, 65 or 70 percent of whatever the current salary is, it's really snowballing. We really try to get our people to think like owners. Everybody should want this, but it's a slow process.

I worked for State Farm for 25 years before I came to GEICO. We used to teach at State Farm that we want people to do the work and to rely on themselves to get it right. There's an entirely different cultural attitude in this company because it has always been an authoritarian type company, and State Farm is just the opposite. People call the president of State Farm by his first name; the employees, the secretary calls him by his first name, the only time they call him Mr. is when there is an outside guest present. There was a whole different attitude in that company than there was in this one. Some of that is changing.

NOLAN: The industry's gone through some hard times in the last few years. Is there someone that stands out in your mind as being the top quality servicer?

MEYUNG: Well, the people that get the high marks are AMICA, USAA, and the top company that does a general national business is State Farm. USAA is a specialized company that writes Armed Services officers and former officers—they're a special company. So those are the people that score high in the *Consumer Reports* ratings, and State Farm is the highest one that does general business.

NOLAN: How about reward and recognition for people that come up with ideas that impact quality. Do you have a process?

MEYUNG: We have a thing called "Make It Easy"—make it easy to do business with GEICO. We have rewards for people, nominees, selections—and there are various levels and every year, periodically, we have an overall corporate winner. We have one for every region and so forth. That is one of the things that we do have. We also publish most of the complimentary letters we get in our company publication.

NOLAN: What do you do with the ones that are complaint letters?

MEYUNG: We have a fairly elaborate process when complaints come in. Profit center managers are supposed to review all complaints and then make sure that they are taken care of. I get complaints. I try to find out if there's a structural problem after we get the matter resolved. The most common complaints we get are for surcharges for accidents—that's the biggest number, the second one has to do with rate increases. Those are our two largest kinds of complaints.

NOLAN: We found by looking at a national survey that maybe 4 percent of the people that aren't happy complain.

MEYUNG: I think that's probably low for insurance companies. I think there's a much higher percentage of people that complain. There is so much in the consumer's movement, the insurance departments advertise for complaints and so forth. There is a study that I saw that a dissatisfied customer will tell ten people and somebody that feels they got great service might tell four.

NOLAN: The whole financial services industry has been taking some heat for quality and for service. Do you have any feelings on why it's taken the industry so long to focus on it and to come around to it?

MEYUNG: Well, I really think the only problem is that someone is buying an intangible and the only time they need service is when something bad happens to them. There's a certain emotional psychological attitude anyway, that makes it much more difficult. It's not like going around fixing washing machines. There's even been some studies done about people who get hit in the rear, they have certain emotional problems. So we're faced with dealing with those people right off, so it makes it really a tough row to hoe to start with.

NOLAN: Do you have a measurable way of looking at whether you've reached your service goals?

MEYUNG: Oh yes. Besides the things we do, the policyholder survey, we also have simply stated in our objective as defined is having a national survey like *Consumer Reports* be in the top 20 percent. But we've said we'll settle in 1987 with being in the top 50 percent. I'm not sure that's precisely it, but that's the way we're doing it. So we might say in 1988 the top 40 percent, and in 1989—they don't run that survey every year, but that's the way we would do it—to move up gradually.

NOLAN: Do you have some intangibles about the attitudes within the organization, what you would like them to be like in five years?

MEYUNG: Well, the only intangible is we'd like for people to act like they are owners. Treat the customers like they would if they were the owners of the company, which they are. Some employees now own a 6 or 7 percent of the company. One man owns 41 percent.

CHAPTER SUMMARY

There were several key points that came through clearly in almost every interview.

1. Quality is the most visible front for financial services companies to compete today. Not only is it the best alternative by which to differentiate, it is the hardest for a competitor to copy.

2. The leadership of the chief executive officer is crucial to success. Many companies say their president supports the effort. This is not enough. The president must be leading the charge and can't turn away from quality for an instant.

3. Training and orientation of every employee is associated with successful cultural

change. The training can be purchased or developed, but should be tailored to the specific company.

4. The customer is the key. Understanding the concept of customer takes work. It is not as simple as it sounds. Truly understanding the customer's expectations requires savvy.

5. Reward and recognition is a critical element, but should be refocused frequently. Failure doesn't come from introducing a recognition process that is ill-conceived. Failure comes when you stop trying to find ways to involve, recognize, and reward employees.

6. Quality improvement is a process. It evolves. A company that stops to smell success will be surpassed by companies who never see the finish line.

3   *Understanding and Achieving Quality*

UNDERSTANDING QUALITY

What Is Quality?

What exactly do we mean when we use the term "quality"? Is it something that we can touch, taste, or smell? Is it real and verifiable, or is it just a feeling we have about something? Are we talking about product quality or quality of service? Can we find a definition that suits everyone, or do each of us have to define it in our own way?

Webster's Dictionary defines quality simply as "degree of excellence." Excellence is defined as "very good of its kind." Combined, the definition would be something like "the degree of good of its kind."[1]

David Bain, author of *The Productivity Prescription*, says that "Quality is in the eye of the beholder. Most often it is a subjective, rather than objective, evaluation based primarily on personal preferences and feelings."[2] The more we study the word, the more we realize that it is very difficult to nail down. It appears to be like works of art. As we have heard so often, "we don't know much about it, but we know what we like when we see it." The same can be said about quality. Perhaps we can't define it, but we know it when we see it.

Product Quality

One way to attack the definition problem is to be more specific in the context in which we use it. For the purpose of this book we are concerned with quality as it relates to financial services institutions.

Unfortunately, narrowing the problem down to financial services institutions doesn't help as much as if we were talking about manufacturing companies. In manufacturing we think of quality in relation to the products produced.

For example, Mercedes-Benz automobiles have long been recognized as quality cars. Almost anyone can look at one and understand why. The style is classic, not flashy and doomed to obsolescence in a few years like many others. The paint is very smooth and thick. It radiates a luster that seemingly will not allow dust or dirt to stick to it. It makes us want to polish it and never drive it in bad weather. The interior is fine. It looks tastefully elegant and feels very comfortable, yet solid. The upholstery's stitching is done to exacting standards and we never see a loose end or an exposed wire inside the passenger compartment. The instruments and switches are engineered to be located in the right places for ease of use. The automobiles are a pleasure to drive. They challenge us to corner a little faster than we normally would and dare us to speed over bumps that would produce rattles in cars of lesser quality. Even the high price adds to its "quality" mystique. Surely a car so expensive must be costly to build. Owning one makes the owner feel special. Even if it is ten years old, driving it helps create the impression that we are affluent, have good taste, and recognize value. The cars hold their resale value better than most others. Here is a product that helps distinguish its manufacturer as a quality company.

Compare this to the manner in which we view quality in financial services companies. We don't automatically think of their products as we do with manufacturing companies. When was the last time that you admired your automobile insurance policy? Were you impressed with the texture of the paper that it was printed on? Perhaps you noticed the clear printing or the color of the ink. Have you ever gotten it out to show it off to your friends and neighbors? Maybe you had it framed and hung on a wall in your study. Likely not.

The nature of the financial services industry is that its products are mostly intangible. We can't see them. We can't feel, smell, or hear them. Until recently, most of the products were represented by pieces of paper with writing on them. Now that the world is becoming more and more automated, even the paper is disappearing. We seldom complete a withdrawal ticket at a bank anymore. Instead, we go to an automated teller machine and electronically complete the transaction. We don't complete forms to transfer money, we simply get on the telephone and punch in the changes. We even pay some of our bills in this manner, rather than the more traditional way of writing out checks and mailing them.

Underlying Value of Quality

Which is the true product, the physical automobile policy or the insurance coverage which it represents? Is the bank passbook savings account statement the product, or is it the safekeeping of the money and the investment that is tied to it? With investment firms, is the product the stock certificate or the investment it represents? Many of us have never seen our actual stock certificates. Our full service brokers keep them safe for us and simply inform us of their status on a periodic basis and whenever we buy or sell them.

The physical manifestation of a financial services company's product is seldom what we think of when we try to define quality. Granted, if it is of exceptionally poor quality because of typographical errors, misspellings, torn pages, incomplete or inaccurate data, and so on, it may negatively shape our image of the company's quality, but the chances are that this will not be the case. Most of these manifestations are fairly simple, or, and such is the case with an insurance policy, they contain somewhat standard verbiage that isn't changed much from one customer to the next. The real product is not the printed policy or the passbook, it is the insurance coverage or the security represented by the passbook.

Hence, one way quality can be defined in a financial services company is by looking at the underlying value its products provide. Does the automobile insurance policy provide enough coverage for the premium paid? In the event of an accident or other loss, does the company treat your claim fairly? When you purchase a bank's certificate of deposit, does the bank pay a competitive rate? Is it fair considering the risk you might face? Do you get expert advice from your broker when he sells you an investment? The commission paid should reflect the quality of the investment advice that is given.

Service Quality

Another element that is useful in defining quality in financial services organizations is that of levels of service. It is difficult to view service as a product because it has no physical being. Nonetheless, it is a product in and of itself. Karl Albrecht and Ron Zemke provide an excellent overview definition for service in their book *Service America—Doing Business in the New Economy*. They note that service has the following attributes:

1. A service is produced at the instant of delivery; it can't be created in advance or held in readiness.
2. A service cannot be centrally produced, inspected, stockpiled, or warehoused. It is usually delivered wherever the customer is, by people who are beyond the immediate influence of management.
3. The "product" cannot be demonstrated, nor can a sample be sent for customer approval in advance of the service; the provider can show various examples, but the customer's own haircut, for example, does not yet exist and cannot be shown.
4. The person receiving the service has nothing tangible; the value of the service depends on his or her personal experience.
5. The experience cannot be sold or passed on to a third party.

6. If improperly performed, a service cannot be "recalled." If it cannot be repeated, then reparations or apologies are the only means of recourse for customer satisfaction.

7. Quality assurance must happen before production, rather than after production, as would be the case in a manufacturing situation.

8. Delivery of the service usually requires human interaction to some degree; buyer and seller come into contact in some relatively personal way to create the service.

9. The receiver's expectations of the service are integral to his or her satisfaction with the outcome. Quality of service is largely a subjective matter.

10. The more people the customer must encounter during the delivery of the service, the less likely it is that he or she will be satisfied with the service.[3]

One interesting aspect of financial services institutions is that they do not fit the traditional mold of "pure service" companies. They fall somewhere in between the continuum with manufacturing on one end and pure service companies on the other. Using Albrecht and Zemke's service attributes as a guide we could form a list of financial service attributes:

1. Financial services companies produce products. They create insurance policies, IRA accounts, checking accounts, and so forth. However, they are unique because their customers don't use the products themselves on a day-to-day basis. Often, once the product is sold to the customer, it is never used again until it expires or matures. Unless the insured suffers a loss, or changes his address, the typical insurance policy is received in the mail and filed away for safekeeping. The same is true of most investment products. The chances are that the insured never even reads the actual policy, prospectus, or contract unless a problem develops while it is in effect.

2. Service, as it pertains to financial services companies, occurs almost always at the point of sale, sometimes at maturity or expiration, and sometimes in between. Since the actual product is not treated by the customer as a "real" product, the service accompanying it becomes a substitute for the real product. The customer's perception of the product is affected more by the services associated with it than by the physical product itself.

3. Products produced by financial services companies seldom differ from those of their competitors. Although the products are similar, the service associated with them can be significantly different.

4. There are relatively few opportunities (points of contact) for customers and financial services companies to communicate. Systems are established to minimize the need for human contact and, as long as the systems work effectively, customers and companies have little need for face-to-face contact.

5. Financial services companies lose customers more often because of poor service than because of poor products. Since the products offered in any market are so similar from company to company, customers are beginning to restabilize. Major new product development during the past few years produced a dramatic re-

shuffling in which customers left their old companies to choose the new products. For example, the development of the Universal Life and interest sensitive products had a dramatic effect on the insurance industry. Deregulation had a similar effect on the banking industry. However, things have settled down somewhat and customers have begun to realize that if a new feature is developed for a product, chances are that their company will soon offer it as an option to them. By the time it would take to complete the paperwork needed to shift companies, they could have the same benefits with their current company. Hence, customers seldom leave because of minor product innovations, unless they are dissatisfied with the attitude and service of their current company.

6. Competition in the financial services area is intense, and customers have become more demanding in their service interactions. They expect their company to satisfy their needs quickly and effectively. Failure to do so often results in the customer shifting to another company. One bad experience carries more weight with the customer than a dozen good experiences. Near perfection is expected, and when it is provided the customer sees it as routine. It is difficult to exceed the customer's expectations.

Reputation/Financial Strength

Often the quality of a financial institution is defined through its reputation. Phrases like "serving America's banking needs since 1909," and "75 years strong" are common. Other companies tout their financial strength: "backed by 3.5 billion dollars in assets," and "one of America's largest providers of group life insurance," are also popular. Unfortunately, size and years in business seem to mean very little in terms of a company's actual ability to provide financial security. In the past few years we have seen many examples of failures and mergers brought on by poor operating results in companies of substantial size and with long histories of profitability. Many investors were caught in the failure of the Baldwin-United Insurance Company. Banks in the Southwest are failing at a rate of several a month.

The deregulation and increased competition of the 1980s have pushed more large financial services organizations to the brink of disaster (and beyond) than any decade since the Great Depression.

Still, size and apparent financial strength continue to be key factors shaping consumer's image of quality.

Image

Another way to attack the problem of defining quality in financial services organizations is to look at the overall corporate image. Financial services companies work very hard at shaping our images of them. Because of their fiduciary responsibilities they often attempt to project images of financially solid, astute, progressive, yet conservative companies that can be trusted with your money.

Picture the Merrill Lynch advertisement of a large black bull wandering through a china shop. Think of the imagery involved. The message is that an investor must be strong in his pursuit of profit, yet mindful that the investment arena is fragile and if one isn't careful it could come crashing down. Or, consider the Prudential Financial Services ads. How many of us want to "Own a piece of the rock"? You can't get more solid than a rock. How about companies that use famous people whom we trust and respect? Bill Cosby sells us on his investment broker. John Houseman tells us about his investment firm, "They make money the old fashioned way—they earn it."

Of course, advertising is not the only way that our image of quality in financial services companies is shaped. We form impressions of quality because of numerous factors. Is it any surprise that the tallest building in most cities is a bank? Never mind the fact that the bank may occupy only a very small part of the building, while renting less expensive space elsewhere. The image of strength and security is promoted through the mere presence of the tall building.

Corporate image is also shaped by the appearance of its employees. Do they look like professionals? Do they act like professionals? Gone are the days when the neighborhood insurance salesman could dress in bold plaid sport coats and white shoes. The agent now represents a company that provides financial security and investment advice. It was one thing to trust this person with your auto insurance. It is quite another to trust him with your life's savings or other investments. Naturally, during this transition period when many companies are making the shift to become full-service financial services companies, we will continue to see the old stereotyped salesman, but their days are numbered. In fact, the new salesman may not even be a man at all, he might be a woman. Women have become more and more common in what was once an all-male domain.

Sponsorships and community involvement are other popular ways by which financial services companies shape our images. In these situations the companies go after specific market segments. For instance, is it any surprise that the Mutual of Omaha Company sponsors a 10K race? Providers of health and accident insurance are naturally interested in marketing to people who are healthy, and who is healthier than a runner? Have you noticed who sponsors much of educational television? It is usually a major financial services organization. Again, they are interested in projecting an image of companies that care about communities and public education.

Another interesting image-building campaign took place with Blue Cross/Blue Shield of Indiana. Most of the Blue Cross/Blue Shield plans are known for their health insurance prowess. But, many of them are branching out into different products and markets. Such was the case with Blue Cross/Blue Shield of Indiana. It first began looking beyond the traditional health insurance business in 1972, when it established Regional Marketing, Inc. to contract with other insurance companies to sell their products. In 1981, Blue Cross/Blue Shield acquired a life insurance company and made it a subsidiary. In 1985, it began to offer property and casualty insurance, with its first product a payroll deduction plan for automobile and home-owners insurance. Although these new operations developed nicely, the Plan was still thought of primarily as a health insurance company. Then, in 1987 the Pan American Games chose Indianapolis as the site for its athletic competition. Blue Cross/Blue Shield of Indiana decided to sponsor the games, and providing all the insurance for the games was the perfect public relations vehicle for their new products. The exposure was excellent and people began thinking of Blue Cross/Blue Shield of Indiana as more than a health insurance company.

Fact Versus Perception

Closely tied to the subject of image of financial services companies is the issue of fact versus perception. Fact deals with reality. Many companies routinely measure quality indicators such as the number of complaints received or the number of errors detected. These measures are monitored by management and represent statistically valid measures of quality.

Perception is not so cut and dried. Perception is defined as what the customer thinks the level of quality is. Frequently there is a major difference between fact (reality) and perception (what it seems to be).

The reality of the situation is that from a competitive standpoint, customer perception is far more important than reality. That is, the facts are unimportant unless the customer is aware of them and believes in them. Some financial services companies have turned this issue into a major competitive advantage. They aggressively market their products and services through full-color brochures touting their levels of quality in various product lines. An excellent example can be found with the First National Bank of Chicago. We will discuss how it uses quality as a competitive advantage later in this chapter.

Summary Definition

John Naisbitt has an excellent summary of what quality is and what it means to financial services companies in his book *Re-Inventing the Corporation*. He quotes New York advertising man Steve Arbeit:

For successful products, services, and companies in the 1980s, quality is what's under the skin of beauty. To the consumer, value equals the sum of quality products, quality service, a quality environment, quality employee relations, and quality community involvement.[4]

Later he adds, "Consumers perceive quality in terms of the whole, not just the parts; a company must offer quality in the totality of its dealings with the public."[5]

Financial services companies that are interested in improving their quality cannot concentrate on just their products, any more than they can focus on cosmetic image building or service. They must address all these issues. Hence, the best definition of a quality financial services company is one which maintains competitive products (not necessarily leading edge), provides high levels of customer service, supports the community within its market, and provides for its employees' welfare.

Summarized, quality to financial services institutions is probably best defined as "the degree to which the customer's expectations are met or exceeded."

Exceeding Customer Expectations

This is a delicate issue, because exceeding customer's expectations is great—as long as the customer doesn't have to pay extra for something he views as having questionable value. For example, relating back to our earlier example of the Mercedes Benz automobile, let's assume a customer is prepared to pay $45,000 for a particular model. He orders it. Later he arrives at the dealership to pick up his car. As he opens the door to sit in it the first time, he finds that the seats are made of an even higher quality of leather than he had expected. In this case he will be very pleased. His positive quality feelings about the Mercedes have been strengthened. He has gotten more than he expected to get for the $45,000 that he paid.

But, let's examine another scenario. Let's say that the customer orders the same car and when he arrives to pick it up the dealer tries to collect an extra $500 for an optional feature like air bags. The customer may or may not see the value of air bags, and exceeding his expectations will result in lowering his image of quality.

What we are saying is that, if customer expectations can be exceeded without negatively affecting their concept of value, then the supplier comes out ahead. The problem with exceeding expected value is that cost increases are usually associated with them. If financial services institutions can exceed customer expectations in ways that do not increase the costs, then the organization has gained an additional competitive advantage.

An example comes to mind. Two banks offer nearly identical personal checking account services. The price, level of service, and quality are all pretty much equal. But, one of the banks has a more sophisticated computer system that sorts checks in numerical order. The other does not. The customer gets high quality in both instances, but one organization exceeds his expectations slightly by offering this additional service. As long as the cost of both banks is equal, the customer will choose the one that exceeds his expectations. He may not be willing to pay extra for the service, but since it is free he sees a value.

Quality Perception

Who decides whether or not a company provides good quality? Whose perception is the most important? Is it the president? How about the executive staff? Perhaps it is the customers. Which ones? Could it be the communities in which the company operates? How about the sales force? Vendors?

To better understand this problem, let's approach it from several perspectives.

The President of the Company:

I think that we probably have good quality because I didn't get any negative feedback at the last board meeting. Also, at last month's meeting with the sales force, several people made a point of telling me what great service they received recently when they contacted the home office for assistance with billing problems. In addition, as I get out and about the community many customers comment on how helpful our employees are and they mention what a pleasure it is to do business with us. I wonder if they're being honest with me? Do they really feel that way or do they just say nice things because I'm the president? Oh well, as long as they aren't complaining, I guess things must be OK.

A First-time Visitor to the Home Office:

This looks like a nice company. The building is impressive and there is plenty of free parking. The reception area is pleasantly decorated and the employees smile a lot. They appear to be well dressed. Yes, this looks like a quality company that I would like to do business with.

A Member of the Community in which the Company Operates:

I read in the morning newspaper that Company X is sponsoring a 10K fun run. They are supplying T-shirts for all participants. It's nice to see such a big organization get involved in community events like this. I'm sure that this will cost them several thousand dollars and many of the participants will never even do business with them because they already use a competitor or they're from out of town. Perhaps I should become a customer. I like the way they do things.

A Competitor:

Boy, that company sure is hard to compete with. They seem to beat us to the punch on all of our new products. We work for months and months to put something together and then we find out that the new product has been offered by them for several weeks. How do they do it? Also, their rates are usually better than ours. How can they hire good people, pay them more than we pay our employees or at least as much, and yet still beat us on rates? Perhaps I should talk to them about a job. They seem to have it all together.

A Sales Employee:

Why can't they seem to get my commission paid correctly and on time? The last business I turned in was error free and complete with all the details, yet it took several weeks for the commission payment to be made. It seems to be a quality company. It offers a main line family of products and most of them are competitive in terms of price and benefits. Service after the sale is good, yet there's that nagging commission problem. If they don't get it straightened out soon I'll have to switch to another company. As a matter of fact, I have a friend who works for our main competition and he's always talking about what a great company he works for. Maybe I won't even wait to see if this problem can be straightened out.

A Nonsales Employee:

This seems to be a quality company. We hire talented, bright employees and every-one knows what they're supposed to do. Because of the open, friendly atmosphere I've gotten to know several other employees. They are all dedicated to doing a good job and providing top levels of service. A few weeks ago I had an opportunity to work on a quality improvement team that was charged with the responsibility of improving service to our agents. We were given specific objectives and turned loose to make whatever recommendations we wanted to as long as they fit within some general guidelines for projects of this type. We made some pretty good suggestions and my manager approved most of them for implementation. Yes, I think this is a quality company. We hire good people, pay them competitively, challenge them to do a good job, and recognize them when they do. I wouldn't consider working anywhere else.

A Mid-level Manager:

I'm not sure whether or not this is a quality company. It used to be. Our products were always considered to be the "Cadillac" of the industry. But lately we have gotten involved with this "downsizing" thing. Senior management seems to feel that we have too many managers and we need to reduce our ranks by 30 percent or more. I just don't see how this can be done. I work hard, and most of the other managers I know are busy all the time, too. Where is this headed? We have been successful for the past 60 years using the same basic management structure. Why all of a sudden does it need to be changed? If we eliminate 30 percent of our managers, our quality will have to suffer. I guess that I'll just sit this one out and take a wait-and-see approach.

The Customer:

Is this a quality company? I guess so. I chose it because it was convenient, its products seemed to be competitive, it has a pretty good reputation for customer satisfaction, and I liked the salesperson I talked with. It's been hard to keep up with all the changes the past few years. Financial services companies all seem to be getting more and more businesslike and less personal. I used to have a free checking account. Now it costs me money unless I maintain a large minimum balance. I used to have small savings accounts for my children. We didn't put much into the account, but at least it taught the kids about the need to save. Now, our bank notified us that they want us to close the accounts because they're too costly to maintain. If we didn't close them they threatened to charge us a fee. What's the world coming to? Is that good service? On the other hand, they do a great job providing the services that are still offered. I seldom have to wait in line and most of the employees seem to be eager to help me. I just don't know.

The First-line Supervisor:

Quality? Sure. I started working here for my first full-time job. It was pretty difficult. I didn't know much about how financial services companies worked and there was a lot to learn in just a very short time. I guess that I did pretty well though. After only about six months on the job I was given a promotion. They came regularly after that, about every six months. Finally, when my supervisor left the company to move to another part of the country with her family, I was asked to supervise the unit. Yes, employees have the opportunity here to work hard, learn a lot, and gain recognition and advancement. I like my job and we offer a good level of service to our customers. This is definitely a quality company. I expect to advance further as long as I continue learning more about the business and do a good job of managing my unit and developing my people.

A Stockholder or Investor:

I've seen better quality in companies. I invested in this company several years ago and it has gone through some tough times since then. The stock price rose a little then dropped to a five-year low. It has rebounded since then, but it's still only up over what I paid for it by a few dollars per share. I could have done better with other investments. On the other hand, I could have done worse. The company now seems to be poised for growth and I understand that the aggressive policy of growth through acquisition is a sound way of expanding market share. I expect the price to increase dramatically over the next few months. I'll withhold my evaluation of the company's quality until I see how I do.

A Vendor:

A quality company? You bet! I've been able to increase my sales by over 30 percent this year because they hired a new purchasing manager who introduced competitive bidding on all orders. His predecessor had a small group of suppliers that he used all the time. Even though I offered the same products at more competitive prices he wouldn't let me in the door. I think that they entertained him a lot and gave him tickets to sporting events and concerts that were in town. I never went for that type of selling. When the new purchasing agent took over, he cleaned house and opened things up for the rest of us.

The Auditors or Industry Regulators:

Quality? They seem to have done a pretty good job. During our last audit we presented them with a list of deficiencies and they have diligently worked to correct them. Of course, they are experiencing some of the same problems as everyone else in the industry, but overall they seem to be financially solvent. Their ratio of operating expenses to sales has risen over the past few years, but actions have been taken to reverse this trend. We are confident that they will be successful. They have always managed to get the job done in the past. Yes, they are a quality company.

The Quality Assurance Director:

We do a pretty good job in the area of quality. My department measures quality levels in a number of departments and reports summary information to management. For example, last night we mailed statements to our customers. Over 97.6 percent of them were processed without problems. The others had to be worked manually. During the past five years that we have measured statement processing quality, it has increased by 10 percent. The employees who have to do the manual processing on the rejects are very happy. All in all, we measure the quality for over 30 operations. Then we compare it to our past performance and that of our competition. Yes, our quality is pretty good!

WHO DEFINES QUALITY?

As we have learned, the issue of quality in financial services organizations is not as simple as it might appear to be on the surface. Just agreeing on a definition is difficult. Compound this with the issue of deciding who should define it and the problem becomes even more confusing.

Who should define it? Let's consider some of the most obvious possibilities.

Industry Regulators. If quality involves the financial stability of an organization, then the chances are that the industry's government regulators will feel that they should. After all, they exist primarily to protect the consumers' interests. If the company becomes insolvent the consumer could suffer; hence, the regulators want to be involved in establishing financial quality definitions.

The "Owners." Most companies were originally formed to benefit a group of individuals. This group differs, depending on the form of incorporation. For example, mutual insurance companies were developed by their first policyowners to provide insurance protection. The policyowners actually owned the company. On the other hand, commercial banks are generally owned by a group of investors or stockholders, and besides providing banking services, the owners expect to make a profit and thus provide a good return on their investment.

Blue Cross/Blue Shield companies are different from both. By definition in their charter they are not allowed to earn profits (beyond a certain level that is established to allow for day-to-day operation). The companies exist for the purpose of supplying low-cost insurance coverage to their subscribers.

Hence, the owners may be different from industry to industry, but in all cases they naturally feel that they should have the right to define quality, should they choose to do so.

The Management Team. Most owners of larger companies choose to assign the daily administrative duties involved in running their companies to professional managers. Given the responsibility of protecting the owners' interests, these managers naturally feel that they have the right to define quality.

The Community. Companies could not exist without the efforts of its employees. More than one company has had to shut down its operations or move because it could not find enough qualified employees to staff it. In exchange for supplying new employees, many communities feel that the companies have a responsibility to the community in which they operate. They certainly should have a say in defining quality.

The Board of Directors. Most financial services companies have a board of directors between the upper layers of management and the owners or policyholders. Their responsibility is to "direct" or guide the management team in decisions that might be important to the owners. Just as the management team feels that it should define quality, the board of directors has a similar claim.

The Customer. If the organization's customers are not satisfied with the quality of products or services then they have what is perhaps the strongest vote of all. They can take their business elsewhere. Customers routinely choose financial services organizations based on a number of considerations, including quality, service, product, price, location, and others. Indeed, the customer could define quality.

Others. A host of others would like to define quality. Consider the outside vendor who wants to supply products or services to the organization. He would certainly like to define quality in such a way that it benefits his interests. Visitors, employees, other layers of management, competitors, and many other interest groups would like to have their say.

Summary

All things considered, again the customer emerges as the one who defines quality. All the "players" are important, the owners, the community, the board of directors, the management team, the regulators, and others. But, if the customers decide not to purchase the organization's products because they are unhappy with the quality level, then the company is doomed to fail. Without customers there would be no need for employees, managers, or a board of directors. Vendors would be unable to sell. The regulators would have no one's interest to protect, and the company would cease to exist. Thus, the community would suffer accordingly. The customer is the king. End of story!

Now that we have a general understanding of what quality is, and now that we understand that the customer is the one who should define it, our problems of definition are solved. Right?

Wrong. We are faced with yet another obstacle. We all agree that quality in financial services institutions requires meeting customer expectations. We also know that the customer is the one who has to define what his quality needs are. The last hurdle to jump in defining quality then is to define who the customer is.

This should be simple. Logic tells us that the customer is the one who purchases the product being offered by the company. Unfortunately, this is not always the case.

WHO IS THE CUSTOMER?

In the course of conducting our consulting business we have many opportunities to present our concepts of quality to executives of financial services organizations. We ask certain questions routinely. One such question is, "Who are your customers?" The answers we are given are often very different. Take the case of a medium-sized life insurance company located in the southern part of the United States.

The president was convinced that his customer was ultimately the consumer—the one who decided whether or not to purchase an insurance product from his company. Hence, all operations in the company revolved around this philosophy. Please the consumer. He is the one who makes the buy/no buy decision and he is the one to satisfy. As a result, the products were kept fairly simple. They were straightforward, and their wording was easy to read and understand. WATS lines were installed to accept customer inquiries, and there was a large customer service department. Turnaround time for any policy maintenance was fast and efficient, and employees were encouraged to give personalized service to customers either on the telephone or during visits to the office.

The president of another life insurance company had quite a different view. His company felt that the consumer wasn't the one to please—the agent was. His company relied on sales from their general agents. Since these agents were not company employees, they had the option of choosing where to "place" the business they sold (to the ultimate consumer). The president felt that the agent was the one who had to "woo" the consumer and, therefore, his company should not spend a lot of money on services that would please the consumer. Instead, this company invested heavily in automation that would make the agent's job easier. They developed a sophisticated commission system that paid the agents faster than most companies do, and they included a commission statement that truly met the agents' needs—something that many companies never seem to be able to achieve.

The point is that just as every organization must define what quality means to them, they must also define who their customers are. The answer to this last question is not easy to find, and many companies have made the mistake of trying to be all things to all people. Our experience has taught us that this is usually a dangerous position and in these times of turmoil in the financial services industry, it can be fatal. Companies need to focus on one, or at the most a few customers. One approach used by companies that believe they serve multiple customers is to organize around those customer groups.

For example, it is not at all unusual for a bank to have both a retail division to deal with individuals, and a commercial division to deal with businesses. By creating separate divisions, the company has in effect split into two companies, each serving its primary customer. However, in order for this approach to be successful, it is important that each division be allowed to operate as an independent business unit, or profit center. This ensures that it can act like a separate entity, even though it is not.

Outside Versus Inside Customers

In theory, all employees serve the outside customer. After all, if the customer doesn't purchase the products offered, the company will not survive. However, only selected employees deal directly with the outside customer. There are a host of back office employees who fill a vital support role who never deal directly with outsiders.

A perfect example can be found in the data processing, or information services, department. The computer may generate some written contact with the consumer, as in the case of a monthly statement. Even though the data processing department may be responsible for the physical creation of that statement, little direct contact occurs between the systems analyst and the consumer. If, upon receipt of his statement, the consumer has a problem or question about it, he is probably steered toward a customer service representative for the answer. Chances are that the data processing professional does not have much knowledge about the customer contact side of the business. His primary responsibility is to develop and maintain support systems for the various products offered. When the customer contacts the service representative for assistance the representative probably uses a computer terminal to research the problem. Hence, he relies on the data processing department.

In this case the actual customer of the data processing department is not the outside consumer, but the internal customer service representative. Ideally, the service representative and the outside consumer will share common goals and the representative will be able to "speak" for the consumer. But, this is not always the case.

Another example is the human resources or personnel department. While it may have more contact with outsiders than the data processing department, it still is concerned mainly with internal employees and outsiders who want to become employees. Again, this is not to say that human resources personnel are not interested in serving the outside consumer. It simply means that the department's focus is more on internal customers.

The same could be said of employees in accounting, finance, investments, actuarial, mortgage services, and a host of other departments. All of them primarily serve internal customers. Naturally, they are interested and concerned about the outside consumer, but their primary focus is internal.

This presents additional problems. In our efforts to understand quality in financial institutions, not only have we had to define it and specify who should define it, but now we find that there is often more than one type of outside customer and a host of internal customers who are concerned about quality as well. We hope these internal customers have a healthy respect for the outside customers, for they create all the support services for the customer contact employees. If their quality is poor, then the support services they offer will also be poor and this will usually result in poor quality of service being provided by the customer contact employees to the outside consumers.

MISCONCEPTIONS ABOUT QUALITY

Much of the problem of defining quality is caused because we have misconceptions about what we think it is. Perhaps a way to help us better understand it is to explain what it is not.

Quality Circles

Quality circles were introduced to Japan soon after World War II. Dr. W. Edwards Deming is generally credited for pioneering their use to help rebuild a country that was demolished industrially. Quality became a rallying point for Japanese workers, and the result is well known to every American consumer today. Japanese products are recognized throughout the world for having top quality.

This was not always the case. There was a time when the label "Made in Japan" carried an image of shoddy quality. "Made in the USA" had the opposite image. If you wanted to buy a product that would last, whether it was an automobile or a toy, you "shopped American."

The Japanese latched onto Dr. Deming's ideas and improved their products and reshaped the world's image of them. In the 1970s the dollar gained in value against the yen, and the two forces, high quality and inexpensive products, combined to give Japanese products a major foothold in the United States. Now, in the 1980s, it appears that the foothold turned into a major share of the market and it is obvious that Japanese products will be around for a long time.

Americans are not ignorant. They realized what was happening, especially in the automobile industry where Detroit slowly bled to death while Japan became stronger and stronger. We decided that we had to know more about how Japan became so powerful, and we discovered "their" secret, quality circles—an American technique, introduced by an American, and perfected by the Japanese.

It wasn't long before you couldn't open a magazine without reading about how quality circles saved Japan. American companies jumped at the concept enthusiastically and circles became the rage of the 1980s. If your company didn't have quality circles in place, then obviously you weren't interested in quality. Company's annual reports touted their use. Marketing literature was rewritten to reflect the renewed interest in quality. Teams were formed at all levels, and many companies made it a mandatory requirement that all employees join a team and participate in quality improvement efforts.

Financial services companies were slower to jump on the bandwagon, but when they did, they did it in earnest. Book after book was written explaining how to do it. Mail order houses sold the "expertise" in ads that appeared in newspapers and magazines along with ads to "get rich stuffing envelopes in your spare time." People with firsthand knowledge of how to do it became "consultants" overnight, and marketed their "expertise" actively. Associations were formed and thousands of companies sent hundreds of thousands of employees to conventions to learn the secrets of how to develop successful programs. It is somewhat rare today to walk into a bank or insurance company that has not at least experimented with some form of quality circles.

Quality became a panacea. It was touted to be the answer to every problem. And, the beautiful part about it was that not only would quality improve, but costs would be reduced in the process! This was almost too good to be true. Think about it, companies could drop their old, tired, often hated productivity improvement programs and replace them with shiny new quality programs. Every employee would be involved and America's work force would reawaken to once again become the gem star of the world. Many productivity programs were old and outdated, often using techniques dating back to the period of early industrialization. They relied on heroes such as Frederick Taylor and his stopwatch and Frank and Lillian Gilbreth and their motion studies. Employees despised them and viewed them as "Big Brother" techniques. First-line supervisors hated them as well, because they involved a great deal of recordkeeping and employees constantly complained that they spent so much time counting that they had no time to get their work done. Middle management was almost negative, because they were caught in the middle between employees and supervisors who despised the system and senior management who felt that it was essential for staffing and expense control.

Quality circles appeared at just the right time and in just the right form. Here was a technique that would improve quality, lower expenses, and turn most employees into dedicated and conscientious workers.

Many companies felt that they had great early success. One could not pick up *The American Banker* or *LOMA Resource* magazine without reading about a firm that improved quality and reduced millions of dollars with their program. Industry conferences became mini–quality circle conferences as company after company stepped up to the podium to spread the gospel of the technique's virtue and of their financial success.

Why then didn't these companies prosper? Some did, but many began to realize that by themselves quality circles had become largely an unfulfilled promise. Many companies pumped hundreds of thousands of dollars into their programs and realized only minor improvements in quality or productivity.

Now that the dust has settled, the general attitude of the financial services companies who have experimented with quality circles reflects the following:

- They are not a panacea. They do not solve all problems. Generally speaking, they are most effective when the focus is on tasks and basic procedural improvements. They are seldom effective in addressing systems, functions, or organizational issues. (See more on this concept in Chapter 4, where we address the work analysis pyramid.)

- They are most effective when someone establishes measurable goals on which circle members and management can agree.

- They often produce "soft" dollar savings. Generally, circles save an hour here and a half hour there. Seldom do they eliminate major blocks of work. As a result, an individual employee may find himself with an "extra" twenty minutes per day. Unless the improvements agreed upon equal at least the equivalent of one full-time employee, the savings are very difficult to realize. Seldom is an entire job eliminated, and the only way to benefit (cost-wise) from recommendations is to take on more work with the same staff until all the "savings" are used up.

- Not all employees are interested in participating.

- Not all who choose to participate are effective.

- They are very effective in creating an increased awareness of quality. Since they are so participative at the nonmanagement, rank-and-file employee level, they help to inform everyone that quality is important.

- They can be quite effective in dealing with problems that are wholly within the control of the participants of the circle.

- Higher-level circles can be formed for middle- and senior-level employees. While these can be effective if all participants are willing to work at it, there are other techniques that were specifically designed for this level that are much more effective.

In summary, quality circles can be very useful when the conditions are right. However, even when this is the case, quality is a much broader subject. Quality circles can be an effective tool for accomplishing some corporate quality objectives, but they are only one dimension of a broad quality effort.

Quality Assurance

Mention the word quality, and most people will think either of quality circles or quality assurance (QA). The technique originated in the manufacturing environment, where it was first used to ensure that manufactured parts fell within preestablished quality guidelines. Elaborate systems have been developed by trained industrial engineers to ensure that standards are met. Nearly every manufacturing plant has someone to manage the quality assurance function.

As manufacturing employees began migrating from the troubled manufacturing industry to the growing financial services industry, some of them brought along their knowledge of quality assurance. Others who made the jump from one industry to the other recognized a need for better quality control and hired engineers to develop programs for them. Now, it is not at all uncommon to see a quality assurance department in a financial services company. In fact, almost all Blue Cross and Blue Shield plans have departments that report quality information on a regular basis to a central source. The data from plans located around the country is then summarized and distributed to each location for comparative purposes.

In most cases, quality assurance programs in financial services companies consist of statistical sampling programs that are designed to measure key quality areas. The emphasis is on the measurement and reporting aspects, although many companies use the data to determine trouble spots and to make necessary adjustments.

Just as was the case with quality circles, quality assurance plays a role in overall quality, but it is only one dimension.

Careless or Malicious Employees

If quality is not quality circles or quality assurance, then what is it? Is it simply a matter of carelessness? Are the stories of workers who sabotage products out of boredom true? No, for the most part they are not. Most employees take their responsibilities seriously. Poor quality is seldom their fault. Of course, there are exceptions. In 1986 a top college football player for a major university in the Southwest told reporters that during the summer months he had worked for General Motors. He and other workers were so bored on the job that occasionally they would put a few extra nuts and bolts inside the doors of automobiles they were making just to pass the time. Afterwards the workers would all laugh about the poor customer who would later have to spend hours and hours trying to find the rattles and then trying to figure out where the bolts belonged. Naturally, GM quickly issued a statement that the football player was lying and that they built high quality automobiles, and that the story was a type of "folklore" with no factual basis. Yet, most of us who have ever worked in factories could relate similar experiences.

Financial services companies have similar stories. In 1981, the file room of a major Midwestern property and casualty insurance company was hopelessly behind. The backlog was caused by a national expansion campaign that the company had successfully launched. The file room employees were not able to keep up with the increased volume and they were frustrated because they were unable to catch up. One innovative employee found a way to relieve her workload. Each day she was responsible for picking up new files in the mail room and transporting them to the file area, where she and others filed them into the shelves. Her solution was simple. She dumped a number of file folders down the elevator shaft each day. This continued until the elevator eventually broke down and a maintenance employee entered the shaft and found the files. Who knows how many customers were lost, because of the lost files?

Events like this can be found in many financial services companies. But, they occur infrequently. Most employees take their jobs seriously, and cases of sabotage and deliberate poor quality are rare. Poor quality occurs for numerous reasons covered elsewhere in this book. While careless and malicious workers can cause quality to suffer, we find that overall they are a very minor part of the problem.

Quality Is a Program

The final thing that quality is not is a program. Programs are usually short-lived. They are started to satisfy a particular need at the time. Interest and support are high. But, as soon as the novelty wears off, they wither and die.

Recently a senior executive with a medium-sized life insurance company attended a conference along with his counterparts from other companies. In general, insurance companies are very willing to share their secrets with one another, and several executives talked about the great success they had experienced with their quality programs. The man was so excited about what he had learned that as soon as he returned to his office he asked his staff to talk with the other companies and implement a similar program. Unfortunately, the man failed to realize that quality is unique for each company and his needs were different from those of the companies he tried to emulate. His company's culture was also vastly different. As a result, the quality program started off with great fanfare and ended a few months later with a fizzle.

The nature of programs is that they are temporary. When they are introduced, the employees who are affected by them often say, "Here we go again." They realize that if they simply give surface support for a short while the program will probably lose its momentum and die. Since their support is not genuine, it becomes a self-fulfilling prophecy and the program fails. It is often difficult to determine whether the failure was because of a poor concept, or the lack of commitment it was given by those who had to make it work.

Quality cannot be simply a program. It is not something that can be switched on and off. It is a way of life. It must be thought of as a natural part of every employee's job. It is never really "started" like a program. It already exists. It may not be at the level you would like, but it is there nonetheless.

Quality can be improved, but not through the use of a program. It must be a process. This may sound like mere semantics, but there is a difference. Programs have a life span. They are born, they thrive, and they die. Processes are a way of life, a way of living. They are an ongoing part of our everyday life. While they may involve a lot of hoopla up front when they are kicked off, the excitement is simply a technique used to give it some visibility. Once everyone understands the basic concepts of the process, it becomes ingrained. Employees become so conditioned to producing good quality that it becomes second nature to them. We call the process a "quality cycle."

QUALITY CYCLE

The quality cycle is our terminology to begin a quality process. It is generic. It can be used by any company, regardless of size or type of industry. It is just as helpful in a banking environment as it is in insurance, mortgage services, brokerages, and others. While the cycle itself is generic, it must be used as a guide to answer questions that are unique to each company. These answers are not generic, and assuming that all companies should answer them in the same manner can be disastrous. It will help you to understand what quality means to your company and how you can manage it effectively and even use it to gain a competitive edge. The following are the major steps in the quality cycle.

Step 1: Define It

Define it. As we have learned, this is not an easy task. What's more, we must define it at the corporate level, and every function must then define it again for their level, in such a way that it blends with the corporate definition, yet is meaningful to that function. This means that the data processing department must have its own definition. So should the accounting, marketing, and finance departments. All functional areas need to develop an understanding of how they support the corporate definition.

One important step in this pursuit is to find out what the customer expects. Then the definition can be tailored specifically to meet the customer's expectations. Many companies rely on surveys to assist in this effort. Questionnaires can be developed that are unique to each function and its customers. Remember that customers can be different for various functions within the same organization, and they do not always have to be outside customers. For example, the customers of a bank's data processing department could be the tellers and platform employees, loan processors or underwriters, or other employees who use an automated customer information system in dealing with outside customers. The human resource department within an insurance company has as its customers every other department that relies on them for personnel-related matters. And, of course, the organization has outside customers who have quality expectations. An example of a typical survey form can be seen in Figure 3.1. These survey forms are sent out to a sample of the customer base, and results are compiled for all those that are returned. Once the company, or a function within the company, knows what the customer's expectations are they can then define quality in such a way that those expectations can be met.

Step 2: Develop a Corporate Philosophy

In order for a company to meet customer quality expectations, every employee from the entry level up to the chair of the board of directors must work to achieve it. As D. Quinn Mills states in his book *The New Competitors: A Report on American Managers*.

A commitment to quality turns out in many instances to be less a technical matter of controls, sampling and inspection, than a behavioral matter in which the attitude of people in all branches and functions of the organization are involved. People have to think about quality, have a commitment to it, and make sacrifices for it. Hence, quality requires a personality change in the corporation.[6]

Buck Rodgers agrees. He was a 34-year veteran of IBM Corporation, where he began his career as a sales trainee and ended up as the vice-president of marketing, with responsibilities worldwide. He wrote a book with Robert

Figure 3.1
Sample Quality Survey

SAMPLE CUSTOMER SURVEY QUESTIONNAIRE

For the Customer Inquiry Department we would like you to rate the collective efforts of the individuals in each area on several performance and quality factors. To do this, circle the appropriate number on the scales below. 1 means poor performance, 5 means average performance, and 9 means excellent performance. Also indicate the relative importance of each performance and quality factor to you, your department or branch on the Importance scale. 1 means not important at all, 5 means average importance, and 9 means very important.

Please ⌐ if you don't know enough about the Customer Inquiry Department
(Proceed to Part B)   ☐

Servicing Factors	PERFORMANCE Poor · · · Average · · · Excellent	IMPORTANCE Not at all · · · Average · · · Very
Accuracy	1 2 3 4 5 6 7 8 9	1 2 3 4 5 6 7 8 9
Timeliness	1 2 3 4 5 6 7 8 9	1 2 3 4 5 6 7 8 9
Courtesy & Cooperation	1 2 3 4 5 6 7 8 9	1 2 3 4 5 6 7 8 9
Competence & Experience	1 2 3 4 5 6 7 8 9	1 2 3 4 5 6 7 8 9
Sensitivity to Customer/ User Needs	1 2 3 4 5 6 7 8 9	1 2 3 4 5 6 7 8 9
Availability of Service	1 2 3 4 5 6 7 8 9	1 2 3 4 5 6 7 8 9
Availability of Information	1 2 3 4 5 6 7 8 9	1 2 3 4 5 6 7 8 9

Overall Rating

General Assessment of Customer Inquiry	1 2 3 4 5 6 7 8 9

Shook entitled *The IBM Way*. He said that Thomas Watson, Sr., set forth a code of behavior when he founded IBM in 1914. The code was reaffirmed when his son, Tom, Jr., became IBM's second chief executive officer. The rules are simple and can be understood by all employees from the mail room to senior executives. There are only three of them. They are:

1. Respect the individual.
2. Give the customer the best possible service.
3. Pursue excellence and superior service.

Rodgers says that the principles lie at the heart of the company's operation, and every action and policy is directly influenced by them. He equates the tenets to muscles. If you exercise them regularly, they grow strong and hard. If you don't, they grow soft and weak. He feels that principles can't be followed in a business unless they are understood by everyone in management and unless they are articulated to every employee. They must be repeated often so that everyone understands how serious you are about them.

IBM conscientiously drives home its philosophical messages in meetings, internal publications and memos, at company gatherings, and in private conversations. None of this would mean anything, of course, if IBM's management did not demonstrate what it means by its own deeds. Management must be diligent, but it works. This corporation's employees understand that not only is the company's success dependent upon faithful adherence to Watson's principles, but so is their personal success. And that means all of IBM's employees.[7]

Companies that want to be recognized for their superior quality must be dedicated to achieving it. Simple definitions or tenets are helpful because they are easily understood and interpreted. Paul Revere Insurance Company realized this when it developed a unique slogan that drove home its message: "Our Policy Is Quality." They played on the double meaning of the word "policy" and did so in a very effective manner. If their internal policies (rules and regulations) encouraged high quality, then their policy (product) would reflect that quality. The slogan is simple and effective. It is easily understood by employees and customers alike.

Step 3: Set Goals

In order to achieve customer expectations, goals must be established and managed. Frank Gozzo, a noted employee trainer who spent much of his career with the Travelers Insurance Company, feels that there is only one goal for quality, and we agree: Zero defects! Many people don't believe that this is attainable, but Frank would always disarm the doubter with the example of a parachute packer. Should his goal for quality be less than 100 percent? If you were going to jump out of an airplane at 5,000 feet, would you be satisfied if your parachute was packed by someone who felt that a 3 percent error rate was acceptable? That means that three out of every one hundred people would jump to their death. How about a doctor? Would you want someone to operate on you who had a goal for quality of less than 100 percent? We think not. Frank has a point. We can and should expect 100 percent quality.

Perhaps Thomas Peters and Robert Waterman, in *In Search of Excellence: Lessons from America's Best Run Companies*, said it best:

The impossible becomes almost possible in the excellent companies. Is 100% quality or service possible? Most would guffaw at the thought. But the answer is yes and no. Statistically, it's no. In large companies the law of large numbers insures that there will be enough defects and breached service standards now and again. On the other hand, a friend at American Express reminds us, "If you don't shoot for 100% you are tolerating mistakes. You get what you ask for." Thus it's possible to be aggravated at failure, any failure, despite the volume.[8]

While statistical perfection may not be possible, the goal must be perfection. This can only be achieved by a tireless dedication of all employees. In his later book, *A Passion for Excellence*, Peters points out:

The smell of the customer and the smell of innovation have nothing to do with some grand design. They have to do with a thousand tiny things done a little better: serving the customer with courtesy and distinction. That distinction requires a commitment to excellence (quality, service, innovation) by all hands.[9]

Step 4: Manage the Contact Points

In their book *Service America*, Albrecht and Zemke ask business to think about the points of contact at which the customer passes judgment on your business.[10] They want you to think about how many opportunities you have to score points with your customers. These they call contact points. They describe a cycle of service that could apply to any financial institution. Take the case of a life insurance company. The cycle may begin when an agent, who may or may not actually be a company employee, first contacts a prospective buyer. This is the first contact point. It may be the most important, because it establishes the customer's first impression. The next contact comes when the application is processed and the company makes a decision to accept the customer as a risk or to deny coverage. The third and subsequent contacts come each time the customer's premium is processed, frequently only once per year. Occasional contacts come with routine changes such as name changes for marriage, change of address, and so on. The final contact point involves the benefit settlement. Over the life of the policy there may have been only as many as ten to thirty contacts, and only one of them was actually face-to-face, and that may have occurred with an agent who actually was not even an employee of the company. The number is less if you consider the possibility that the insured will allow the policy to lapse.

The point is that most financial institutions have a very limited number of chances to impress the customer. They must treat these contact points as opportunities. Even though the contact might be something as mundane as a change of address, the opportunity to create a positive impression must be cherished and not allowed to slip by.

Step 5: Measure Success

As is the case with any endeavor, it's important to know how successful you are in your efforts. You must periodically measure your success. One effective way to do this is to repeat the survey questionnaire that was discussed in Step 1. This can be done either with the same customers as were used the first time, or with new customers. Chances are that you would not want to poll the same group of customers more than two times within a period of a year or so, but it might be useful to do so twice just to see if their perceptions changed as a result of your quality efforts.

Harold Geneen and Alvin Moscow suggest another way to measure your success.

When all is said and done, a company, its chief executive, and his whole management team are judged by one criterion alone—performance. Lost and lay forgotten are the speeches, the lunches, dinners, conventions and conferences; the public causes endorsed and supported: all those supposedly key contacts with important people. What remains is the record of the company and its performance.[11]

Quality companies produce quality earnings. The simplest measure of success is to look at the bottom line.

Step 6: Use Quality as a Competitive Weapon

Achieving quality is not easy. It takes a huge commitment and requires almost constant attention. But, once it is achieved, don't fail to capitalize on it. Use it as a competitive weapon. Figure 3.2 is an example of how First National Bank of Chicago does just that. Quality is monitored in key areas on an ongoing basis and it is summarized, graphed, and printed into a booklet for distribution to customers. The booklet is called *The Quality Performance Chart Book*. It includes a statement about the bank's commitment to quality, a brief history of the bank's quality efforts, and charts illustrating performance levels achieved in various functional areas. The book is very well done, with multiple colors, glossy paper, and a spiral binding. It depicts an image of high quality.[12]

Quality companies capitalize on their achievements.

ACHIEVING QUALITY

While the quality cycle explains a general framework for developing a quality process, it doesn't go very far in explaining how quality can be achieved. There are as many methodologies for achieving quality as there are companies. But the best quality processes incorporate a set of basic tenets that are managed to.

David Bain defines two important tenets in *The Productivity Prescription*.

Equating quality with customer satisfaction, the quality of the organization's outputs as perceived by the customer is nothing more or less than providing them "what" they want "when" they want it. Quality = what is wanted + when it is needed.[13]

Figure 3.2
Quality Graph from First Chicago Bank

CHECK COLLECTION

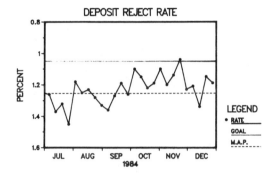

Our Check Collection Business Unit processes 20 million checks each month. Every check must be sorted and the magnetic ink line read to capture the dollar amount, account number, and the bank on which it is drawn. Any item that cannot be read for dollar amount or bank number is rejected. During the second half of 1984, performance was impacted by additional reject cash letter volume.

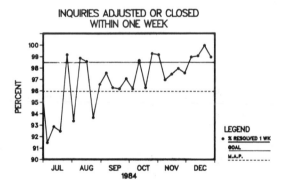

The goal of our Customer Service Unit is to have 98.5% of all inquiries adjusted or resolved within one week. This includes photocopy requests, account adjustments, and inquiries on encoding errors. Our performance was affected as we adjusted to check volume increases of more than 20% during July through September.

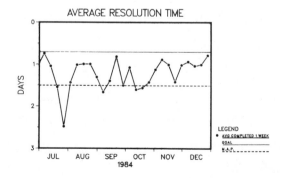

For inquiries adjusted or closed within one week, we strive to maintain an average resolution time of .7 days. Our resolution time increased from July through September because of the additional volume referred to in the explanation of the previous chart.

Bain equates the "what is wanted" with accuracy, and the "when it is needed" with timeliness. This modifies his equation to "Quality = Accuracy + Timeliness." We agree. To fail in either area results in poor quality. If an accurate product is delivered late, it may be useless. Conversely, to deliver a product on time, but one that is in error, might also be useless. Hence, both accuracy and timeliness are critical.

Six Essential Tenets of Quality

While these two essential tenets are important, they do not go far enough. We have expanded them to include four more. When all of these are achieved, you can rest assured that the highest possible levels of quality will be achieved.

The following are the six essential tenets of quality:

1. Accuracy
2. Timeliness
3. Simplicity
4. Consistency
5. Attitude
6. Cost

The remaining chapters of this book are dedicated to developing a better understanding of these concepts and how they will ensure high quality.

CHAPTER SUMMARY

The following are the key points made in this chapter.

1. Quality is very difficult to define. Each company must define it for itself. A host of issues must be analyzed, including: product quality, underlying value, service quality, reputation and financial strength, image, fact versus perception, and various perspectives.
2. The best generic definition of quality is "The degree to which customer expectations are met."
3. Customer expectations can be exceeded as long as the customer perceives the difference as having value and the cost of the basic product is not increased.
4. Customers ultimately must define quality, although a host of other groups would like to have input to the definition.
5. Customers can be inside as well as outside the company, depending on the level of organization being discussed.
6. Quality is not quality circles, quality assurance, careless workers, or a program.

7. There are six steps to a quality cycle. They can be used as a guide by any financial services company to get started with their quality process.

8. Quality is achieved by following six basic tenets. They are: accuracy, timeliness, simplicity, consistency, attitude, and cost. The remainder of this book is dedicated to these tenets.

NOTES

1. *Webster's Ninth New Collegiate Dictionary*, (Springfield, Mass.: Merriam-Webster, 1986).

2. David Bain, *The Productivity Prescription* (New York: McGraw-Hill, 1982), pp. 113–139.

3. Karl Albrecht and Ron Zemke, *Service America—Doing Business in the New Economy* (Homewood, Ill.: Dow Jones-Irwin, 1985), p. 27.

4. John Naisbitt and Patricia Aburdene, *Re-Inventing the Corporation* (New York: Warner Books, 1985), p. 68.

5. Ibid.

6. D. Quinn Mills, *The New Competitors: A Report on American Managers from the Harvard Business School* (New York: John Wiley and Sons, 1985), p. 298.

7. Buck Rodgers and Robert L. Shook, *The IBM Way: Insights into the World's Most Successful Marketing Organization* (New York: Harper and Row, 1986), pp. 1–21.

8. Thomas J. Peters and Robert H. Waterman, Jr., *In Search of Excellence: Lessons from America's Best Run Companies* (New York: Harper and Row, 1982), p. 181.

9. Thomas J. Peters and Nancy K. Austin, *A Passion for Excellence: The Leadership Difference* (New York: Random House, 1985), pp. 414–420.

10. Albrecht and Zemke, *Service America*, pp. 1–18.

11. Harold Geneen and Alvin Moscow, *Managing* (New York: Doubleday, 1984), p. 33.

12. First National Bank of Chicago, *The Quality Performance Chartbook*, July–December 1984 (Chicago: First National Bank of Chicago), p. 2.

13. Bain, *The Productivity Prescription*, p. 114.

4

Simplicity: The Improvement Process

Every time we've examined a quality issue we have found a way to reduce costs. A lot of people think quality costs money. The exact opposite is true; poor quality costs a lot.[1]
—G. Christian Lantzen, Vice-Chairman and Treasurer, Mellon Bank

Examining the simplicity of quality issues requires a series of structured improvement processes. A full understanding of how to integrate traditional improvement techniques into a company's quality plan takes time to research, discuss, and evaluate.

Charles Soule, executive vice-president of Paul Revere Life Insurance Company and cochairman of their Quality Steering Committee, attributes much of the success of their nationally acclaimed Quality Has Value process to "just messing around with quality." It took a group of executives hand-picked by the president, Aubrey Reid, months of reading, traveling to leading edge companies in the United States and Japan, and mulling it over before the committee arrived at their overall plan of action. They continually fine-tune and add pieces that address overall quality improvement as they make sense.

Not every firm has taken this approach. Some organizations have hired quality specialists with experience at other organizations to come in with a designed program that has proven successful in the past. Fireman's Fund Insurance Company brought in Anthony Draper, a quality expert from American Express in England, and began gaining control of their quality problems by establishing quality standards in each of their branch offices throughout the United States. The Travelers Insurance Company started with a traditional Quality Circles Program called ITI (Improvement Through Initiative) targeted at involving the employees in a bottom-up approach.

In fact, most financial services organizations have tried some form of improvement process in an attempt to keep up with the competition, and in reaction to the overwhelming positive press on the subject of quality as a strategic issue.

Any organization that has made an attempt to initiate a quality improvement process should be applauded. Five years ago little was written about the subject. Quality suggestion programs and quality circles were in vogue.

Quality control programs were initiated in companies to track and control errors. In 1982, for instance, Minnesota Mutual Fire and Casualty Company developed a comprehensive quality assurance program designed to detect, correct, and prevent errors. Preventing errors was the additional component which worked at improvement using traditional systems and procedures analysis as a basis. The program was very successful.

With each passing year, organizations have become more sophisticated about quality. The media has played up quality as more than a control or circle program. In fact, successful financial services organizations have proudly and openly discussed their formula for success. There are a few companies that regard quality as a fad. They point to the failures of quality circle programs, and relate it to quality in total. We hear cynics say, "Why do we need to even discuss quality? We tell our employees when they are hired that part of their job is to look at ways to simplify it. In fact, it is in the job description." It is humorous to hear that job improvement is in the job description, yet just as often employees are not provided with any training as to how to make the improvements.

This chapter is about simplicity. In a quality process the improvement techniques get a tremendous amount of attention. Simplicity should not be limited to the tasks and transactions within the company. It should include improvement in tasks, systems, functions, organizations, and the strategic planning which drives the organization.

Simplicity is most effectively gained by blending techniques that fit the organization's overall quality strategy in terms of timing, participation, and practicality. We recognize that the starting point has already been reached by the majority of companies, but hope that a presentation of the ideal conditions will be meaningful for those organizations trying to evolve their process, as well as those starting out.

To gain an understanding of how each quality improvement technique fits the overall process we will present an often-used concept of the improvement pyramid as illustrated by Figure 4.1. This figure distinguishes between the various levels of an organization. It starts with tasks as the basic transactional level of work. At this level the improvement technique is quality teams involving employees and managers. The next level is the systems (both human and automated) which link the tasks throughout a work stream to either create financial or informational outputs. The improvement technique used here is systems analysis, and the involvement is

Figure 4.1
Organization Pyramid

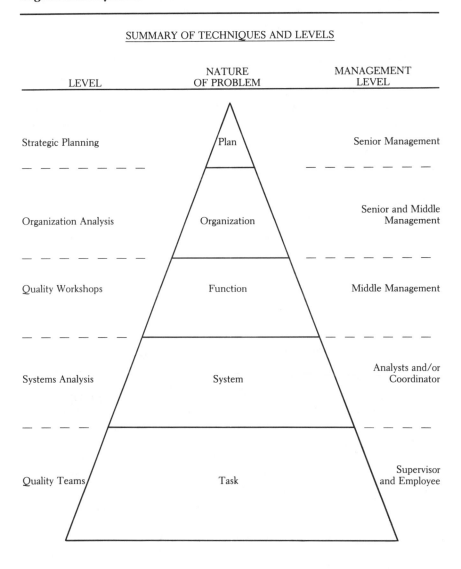

SUMMARY OF TECHNIQUES AND LEVELS

LEVEL	NATURE OF PROBLEM	MANAGEMENT LEVEL
Strategic Planning	Plan	Senior Management
Organization Analysis	Organization	Senior and Middle Management
Quality Workshops	Function	Middle Management
Systems Analysis	System	Analysts and/or Coordinator
Quality Teams	Task	Supervisor and Employee

either by what is called internal consultants or, in quality jargon, quality coordinators.

The next building block of work is called a function, which is an organization of systems, usually by product line or a specialty group delivering specific support to the organization. The improvement technique we use at this level of the organization is quality workshops (functional analysis), and the involved company members are middle managers responsible for the function, customers external to the company, and users or key interface personnel at the middle management level within the organization.

As we proceed up the pyramid, the next level is organizational. This, of course, is how we structure people to deliver work. The analysis technique we use is organization analysis, and the level of involvement includes each member of senior management down through supervisors. Overriding the entire pyramid is the corporate plan, which is attained through strategic planning. Again the process includes the hierarchy of decision makers within the company.

Keeping each component as simple as possible will result in higher value, efficiency, and effectiveness directed at achieving the customer's objectives. Where should we start? Taking the ideal condition, it makes sense to be sure that we are doing only right things before we start to improve the way we do them. The fact is that many financial services companies have built in excessive functions over time and end up doing many things very well that should not be done at all. Therefore, we will start with a technique designed to streamline functions. As we proceed through the chapter we will introduce the organization of quality through quality steering committees, to training quality coordinators and quality team facilitators. Each plays a role and interacts to make quality a reality.

QUALITY WORKSHOPS: DOING ONLY RIGHT THINGS

Quality workshops involve the middle management level of the organization in a process designed to change their fundamental thinking processes about work and quality in addition to achieving the expected tangible improvements.

The workshop organizes the decision makers of a process, along with the key customers and users the function serves, to conduct the analysis. The benefit of including customers and users is that they provide instantaneous feedback and enhance the development of understanding by all parties in the service cycle. Some management teams are fearful of including the customer, because it appears to require them to admit the weaknesses of their current functions. In reality, the customer is not exposed to every detail of analysis, but plays a vital role when rating the relative importance and reliability of work components.

As an example, a large commercial bank in New Jersey had a policy of submitting statements to commercial customers five days after the end of the month in order to attract potential customers with a service-level advantage. When the bank started the quality workshop process and asked the existing customers to rate this aspect of service in terms of importance, it was rated very low. Further analysis revealed that most of their customers had multiple bank relationships and their five-day statement was simply held aside until the other banks' statements came in (usually ten days later), and reconciliation could be accomplished for all the statements at one time. The customers identified an area of low value. It cost the bank an additional $200,000 annually to speed up their service level, and it wasn't wanted or expected by the customers. Without the customer's input the bank would likely have continued the practice under the misconception that they were providing excellent service.

Technique Basis

The analysis technique used most successfully for the management workshops is derived from value analysis. In fact, the concept of value is so strong in the quality process that Paul Revere Insurance Companies called their entire quality process "Quality Has Value." It is important to note here that terms can be deceiving. The value analysis technique was originally designed to improve the value of manufactured products. Larry Miles, recognized as the father of value analysis, experimented with and put form to the technique while working for General Electric in the early 1950s. In Japan the technique is revered, and annually a Miles Award is presented in his honor to the company making the most substantial improvement using the technique.

Much more has been written about W. Edwards Deming and Japan's Deming Award, but the reason for pointing out the awards is to emphasize that the technique is powerful when used effectively, and is highly regarded internationally.

When applied to the functions of financial services organizations, the application must fit the total intentions of the company's quality movement. Adaptations of value analysis such as overhead value analysis and activity value analysis do not focus on the customer through active participation, and do not use a consensus only format. While these techniques may meet the cost reduction goals they were adapted for, it is limiting and ill-advised to apply them as part of a quality improvement process.

Quality improvement requires the structure that analysis techniques provide and the openness of communication and ideas provided by a workshop format. Many organizations have not included this major aspect of quality improvement only because little is written on the subject, and the technique's goals appear to be similar to other planning and problem-solving vehicles they are using on a day-to-day basis. In many cases these substitute techniques don't include the customer in the process.

How can you introduce a major quality improvement process without considering the customer's expectations and perceptions? A senior vice-president of a major Northeast regional bank who heads up their quality improvement process explained to us that his managers take off their banker hats and put on their customer hats when looking for improvements. We ask, but isn't this what all managers do when designing products and services today? Don't they do this when they manage their functions on a day-to-day basis? We believe they do, but even with years of experience managers can misconstrue the customers' expectations just as the bank in New Jersey did when it decided to provide five-day service times for statement rendering.

How many customers should we involve? How much time will it take them? Should we involve them for the entire process or at key points? The answers to these questions are not easy. It depends on the function being analyzed. When we analyze a claims payment function in a property and casualty insurance company, the customer may be the insured; when we look at a human resource function, the customer may be all department managers served within the company. Each function has its own distinct customers.

A senior vice-president of a Midwest property and casualty company stated flatly that "Every employee in our company knows who the customer is. It is the policyholder. There are no other customers." In this company the focus is honorable and leaves little doubt who the employees are all bound to serve, but limits the direct interaction of support functions within a company. Data processing operations ultimately serve the end customer, but their direct customers are often departments who serve the end customer. In the quality improvement process we need to identify the customers who demand the time and other resources of the function analyzed. For this reason each set of workshops will have different dimensions.

Workshop Organization

Generally, each workshop will have five to eight full-time members. In addition, customers, key interface support staff, and other outside resources (vendors, industry association experts, and other companies' competing or noncompeting managers) will be brought in as the stages and information needs dictate. Senior management generally identifies the decision makers to participate in the workshop, with the agreement of the steering committee. Additional internal resources and customers are also agreed upon by the steering committee in advance. As you can imagine, the quality process with all aspects of organization, improvement, and evolution, if accomplished, will require a commitment of time to do it right. The steering committee will be meeting for four or so hours per week with untold outside hours of reading, visits, research, courses, and conversations. The allocation of senior management time is what sends a message to the rest of the organization about the company's seriousness in improving quality and becoming known as a quality organization.

Once the workshop members have been established, the team needs to get oriented and allocate time to the workshop process. Generally, a workshop will consume 40 hours or so over a six- to eight-week time frame. Some functions will require more time, depending upon the impact that the subject will have on present and future earnings of the corporation.

For example, a workshop examining a function such as credit life marketing will have more strategic implications for the company, since it directly interfaces with outside customers and is responsible for business development, than a workshop examining premium accounting. The time needed to successfully analyze the quality of each function will depend on the issues, the level of the workshop participants, and the abilities of the facilitators involved. Usually, the functional workshops are cofacilitated by an internal resource (referred to as quality coordinators throughout this text) and an experienced outside consultant.

The process focuses on the concept of essential purpose. More precisely, the essential purpose of the function to the function's customer or user. When the function was originally organized, what was the essential purpose? Is the essential purpose as critical in today's environment?

Essential purpose is not an easy concept to reach agreement about, nor is it currently the basis for decision making in most companies. In a Texas life insurance company a marketing support function called "advanced underwriting" was hung up for hours on determining their essential purpose. At one point a member of the workshop stood up and said, "Let's get on with this. Everyone here knows that our essential purpose is to increase profits." With this the facilitators placed "increase profits" into the essential purpose slot and said, "Well, that's settled, now we can get on with the analysis. This function's essential purpose is to increase profits for the organization. Profits include investments and the income derived, all costs including claims, and direct expenses in addition to the income from premiums paid. Correct?" This exchange got the workshop to focus on their specific purpose, which was to increase sales in a specific market segment.

Functions similar in name will have entirely different essential purposes, depending on the direction of that company's senior management team and their strategic plan. When examining the essential purpose of a commercial bank's collections function a consumer-oriented bank may agree that "maintain the customer" is the essential purpose, while a profit-driven, commercial-oriented bank may agree to "collect receivables" as the essential purpose. What we are pointing out here is that no two company's functions are transferable. More importantly, the essential purpose should be thoroughly discussed and agreed upon by the management of the function to get orientation and full benefit from the analysis.

The next thing the workshop does is to order every component of work currently performed by the function using a unique diagramming technique developed for value analysis at Univac, called F.A.S.T. diagramming. It works using a test of why we do things, then how we do them. What the workshop discovers is that there are many things they do that have nothing to do with the function's essential purpose.

At this point the customer's contribution becomes critical, because each component of work is rated to determine how important it is to the customer and then how well the current function's employees perform it in the customer's evaluation. Direct customer participation is desirable for this part of the analysis, but some companies supplement the customer's participation and contribution with survey information. At this point a picture unfolds, and the workshop participants can start to understand their current condition in the customer's eyes. The workshop then costs out every component of work based on actual dollars spent on the function.

The function is now segmented into a group of things that, in the customer's eyes,

1. Are *very important* that we *do very well*.
2. Are *very important* that we *don't do well*.
3. Are *not important* that we *don't do well*.
4. Are *not important* that we *do very well*.

Remembering that quality is based on what the customer expects, this process will isolate things that you do very well that need not be done at all. Financial services managers are always skeptical about this concept. "How could we have added functions that are not necessary? We are regulated for much of what we do in our business." Remember the example of the bank in New Jersey that added overtime and temporary costs to provide five-day service. In the customer's eyes the bank performed statement rendering very well, but it (the five-day service time) was not necessary or important.

At this point the group becomes creative, asking questions like, "Do we need to do this at all?" or "Should we be doing these things other ways?" The ideas are generated using many different techniques.

One approach that has been extremely popular is one outlined in an AMA Management Briefing by James F. Bandrowski, entitled *Creative Planning Throughout the Organization.*[2] In this briefing a section on "Techniques for Imaginative Strategic Thinking" outlined a series of creative steps that we can capsulize by calling them "leap to the ideal." The concept starts with what is ideal (in our use, for the customer), and then works backward to the current environment. Taking creative leaps eliminates the barriers of regulation, corporate policy, target market, systems support, or any such inhibitors to quality ideas. As with most other creative approaches the workshop members are encouraged to produce a great volume of ideas. The environment to elicit the ideas is an important factor as well. The environment should be open, spacious enough to get up and pace around, bright, at a comfortable temperature, and devoid of distractions like the telephone. Some companies have moved creative sessions off-site to a conference center to get the ideal conditions. Just imagine being cramped, in stuffy quarters, and being asked to concentrate only on creative solutions for servicing your customer. It is just not effective.

Another important factor in the creative equation is trust in the facilitator. One reason why companies use outside consultants for this aspect of their quality improvement process is that the consultant is neither biased by the company's past nor the future. Neutrality is essential to trust. The consultant does not personally gain from shifts in service delivery, organization, or support design. We should note here that one aspect of the consultant's value is in the perception of being totally unbiased. A facilitator who comes across as having ulterior motives will be scuttled by the workshop members. The issues the workshop is brainstorming will ultimately affect their customers and the way the company is organized to deliver services.

Internal quality coordinators assist the consultant with the workshop process. It is an important role in the overall quality process, and should be staffed with a highly regarded person. At Connecticut Savings Bank the coordinator for the Operations Division was a vice-president of operations. Esther D'Albero's background includes extensive banking operations experience, a can-do attitude, and she is well respected by her peers. At Paul Revere Insurance Company the coordinators were director-level personnel. Bill Domings, now the director of organizational development in Human Resources, had an extensive background in systems design and had worked ten years with the company overall. We have seen examples at banks and insurance companies where people were utilized who either were not fully productive but had the time in their schedule to assist in the workshop, or for whom the company was trying to find a position the person might be capable of handling. We strongly advise that companies use only their most capable, well-respected employees in the role of coordinator.

The coordinator works as an extension of the consultant. He or she knows where to go in the organization to obtain key information, and has access to key personnel. He or she assists the facilitator with documenting each phase of the process, and ultimately becomes responsible for assisting the function's management with implementation of workshop recommendations. In many organizations the coordinator reports directly to the Quality Steering Committee on implementation progress. The coordinator's additional role is to conduct systems analysis when necessary.

This creative phase can have other inhibitors. We have seen instances when the manager of the function had been in his position for over fifteen years and had, in fact, originally designed the workflow, controls, job design, and work distribution. This manager had talked to other participating managers who reported to him, and had stated flatly that there were some issues that were strictly out of bounds. The idea was established with his managers that the facilitator did not have the benefit of fifteen years of experience with this function and that the workshop members should take their lead from him on issues of policy. The reality often is that the manager has had one year of experience fifteen times, as the old saying goes.

The facilitator's role, of course, is to examine each aspect of the function without regard to current policy or regulation in order to expand the thinking of the team. When faced with stonewalling, one approach is to use the nominal group technique developed by Andre Delbeseq and Andrew Van de Veer in 1968. This approach gives the facilitator some control over the workshop team, since the idea generation is conducted silently. Each member is asked to identify a list of ideas in a designated period of time (five to ten minutes). When the time has expired, the ideas are recorded in a round robin fashion, starting with one member and rotating around the room until the lists are exhausted. A skillful facilitator will start with the workshop participant next to the negative influence and rotate away from that manager so that he or she speaks only after each other participant has offered an idea. The ideas are recorded on a list by the facilitator or co-ordinator. Once the ideas are exhausted the facilitator goes back over each idea to clarify the meaning, importance, and logic behind it. Discussion is controlled by the facilitator so that heated debates are minimized. At a later point the ideas are thoroughly discussed before evaluation for recommendation and implementation.

There are times when the facilitator has to go outside the workshop process to talk privately with members to open the flow of ideas. There are also times when outside discussion doesn't solve the problem, and a change in the makeup of the workshop team is required. This is highly unusual. It happens only 3 percent of the time, but if it happens in the first or second set of workshops the company will need to handle this sensitive problem in a decisive manner.

We should also point out that having participation in the workshop by employees from key interface functions and customers helps to limit the effectiveness of such sabotage.

The rules established in the creative process should generally follow the classical brainstorming format developed by Alex Osborn in the late 1930s.[3] The rules are as follows:

1. No Criticism. This is hard to enforce, because members will initially laugh or let out shrieks. Even after the violator is warned, facial expressions will give away true feelings about an idea. Some facilitators devise a monetary penalty that violators will pay to be used for a party at the completion of the workshop process. The facilitator's job is to discourage "know it all's" and, in the process, encourage idea generation. Discussion of regulations and corporate policy are evaluative measures and should be left to that phase of the workshop process.

2. Wild Ideas and Freewheeling Are Encouraged. The blue-sky idea may not be one that is ultimately implemented, but it might lead to other ideas along the same lines at a later point in the process. The workshop members should feel freedom of expression and often find that this is the most fun aspect of the workshop.

3. Piggybacking on Another Member's Ideas Is Encouraged. Several presidents of companies have told us that the workshops produced team building that they hadn't anticipated going into the process. It has a lot to do with the joining of ideas for an effective solution and the understanding of other members' thought processes that comes about by working on the quality of the function in an open environment. The objective of the process is to get ideas on the table in volume. One of the founding principles is that quantity breeds quality.

Another aspect of the creative process is to provide a period of incubation. Facilitators often shorten sessions from the normal three to four hours a session to two hours. This creates the need for more sessions in the creative process and time for the subconscious to work on additional ideas or enhancements of existing ideas between sessions.

Analogies are often used as a creative methodology. There are several general categories, as follows.

1. Personal Analogy. In this process the workshop members imagine themselves as the loan application finding its way through the new business, underwriting, closing, operations, central information file, file room, and accounting departments to pick up information and deliver it on its path. The members become immersed in the subject and see and feel the shifting of information and approval in a new way.

2. Direct Analogy. In this process the relationships are drawn as a simple, straightforward comparison. One example is a human resource insurance operation brainstorming how to find a way to distribute general and personal information to employees about their benefits. The human resource function found it difficult and expensive to maintain the information base and provide options to inquiring employees in a home office with many thousands of employees. An analogy was drawn from banking, where freestanding ATMs (Automated Teller Machines) linked to the central computer are able to dispense information, shift money from one account to another, and print a hard copy of the transaction. This vehicle had the added value of confidentiality an employee at the other end of the telephone did not have.

Another inhibitor to the creative process is the notion that the participants are business people and have selected a field of work that is driven by facts and analysis, but not creativity. The facilitator must work to overcome these fears. One way is to give an example of a creative person like popular songwriter Paul Simon, who structures time for writing songs similar to the workshop structuring time for coming up with ideas for the function they are analyzing. In the article "The Sounds of Simon" found in the Winter 1987 edition of *Quality* magazine, it points out how he also works at his craft in an analytical and somewhat structured way, building on past success and trying to improve. The facilitator in the workshop process is responsible for limiting self-doubt and pushing the team along to generate the ideas regardless of the roadblocks.

One potential roadblock to the creative process in the quality workshop process is the level of the workshop member in the organization. The closer to the task the participant is, the harder it will be for him to deal with ideas at the functional level. There is a need to use other improvement techniques such as work simplification to involve the person who is performing the task in the generation of the ideas. With this workshop process we are looking for participation of managers responsible for the output of the function, not the processing of activity. The quality teams to be discussed next will involve transaction-level employees in ways to improve the tasks.

It is also important to note that the ideas are not always going to be unique, but could be concepts discussed in earlier years and disregarded because of other software, hardware, political, or technological barriers at that time. It may be simply that the idea was not properly researched and thoroughly analyzed at that time.

It is important to understand that there is a role in the process that the facilitator must live within, and rules that he or she must abide by. First of all, the facilitator should bring additional information to the group, but never list his or her own ideas on the master list. Information may include vendors to contact, other organizations in the industry to contact, books and periodicals to read, and associations to contact. This adds the value of the consultant's knowledge to the process, without the idea becoming the consultant's. It seems like a fine point, but when the workshop ideas are generated by the consultant directly, ownership shifts away from the managers.

Another factor to keep in mind is that a challenge may be the spark that moves a workshop to successful completion. We have observed cases where the workshop members stopped participating and announced that they couldn't come up with one good idea to improve quality for the customer. After trying some preliminary tactics, the facilitator may agree with the workshop members. At this point the facilitator may suggest that they end the workshop entirely and report to management that the members believe that there is not a better run function in another company throughout the country. The facilitator will further suggest that he will contact the Quality Steering Committee members that day to schedule another function that is anxious to get started.

As you can imagine, this tactic cannot be used in every stalled situation to be effective. It will work to get the members to focus in on their overall responsibility to the quality process.

Another rule that is often misinterpreted by facilitators is to keep ideas and discussion by the workshop members confidential. Interpretation of this concept can be critical to workshop success. Facilitators who are strict with the policy limit outside direction on new concepts, and create anticipation by senior managers responsible for the function organizationally. There should be a flow of critical information, but not of what could be considered flip remarks and gossip.

A facilitator working with a marketing function in a life insurance company realized that one of the reasons that the company was unsuccessful "recruiting producers" was because of the way regional managers were compensated. As one regional manager stated it, "They pay us now for warm bodies." The facilitator, working outside the workshop without stating the source, mentioned the comment to the chief actuary and chief marketing officer. One of the solutions (change compensation to the general managers) would require their approval, and the sooner the better. The workshop members were grilled to see who made the comment, and the next session was spent rebuilding confidence and explaining why the quote was used. In the facilitator's mind a quote from a regional manager along those lines provided positive shock value to the senior managers. In reality, the facilitator should have used facts to open the discussion and not a direct quote from a workshop member.

Another role of the facilitator is to keep the objectives set by the steering committee in view during the creative process. This will often stimulate members to rethink their functional components "through other windows." For example, UNUM Life Insurance Company had recently developed a new processing system and had dedicated systems and programming resources for the following year to test and bring up the application. When quality objectives were originally established the functional managers were asked to improve quality with ideas that would not negatively impact the new software system's implementation. This somewhat inhibiting factor was used by the facilitator to seek deeper functional answers.

People often look to automation as the primary way to reduce manual handling, and therefore improve timeliness and accuracy. We have seen instances where it is beneficial to state as an objective to not rely solely on technology as the quality answer.

In the October 1986 issue of *Fortune* magazine, in a section dedicated to quality, the chairman and CEO of American Express, James D. Robinson, III, was quoted as saying:

Technology is only part of our fabric, not the whole cloth. We have a two-part pledge to customers: first, to promise only what we deliver; second, to deliver what

Figure 4.2
Decision Matrix

Decision Criteria / Weights	Service Improvement	Accuracy Improvement	Unit Cost Improvement	Short-Term Implementation	TOTAL
Alternatives	10	8	7	6	
Automation Vendor X	50 [5]	32 [4]	7 [1]	24 [4]	113
Forms and Procedural Redesign	40 [4]	32 [4]	35 [5]	30 [5]	137

we promise. And, we deliver our services one transaction at a time. It is our well-trained employees who make this technology work—who ultimately deliver what we promise.[4]

We feel that presenting senior management's goals and philosophy to employees in the case of a public statement like Mr. Robinson's, and in workshop situations in companies like UNUM Life, will keep the ideas of the managers in line with the ideals of management. Quality is not limited to the system and the answers should encompass each component of work driven by the function.

Evaluation of the ideas takes several forms. The creative process was set up to allow consideration of many ideas that could have been eliminated earlier if the "apple pie and motherhood" test of illegal, immoral, and unethical were applied. A first pass of the evaluative process should reduce the ideas to be dealt with significantly.

Another method of evaluation is called Advantage-Disadvantage. It is based on criteria and standards developed for those criteria by either the management of the function or by the steering committee. The advantage-disadvantage technique basically rates each alternative as an advantage or disadvantage against the criteria with a basic check mark. The columns are totaled to determine which of the alternatives has the greater number of advantages.

A more complex version of this technique is called the decision matrix approach as illustrated in Figure 4.2. Using this approach the decision criteria are weighted by the steering committee against each other. As an example, "service improvement" may be weighted by 10 (on a zero to 10 basis), "improving accuracy for the customer" might be weighted by 8, "unit cost" may be weighted by 7, and "short-term implementation (less than one year)" may be weighted by 6. The workshop would then evaluate the ideas against each criteria and score them on the basis of the following:

> 5 = A great advantage to the standard
> 4 = Achieves the standard
> 3 = No impact on standard
> 2 = Negative impact on standard
> 1 = A great disadvantage to the standard

To continue the example, let's suppose that one solution to solving a service problem in the platform function (new accounts) at a bank was to fully automate the process with a specific vendor. Another situation was to simplify the forms and to package the product so that the customer completes the basic information one time, and supplemental staff completes the duplicate information onto the necessary documentation.

The manual simplification would take eight months of analysis testing, forms design, training, and staffing. In our example the automated solution would take one year and four months. The manual alternative would reduce the basic account opening process from twenty-two minutes to fourteen, while the automated process would reduce the time required to eight minutes. The unit cost of the manual process would be reduced by 30 percent over three years, while the automated unit cost would increase by 15 percent because of initial hardware and software costs. The accuracy of the manual process would be improved from 94 percent to 97 percent through simplification and streamlining, while with the automated system accuracy would increase to 98.5 percent. Using the matrix approach workshop members would find that the manual improvement process would score higher than the automated alternative by 24 points.

This approach is time consuming, but it is beneficial when dealing with alternatives with a major impact. One key is that the evaluation is directed by senior management through the criteria and weights. The workshop members then agree upon the ideas through a structured process that limits emotion by dealing with facts.

There is an evaluation concept that many companies decide is beneficial to the quality workshops called consensus decisions. One potential problem with the concept is that it can be misunderstood. Some companies feel that if they employ a consensus decision process it will imply that they advocate consensus management.

The term consensus, by definition, means "solidarity in sentiment and belief," or "unanimity."[5] The general use and understanding of the word in management applies to situations where everyone agrees. In the quality workshop environment it can be beneficial to use a consensus process if the facilitator successfully avoids the disadvantages. One disadvantage is that the workshop can take twice as long to accept recommendations. There is also the potential for misuse of the consensus process. The workshop cannot agree to overrule higher management goals or guidelines, or to take on additional responsibilities like determining who should be involved in their workshop presentations. These issues are beyond the scope of the workshop members, and, regardless of unanimous acceptance, have no bearing on general management decisions.

In a consensus process decisions are not reached by taking a traditional vote. The decisions are reached when, through discussion, it is apparent to all of the members that everyone is willing to accept the decision. The fine point here is that they are willing to accept the decision, not that they necessarily totally agree with it. When there is trust in the workshop and the members understand that they are gathered to improve quality for their customer, members are willing to accept alternatives with which they personally do not completely agree.

The consensus process is readied by simply asking if anyone is opposed to the alternative. If no one speaks up, the decision is considered final. The question can also be asked if everyone accepts the decision. In a true consensus process any member of the workshop can ask the question when they feel that the timing is correct. The facilitator is in control by making sure that acceptance is within their scope.

The recommendations are fine tuned prior to presentation to the Quality Steering Committee and implementation. In many cases the authority to implement is within the scope of the workshop members. When this occurs the workshop does not wait for implementation. They do document each recommendation, listing the expected benefit in timeliness, accuracy, productivity, and cost. Each member of the workshop signs the formal list of recommendations as an indication of participation and support. Typically the group presents their improvements to the senior officer of the function first, both as an informational courtesy and to gain support for implementation of the recommendations outside their scope.

The members then repeat the presentation process to the Quality Steering Committee. We find that the workshop presentations reinforce senior management commitment and active participation in the companywide quality effort. The middle managers appreciate the time given to them. They get immediate gratification from the senior executives in their own division and exposure to executives they may never get a chance to work with otherwise.

QUALITY TEAMS: DOING THINGS RIGHT

The term and concept of quality teams was popularized at Paul Revere Insurance Company in their overall Quality Has Value process, started in

1983. Although they were not the first to use a full participation concept, their management realized that a departure from key quality circle principles was in the best interest of their employees, their management, and their customers.

Pat Townsend, director of Quality Team Control for Paul Revere, has chronicled the first three years of their successful quality process in a book entitled *Commit to Quality*.[6] He points out that at the time that his management team was researching the right approach to adopt for a full-scale quality process, the slant in quality circle periodicals was beginning to shift from magic cure to passing fad. Charles Soule, cochairman of the Quality Steering Committee, says modestly that "We were very lucky to select approaches that worked." We believe that the only fortune Paul Revere's management had was to gather a team of executives who were not afraid to do their homework. The safe approach would have been to stay within the traditional quality circle principles.

The key departure was full participation. Paul Revere's management believes that to become a quality company everyone must be involved. Quality circle advocates believe that the freedom to choose to participate or not is essential to getting organizational trust and ownership in the recommendations. History has shown that success will be limited using this approach. In the United States' work force less than 15 percent of the employees in companies where quality circles are active actually participate. It is also estimated that 50 percent of the quality circle programs that have been started in white-collar environments have subsequently been canceled.

In October 1986, at the International Association of Quality Circles' (IAQC) State of the Art Symposium, six hundred members discussed how to improve the effectiveness of their circle programs. In a financial services organization breakout group a member of the IAQC Committee raised the question, "Why is membership declining in our association even as the popularity of quality in general is on the rise in the United States?" The discussion focused on three major issues as contributing factors. First of all, most senior management teams are looking to involve everyone in the company. Second, the issue of rewards is creating problems. The third major issue focused on the need to document and track service improvement, accuracy improvement, and cost reduction.

Many quality circle advocates oppose using monetary rewards for circle members. They believe that rewards are too often based solely on cost reduction, service, and accuracy improvement and are, therefore, a manipulative tool of senior management. They fear that employees will be directed by the rewards and that the concept will change from a purely bottom-up to a top-down approach.

The issue of quantifying results is also looked upon as manipulative by quality circle advocates. We found that the majority of the circle program mangers present in our discussion group believed that the act of tracking directs the circle members to come up only with ideas that will have measurable impact. Quality circle purists believe that any deviation from the basic principles will lower the success rate of a circle program. The reality is that senior executives are likely to view time allocated to a process with quality ideals and no quantifiable benefit as frivolous.

Using the quality circle approach there is often a "them and us" conflict between circle members and nonmembers. That situation does not exist with a team process, since everyone is a member. One problem that currently exists for companies serious about quality improvement occurs if a previous circle has failed and there is a stigma attached to the failed process. Senior executives wonder how employees will respond to a request for full participation in a process that failed when the circles included only those employees who were most interested in improvement.

In fact, the head of the quality circle program at one of the world's largest insurance companies flatly stated that "Middle management is distrustful of our limited effort today. A full-scale program would be sabotaged immediately." Middle management must feel confident and must also have an active role. This is precisely why the combination of quality workshops composed of the management team with quality teams composed of the supervisors and employees has been so successful.

We have found that some companies are bound by the momentum of quality programs they have announced and outlined for their staff, but realize will fall short without a dramatic change. One large property and casualty insurance company in Philadelphia has invested energy, time, and money into a process that stops just short of becoming successful. The senior vice-president charged with quality improvement for the organization told us that the training they have received to date "has taken them to the edge of the cliff and shown them the promised land, but has not given them a clue how to get down." They have had what he calls "inspirational training," but very little guidance in the area of structured problem solving. To his benefit, he is actively researching how to get results instead of letting the current circle process run its course.

Quality Team Training

The format for quality teams is not dissimilar to that for quality circles. It is based on a working unit and is often led by the supervisor of that unit. Teams are composed of eight to ten members. The frequency of the meetings is left up to the group, but a basic guideline is one-half hour a week, or an hour every two weeks. The team leader is responsible for:

1. Leading the meetings to productive ends.
2. Coordinating activities of group members working on selected problems.
3. Guiding the team through effective problem solving and decision making.

4. Verifying that the team has the authority and responsibility to implement the solutions they have developed.

Often the team leaders have not been previously schooled in the skills required for the team process. The training should be flexible so that seasoned supervisors who have had specific training would not be required to sit through modules they have taken in the past. Basic team leader training consists of a corporate overview of the structure of the quality process. The goals of each component and the corporate goals should become working information. The skills training should include facilitative behaviors for successfully running meetings. They should also be schooled in a team problem-solving model. We find that work simplification training is extremely beneficial to the team process.

Another skill is in training for action planning and follow-up. Some of the basic ground rules appear to be common sense, but as Frank Gozzo, a former trainer at the Nolan Company and long-time Travelers Insurance Company work simplification specialist, often stated, "What is common sense (or knowledge) to one person may not be common sense to the next. It is all based on individual experiences." For this reason it is good to set the stage by establishing ground rules and a standard approach.

The training often takes place as a phased-in exercise and so should the organization of the teams. There are several reasons for this, but the primary one is to be able to coordinate with the quality workshops.

QUALITY TEAMS: PROBLEM IDENTIFICATION

Another departure from quality circles is where problems come from. In a traditional quality circles environment the circle leader will ask a question like, "What are we spending time on that, if improved, would help us to become a quality organization?" Or, "What could we do to reduce errors and improve service time?" Circle members would identify and write down their interpretation of a specific problem in a condensed format. Each problem is collected to clarify and create a master list. At this point problems are sorted by those that are within the power and scope of the circle, and those that are outside the power and scope of the circle. The problems within their scope are then weighted according to their impact on quality to arrive at their first problem.

In a company with simultaneous quality teams and quality workshops, the workshops will feed problems to the teams which are task-oriented and require additional analysis for improvement. This is a departure from quality circles since problem identification and selection is intended to be a bottom-up process.

QUALITY TEAMS: PROBLEM ANALYSIS

Once the team has determined the problem to be addressed, they are set free to come up with a solution that best suits the needs of the customer and the abilities of their unit. Various structured problem-solving techniques can be used, including the traditional work simplification technique.

The first step is to gather, record, and verify the facts impacting the problem identified. They will be collected in various ways, including: interviews, questionnaires, logs, and existing printed or written records. A traditional collection and analysis device is the flow process worksheet. It helps to organize the sequence of the task and characterize the steps into definable and recognizable terms. Another tool is a workplace layout so that the path can be visualized.

The next step is to analyze the facts through a standard questioning process. The questions follow the "What?", "Where?", "When?", "Who?", "How?" format, with "Why?" after each. The simplicity of the questioning process is beneficial to getting large numbers of people trained in a short time.

The analysis is followed by a creative process not unlike what we have described previously, but focused on a more concentrated area. Analysis is followed by synthesis or the evaluation of alternatives and development of preferred solutions. Of course, the sale of the ideas and implementation are what completes the process. Submitting ideas for implementation can become a mammoth undertaking for a company with dozens of regional or branch offices with duplicate areas where teams could be solving the same problems. How do you apply credit and reward members? Is the approved idea at one branch implemented at all other branches? What will be the criteria for the decision-making process: time service? reduced errors? lower costs? or first received?

ORGANIZATIONAL ANALYSIS: DOING THINGS AT THE RIGHT COST

The expansion of managerial and professional levels over the past ten years is now catching up with the financial services industries. Companies considered "top heavy" have difficulty with daily execution because of an expensive communication chain. Employees get mixed messages and often the interpretation of information from managers they are reporting to becomes a guess. In many cases managers make a determination that there is no need to further free communication (either up or down). Employees become frustrated and cynical toward their leaders. This is not an ideal condition for establishing a quality culture.

When senior executives are faced with this problem they are often too close to the individuals who report to them to objectively analyze an improved structure. We have seen companies eliminate organizational layers on their own, but not reduce costs because additional staff positions were created or titles were changed without responsibility shifting. To reliably solve organizational problems specific analysis techniques are employed.

First we should define what organizational analysis is. In Van Nostrand Reinhold's *Encyclopedia of Management* it is defined as:

The analysis of objectives, of the environment, and of the human, physical and functional assets of a company in order to arrive at the most effective design of a human system for the transfer of human creative power from the organization's ultimate authority to eventual accomplishment of its established objectives.[7]

Stated simply, it is how you structure the right people to get required work accomplished effectively. The techniques employed to accomplish recommendations that are practical are structural analysis, span of control analysis, and an assessment of personnel.

Quality is often the basis for making dramatic organizational shifts. As companies become large (3,000 to 7,000 employees), subsidiaries or strategic business units are sometimes formed to place the ultimate responsibility for each product line in the hands of the senior staff responsible for profitability. Depending on the existing corporate culture, this change can drive competitive forces to work against the organization in total. We have repeatedly seen creative product line managers force job design changes (under the banner of job enrichment) to create super clerk positions. This new, do-every-task position rates higher under standard job evaluation criteria, thus enabling one subsidiary manager to entice the most proficient clerical and technical specialists away from his or her peers in the holding company. Of course, the condition is most pronounced when the various product lines' operating staff is located in the same city. The subsidiaries in turn create new super positions to protect and rob back their experts. It can take years for companies to realize that a significant portion of their increases in unit costs are self-inflicted. Compensation consumption can be controlled, but often it is a reflex policy established long after job ranges and employee expectations have been raised.

Structure

Structural analysis evaluates how the major operating support and marketing functions will be controlled and integrated. Should we be centralized or decentralized in our processing? Should we give our product manager autonomy through self-controlled subsidiaries as discussed earlier? Another consideration is the use of matrix management to direct reporting relationships. The dangers are that a management team locks onto one concept as the best or only way to get the job done.

Rarely is one approach appropriate across the board or for an extended period of time. As an organization gets larger or smaller, their organizational needs will shift. For example, if a property and casualty company is located in the Southwest Untied States and effectively supports their agents and policyholders through a centralized operation, will it be able to be as supportive (in timeliness and accuracy) if it expands to the Eastern United States? An even larger question centers on whether customer expectations will be the same in those new markets even if we determine that we could deliver the same support to the East as we do to our present customers. The structural organization analysis is linked to the marketing plan and needs to be assessed whenever market changes are considered.

Span of Control

It is amazing to see how we expect managers and supervisors to deliver quality service through their employee development and direction without giving consideration to the stability of staff and product. In dynamic growth organizations, like mutual funds processors, mortgage companies, and any financial services organization heavily dependent upon interest sensitive products, volume has in many cases expanded faster than the support people can be trained. This puts more pressure on inexperienced employees to get the work out using overtime. It also drives middle managers to utilize outside service bureaus and temporary staff. Pressure on existing staff creates higher turnover and the spiral leads to poor quality. Management will often throw additional personnel at this condition because the backlogs are unacceptable. We have seen situations where managers have a 75 to 1 span of control in health care claims payment. The mangers were expected to prepare two formal employee evaluations annually, in addition to their training, supervision, and planning responsibilities. As you can imagine, the manager could not get around to know her employees.

We have also seen companies with flat production, experienced personnel, and a clerical span of control of 5 to 1. Neither situation is good, and neither one makes sense. Span of control can logically be expanded by redesigning specialty jobs to include an interfacing work unit, or by simply grouping related units by eliminating a layer of supervision.

Many companies use outside assistance with span of control models developed for their industry. The models take into consideration each company's and unit's characteristics, including training, growth, turnover, degree of automation, skills requirements, meeting needs, employee development, and the critical impact of performance. When executives are presented with a range for a group of clerical, technical, or professional positions which will ultimately serve the customer and the stockholder better, then the remaining issue is how to implement.

Quality is best achieved through honesty, communications, and caring.

Companies that have purged management without considering the psychological impact on their remaining staff have found that the scars of mistrust are not eliminated with time. Black Fridays become corporate folklore and outlive the managers who initiated the change process. Golden parachutes have softened the process, as have the use of professional outside placement firms. It is difficult to be considered a quality organization if the actions taken toward well-intentioned employees are undignified. One life insurance company we worked with in Boston was concerned because employees were still sensitive to a major organizational change that occurred eighteen years earlier. At a bank in North Carolina, some executives still talk about the loss of talent, skills, and knowledge that was inflicted in a purge fifteen years ago. We will expand on the link between quality and attitude in a later chapter.

ASSESSMENT OF STAFF

One of the more difficult aspects of organization analysis is getting the right person into the job. It sometimes requires development of the individual currently in the position. Other times the individual in the position was the best technician and even after development as a manager, can't let go of simply doing the work. Other managers were capable of managing in a small company at a time when the products and services were few. As the company expanded they were unable to deal with more complex management issues. In fact, some managers fail to realize the impact of their decisions or lack of decisions. One company converting from a mutual organization to stock ownership lost millions of dollars on the conversion because the senior financial officer missed deadlines and a window of investment opportunity while the market was intrigued with emerging savings institutions. Some executives are effective in day-to-day management but are not innovative leaders.

The assessment of staff is best accomplished using a structured interview process. Most models are built around questions relating to leadership skills, organization, planning, getting results, decision-making ability, communications skills, and potential for advancement. The process of interviewing each level of management is time consuming. In an unbiased format, assisted by personnel records, the interviewer will assess each incumbent against the requirements of the position. Typically, incumbents are scored in comparison to their level within the company and throughout the industry. Each manager and supervisor is assessed using the structured process by the manager they report to and by up to six people that report to him or her. A structured interview designed by industrial psychologists relates the responses to establish potential strengths or weaknesses. Additional interviews are often required to confirm "red flags." The scoring shown in Figure 4.3

Figure 4.3
Management Profile Summary

ROBERT E. NOLAN COMPANY

MANAGEMENT PROFILE SUMMARY

DATE: 12/12/87

NAME: JIM MORRIS   TITLE: SENIOR VICE PRESIDENT

RECOMMENDED SPAN OF CONTROL: 3-6

COMPOSITE MANAGEMENT EVALUATION SCORE

8.1 — 10.0	SUPERIOR	—
7.0 — 8.0	AVERAGE	— 7.5
6.0 — 6.9	SUSPECT	—
0.0 — 5.9	VERY SUSPECT	—

INDIVIDUAL'S RELATIVE INDICES OF MANAGEMENT ATTRIBUTES

Relative Ranking	Advancemnt Potential	Communictn Skills	Decision Making Skls	Get Desired Results	Organizatn/ Planning	Leadership Skills
HIGHEST		X				
HIGH				X		X
MEDIOCRE						
LOW	X		X			
LOWEST					X	

INDIVIDUAL VS. COMPANY MANAGEMENT ATTRIBUTES

Relative Ranking	Advancemnt Potential	Communictn Skills	Decision Making Skls	Get Desired Results	Organizatn/ Planning	Leadership Skills
HIGH		X				
MEDIOCRE				X		X
LOW	X		X		X	

---

becomes an impartial base and is supplemented by the expertise of outside professionals.

The three techniques, although separate in practice, should be conducted during the same time frame to take advantage of combinations.

Organization analysis is often the last improvement technique conducted. The quality workshops discussed earlier tend to sort out some of the more obvious structural and span of control issues. Tom McCabe, senior vice-president of First Fidelity Bank in Newark, New Jersey, while presenting the results from Quest for Quality, the bank's quality process designed to improve the Bank Operations and System Division, confirmed this point at a Bank Administration Institute (BAI) conference in January 1986. He was quoted as saying, "The major unexpected benefit from the quality workshop process was our organizational change." The workshops identified problems and presented solutions. They were also able to see managers interact with customers and peers to solve problems.

Structured organization analysis is the improvement technique sometimes excluded because of an underlying fear that the staff will not view it as an improvement in quality. Aubrey Reid, the president of Paul Revere Life, who was reluctant at first primarily for this reason, told us recently that he has implemented every one of the recommended changes resulting from structured organizational analysis, and that it did not disrupt his management teams' commitment to quality.

SYSTEMS ANALYSIS: DO THINGS ON TIME

Earlier we discussed how the quality coordinator had a significant role assisting with the workshops and conducting additional analysis where necessary. Systems analysis is sometimes required to look beyond the function or departments which directly interface. The quality coordinator or internal consultant will add value to the component of analysis, since they have training in automated and manual systems analysis and an understanding of the profitability impact with regard to cash flow.

For example, trained systems analysts at a property and casualty company in New Jersey were able to identify a series of problems creating a backlog of over one month in new business. The accounting managers were not concerned that processing was backed up. They argued that billing dates are not altered by the backlog. In reality, the agents submit payments two weeks after receipt of billing at this company. One month's backlog in receipts is ten million dollars. The systems analysts cleaned up the backlog so that bills would be mailed earlier and, therefore the company would have the use of ten million dollars to invest that previously was being held by agents.

The analytical technique examines each characteristic of the system.

1. Its mission: why it is done.

2. Inputs: required information to drive the system, including the source.

3. Output: what is produced.

4. Sequence: the steps of the system, including delays and files.

5. Environment: external factors influencing the system.

6. Equipment: including automated components.

7. Human components: required skills and expected productivity and quality.

If the scope of the system is too narrow, then the analyst will be covering ground which may be addressed by the quality teams. The greater the scope the more important knowledge of broader industry issues is necessary. For instance, an inexperienced analyst may not consider the implications of deregulation on state boundaries and how acquisitions could influence incoming volumes and account hierarchy.

The quality coordinator should be selected from internal candidates who are considered knowledgeable and unrelenting. These candidates are likely the people you would least want to lose. The quality coordinators should be those people you would never consider because of their importance in getting major projects implemented. In a real sense there will be nothing more important to the company's survival than the quality improvement process.

CHAPTER SUMMARY

The following are the key points made in this chapter.

1. Each company involved with a full-scale quality process will discuss the results in terms of how their employees felt and their customers feel about them today. The truly committed organizations will not be limited by what has been attempted in the past, but will be driven by what it will take to go forward.

2. To improve, an organization has to involve each level of the company in improvement geared to their responsibilities and their abilities. Table 4.1 is a summary of these levels and the techniques required.

3. The techniques blend to pass improvement potential onto the group where change should be initiated. Quality workshops pass task improvement analysis on to the quality teams. Quality teams pass potential systems improvements on to the quality coordinators, and the quality workshops initiate organizational change, then pass additional potential on to the senior managers who will deal with it. As long as the Quality Steering Committee is active and alert the process will improve trust, which is critical to the longer term cultural changes anticipated in a quality process.

NOTES

1. G. Christian Lantzen, in "The Quality Imperative" (special advertising section), *Fortune*, October 1986, p. 41.

2. James F. Bandrowski, "Techniques for Imaginative Strategic Thinking," *Creative Planning Throughout the Organization*, AMA Management Briefing (New York: AMA, 1985) p. 21.

3. Alex F. Osborn, *Your Creative Power* (New York: Scribner's, 1952), p. 269.

4. James D. Robinson III, in "The Quality Imperative" (special advertising section), *Fortune*, October 1986, p. 52.

5. *Webster's Ninth New Collegiate Dictionary*, (Springfield, Mass.: Merriam-Webster, 1986).

Table 4.1
Summary of Organization Levels and Improvement Techniques

LEVEL	NATURE OF PROBLEM	MANAGEMENT LEVEL
Organization Analysis	Organization	Senior & Middle Management
Quality Workshops	Function	Middle Management
Systems Analysis	System	Quality Coordinator/ Internal Consultant
Quality Teams	Task	Supervisory Staff

6. Patrick L. Townsend with Joan E. Gebhardt, *Commit To Quality* (New York: John Wiley and Sons, 1986), p. 14.

7. Carl Heyel, ed., *Encyclopedia of Management*. 3d ed. (New York: Van Nostrand Reinhold Company, 1982), p. 797.

5   *Accuracy*

Companies that look at accuracy as transaction oriented will achieve improvement results only at that level. Success means starting with policies and reviewing support systems. It is not only what was incorrect, but also what was omitted. In the service sector, if you focus on transactions, what you will end up with is a quality control system, not a quality organization.

—Robert E. Grasing

Accuracy is the popular term used today with a quality process because it focuses on what went right. Most quality control efforts focus on errors or defects.

HISTORY

Zero Defects as a program was initiated in manufacturing at the Martin Company in 1962. It was intended to motivate each employee to concentrate on improving their production quality. The shift to error prevention was not intended to eliminate error detection and correction. It was a new emphasis on performance and a realization by every department that their output was someone else's input. Examples were given to employees to illustrate how a seemingly small error in one department will multiply throughout the organization.

Zero Defects was popularized by the Department of Defense in 1964, and soon thereafter thousands of plants throughout the country were employing similar programs. As with many new concepts or programs, companies established their own identities with slogans and catchy names. Westinghouse established the EFP, or Error Free Performance program, and used techniques that have been incorporated into many of the successful financial services organization's efforts twenty years later. In publicizing EFP, Westinghouse asked their employees to sign a large scroll pledging themselves to error-free performance in their daily work. Figure 5.1 shows how UNUM Life Insurance Company has incorporated this concept into their quality process. In fact, at UNUM the employees often highlight their own names on posters placed near their work units to emphasize their commitment to quality.

Another interesting concept at Westinghouse was a checklist classifying types of errors. Their original list can be used as a starting point for any company interested in quality performance.

1. Failure to do things according to plans.

2. Work that for any reason requires rework before delivery.

3. Work that is acceptable in all respects except that it could have been done for less cost.

4. Work to quality standards below those required by the customers or by the company.

5. Work to quality standards above those required by the customer in all cases where there has been a determination that the customer's standards are sound and practical.

6. Failure to perform detailed tasks as required by the schedule.

7. Failure to pre-plan work in detail and failure to instruct each worker in these details. Failure to maintain surveillance and follow through while work is in progress, so that necessary corrective action can be taken before the work is completed.

8. Failure to manage cost effectively.

9. Work that is otherwise acceptable, but in some way encourages the commission of errors by others, or results in higher costs or in late delivery.

10. Items in cost estimating that lead to higher quotations than are actually justifiable.

11. Omission of items from cost estimates.

12. Failure to meet budget.[1]

The conversion of concepts from manufacturing to financial services is surprisingly easy. Westinghouse's point number ten converted to financial services relates to the work of underwriters, and even actuaries in insurance companies. In banking it relates to commercial lenders, their credit departments, and in a broader sense the loan policy committee. Lenders and underwriters are bound by *policy*, which we will discuss as one of the major components of accuracy. The other components of accuracy we will cover in this chapter are *systems* and *procedures*.

Before moving on to these subjects we should examine the Westinghouse list and draw some comparisons. Points 3, 5, 8, and 12 focus on the rela-

Figure 5.1
Error Free Performance (UNUM Life)

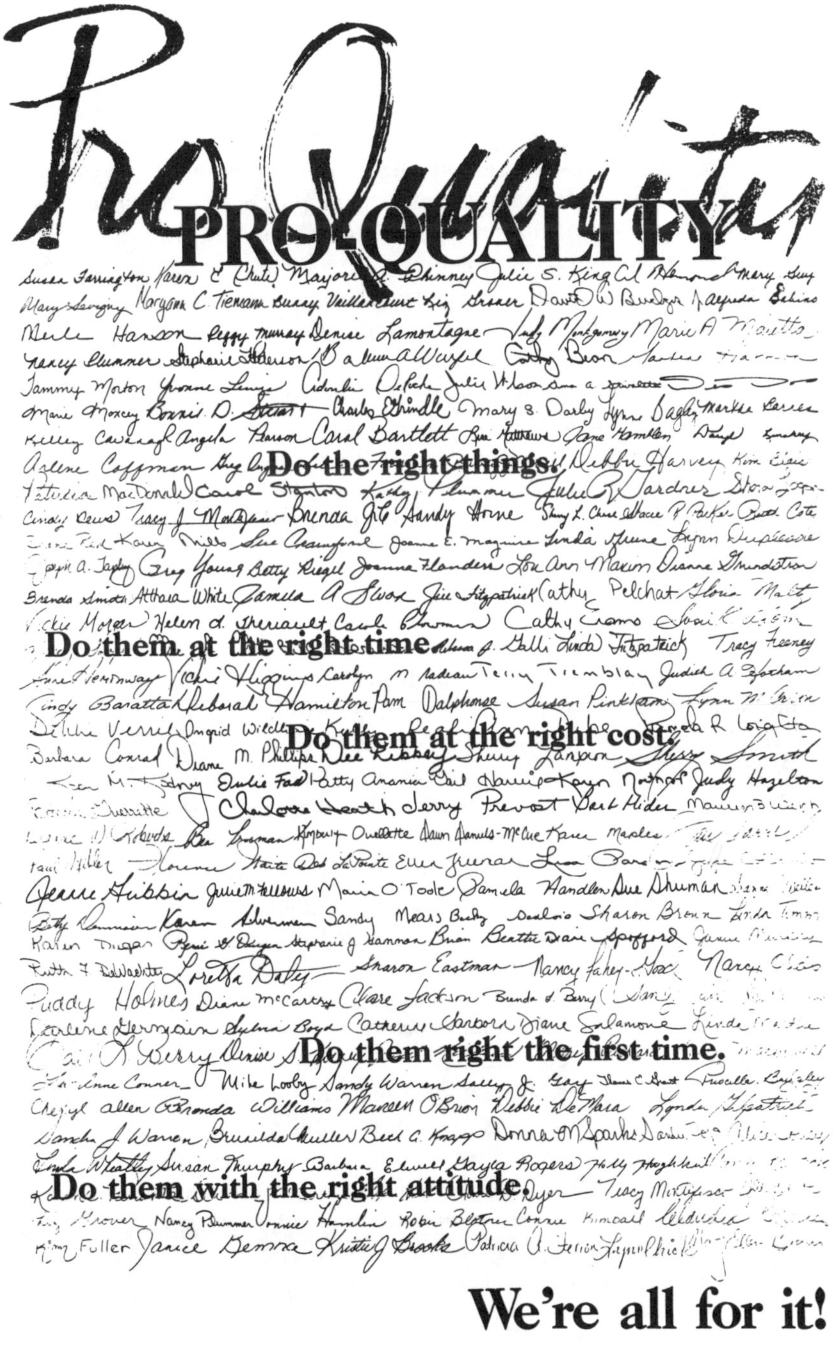

Pro-Quality

PRO-QUALITY

Do the right things.

Do them at the right time.

Do them at the right cost.

Do them right the first time.

Do them with the right attitude.

We're all for it!

tionship between quality and cost. Many financial services organizations have avoided discussing the cost relationships when introducing their quality efforts for fear that employees will view it as another cost reduction program dressed up as something good for the employees, management, and customers alike.

Communications will overcome the employees' skepticism and fear. Otherwise, intelligent employees identify, by omission, cost reduction as the hidden agenda, and the organization is forced to explain why it was not discussed. Paul Revere, as an example, played down cost reduction throughout most of the written communication, but purchased Phillip Crosby's *Quality Is Free* for each supervisor and manager as a quality primer.[2] Although the book is directed at manufacturing situations, Crosby sets forth a plan for reducing the cost of quality. The Paul Revere employees who read the book therefore expected to reduce costs as quality was improved as a natural by-product of their efforts.

Westinghouse points 6 and 9 focus on the issue of timeliness. We will deal with timeliness separately in Chapter 6. We feel that it is becoming more important as a quality factor as our culture in the United States evolves. Teller lines in banks typify cultural changes and differences. In Mexico City retail bank customers wait in line for routine teller transactions for their entire lunch hour. It is not uncommon to see customers eat lunch in line. In major cities in the United States, lunch hour lines reach twenty minutes. The more demanding customers are driven away, because many would not dream of waiting in line for more than five minutes.

Banks have attempted to retain high net worth customers by devising schemes to deflect low-balance, high-activity customers away from the teller lines. The most publicized attempt was made by Citibank in the early 1980s, when they decided to use a minimum average balance system to determine if customers would be charged fees for transactions handled by a live teller. The alternative was to use the automated teller machines (ATMs), which would accomplish two results for the bank: smaller teller lines for high-balance customers; and lower cost because of higher utilization of the teller machines. Customer and consumer group backlash ended the experiment.

In a similar attempt, Goldome Bank established a separate delivery system in 1984, designed to segment high-balance customers. The system was tiered by average customer balance. The majority of customers would continue to receive the service levels that they were accustomed to. A separate line was established for higher balance customers designed to give them even better service. A third service system was established for customers with extremely high balances, involving an office environment that was much more like personal banking. The system had a few drawbacks, including segmenting wealthy people into a separate line and, in some cases, making them feel like they were singling themselves out. The cost effective success of the campaign depended on deflecting some of the lower average balance customers to ATMs. This is an extremely difficult task to accomplish with an elderly customer base or one not accustomed to using charge cards.

The point is that as the United States' population ages and consumers accustomed to using credit cards and debit cards become a greater percentage of the overall customer base, timeliness and convenience will continue to be a critical element of quality.

The remaining points on the Westinghouse checklist pertain to procedural errors or job-related (training and supervision) errors which are typically checked in quality control systems.

POLICY ERRORS

Some organizations establish internal policies with regard to their existing customers or the underwriting of new business which, when examined as an element of quality, would surely be changed. The unanswered question when these policies are uncovered is always how many good customers have we alienated and lost as a result of this policy.

Avoid Alienating Existing Customers

We will use a 1986 credit line campaign by Chase Manhattan Bank to emphasize our point. In late 1986 Chase Manhattan mailed a letter to selected VISA cardholders offering a line of credit. One customer signed and returned the document requesting a $5,000 line of credit. Chase did not ask for current income levels with the return document. In fact, at no point did they ask or find out what the cardholders' current income was. One cardholder's income had tripled since applying for the basic card several years earlier. In the past six months, the customer had purchased a new house and opened several store credit cards at specialty stores (like Nieman-Marcus, Roots, and Narragansett Clothing) while making holiday purchases. Within three weeks the customer was rejected by Chase on the basis of "too many requests for credit for a given time period." Chase didn't find a credit problem from the bureau, nor did they send a standard application to secure the new income figures. The customer quietly let his card expire and moved it to another bank.

Was this a problem with bank policy? Yes, but without a comprehensive quality process it is not a problem that would be detected, corrected, or prevented in the future. Chase compounded the problem by trying to cross-sell MasterCard to the same customer before the VISA card was dropped. The error was in design and judgment. If you checked Chase's accuracy records for their credit line mailing solicitation you would find that the credit analyst was likely within loan quality guidelines for that transaction.

Ensuring accuracy is more than checking to see if the transaction has been completed within the company's guidelines. More important, it is determining if the specifications themselves and the trailing customer correspondence meets the customer's expectations. Is this example unusual for big banks? Unfortunately, it is not. Managing the customer contact points is not an easy matter for the multiple profit centers working as independent Strategic Business Units. A quality organization questions the logic of their procedures and is very careful to reject business based on cause.

Limit Technical Jargon

UNUM Life Insurance Company has established quality control on outgoing policy correspondence. The unit's primary responsibility is to ensure a customer's understanding of letters from underwriting in their Individual Disability strategic business unit. The control unit reads correspondence for clarity. Will the customer understand why we have denied the policy? Have we been cordial as well as clear? Have we recommended alternatives? This practice indicates why this organization is considered one of the top quality life insurers in the country. Ideally, from a quality standpoint the underwriters would be trained to write without using technical terminology. In fact, the control unit may not be necessary in a stable growth environment. It is evidence that the management at UNUM is committed to customer quality.

Scrutinize Profit Versus Service Decisions

Do you ever wonder why some banks issue food stamps, while others do not? Some bank executives would say that it reflects the bank's social commitment. In reality, it is most often related to the level of deposits the states and municipalities hold with the institution. The food stamp issuance decision becomes a financial issue without primary consideration given to how it will impact commercial and retail customers. Who will wait in line longer on the third of the month? They will be the bank's customers that the branch was constructed to support. This policy decision often negatively impacts quality and is an indicator of the company's true commitment to quality.

Punishment and Fear Breed Failure

Policy decisions often stress one aspect of quality over another to the detriment of customer satisfaction. One of the major life and health companies has had a long-standing policy with regard to claims payment. A five-day internal turnaround time is mandated. This service time is tracked, and has actually become a compensation factor for senior managers responsible for the areas. Employees refer to the fifth day as "the line," since there was physically a bold line on the service report showing how much backlog

Figure 5.2
Transactional Service Equation

CUSTOMER SERVICE

Customer Service Time	=	Customer Wait Time	+	Procedure Processing Time	+	Transaction Control Time

Example A

6 Minutes	=	3 Minutes	+	1.5 Minutes	+	1.5 Minutes

Example B

6 Minutes	=	1.5 Minutes	+	1.5 Minutes	+	3 Minutes

The wait time is influenced by the number of services available without change to the basic procedure.

was approaching it daily. The employees live in fear of going over the line and, in fact, admit to processing work incorrectly just to get it out on time. One supervisor lied about the backlog and was fired as an example to other employees of what would happen when management was deceived.

The message here is that quality is not a single element issue. Corporate policies not well thought out, even though at face value they appear to be directed at customer satisfaction, often are counterproductive to the quality process and negatively impact systems.

Avoid Individual Expense Category Myopia

Sometimes executives focus on one problem and institute corrective action which in turn generates a greater problem. For example, a savings bank board of directors in a metropolitan-based company was alarmed by the level of losses due to fraud at the teller station, and decided to adopt a policy to stop the problem. To decide how it would be accomplished they gathered regional managers together to brainstorm the issue from a control standpoint. This should be a red flag to quality- and service-oriented companies. As you will see in Figure 5.2, basic procedures control and cost are the elements that make up a transactional service equation. When you increase controls the overall service wait time will be increased unless you add more resources to pick up the slack. The regional managers decided to lower the floor limits on transactions. This is the dollar amount a teller is authorized to approve without going to a supervisor for a signature. The bank's limits were dropped to the point where tellers were going to supervisors on 62 percent of their transactions. The average customer completed two transactions each time they visited a teller, which in turn resulted in the teller needing supervisory approval 86 percent of the time. The following year losses due to fraud were down 50 percent. Losses went from $80,000 down to $40,000. The directors were pleased. A closer analysis revealed that operating expenses to support the additional checking and longer transaction time increased by over $300,000. In addition, the average individual transaction time rose substantially. Where was the consideration for the customer in the original decision? The solution was originally evaluated strictly from a control standpoint, and the solution achieved their aim. How often do organizations establish a new policy because a senior officer received an irate telephone call or letter? The answer is, too often.

SYSTEMS ERRORS

Systems errors are easier to detect with a comprehensive quality process, yet the integration of human systems and automated systems often leads to quality failure. As an example we will consider the case of CNA Property and Casualty Company and a policyholder in 1986.

The policyholders owned a house which was insured with CNA for over $200,000. In late 1986 the insureds purchased a second home valued under $100,000 and applied for coverage through their agent. The coverage was to correspond with the closing date on the second home. The insureds asked the agent about the payment amount and were assured that they would be billed as soon as the paperwork cleared the new business department at CNA. "Not to worry, you're covered." The next the insureds heard from CNA was a letter denying them coverage past a date three weeks later, and asking for payment for their exposure during the interim period. No reason for denial was provided. The insureds promptly placed their coverage for both properties with another insurance company and demanded an explanation from CNA. The agent, the state insurance commissioner, and the insureds each tried to determine what had happened. The underwriters at CNA responded that they couldn't find the file and had no idea what the problem was. In any event, to rectify the inconvenience to the insureds they dropped their demand for payment of coverage on the second house for the two-month period. Two months after this quality gesture, the insureds received another bill from CNA demanding payment for the coverage.

This example is not intended to be an indictment of CNA. It is simply one real-life example of why financial services companies are not retaining customers simply with an attractive payment rate. The human and automated systems in place created anxiety for the customer by processing the application slowly. Then, they caused panic to their customer when he was told that coverage would expire within three weeks, and confused him by not explaining why the coverage wasn't extended. Finally, the situation escalated to anger when the customer's inquiries were met with, "I don't know. We can't find the file." CNA lost two pieces of business, and they still don't know why.

Improper systems design is often the culprit for our otherwise well-meaning organization. Often the system has not been designed to catch errors that will directly impact the customer. In banking, the new accounts or platform area has traditionally been the source of customer complaints. "The lines are so long that I can't open a simple savings account during my lunch hour." "Changing my Certificate of Deposit from a three-year to a one-year took me thirty minutes and the bank had all the information they needed on hand." "The customer service representative made me fill out another signature card. They must have twenty of them for me by now."

Automation Is Not the Only Answer

To resolve this long-standing service problem various vendors have developed systems designed to recall customer information electronically, update the new account information, and display new account information for the customer prior to automatically printing the required documents. Frequently with these new systems edits are not worked out to prevent errors. While reviewing a major new automated system we found six obvious places where errors would not be detected on opening a simple demand deposit account (checking account). In one case the system allowed the customer service representative to send a Form 1099 to the customer and spell their name incorrectly, even though the name was already in the file correctly.

Attention to detail on systems pays off in the long run with customer satisfaction. Major systems should not be tested on live customers. Often, in the rush to provide better service, companies "switch on" systems that will cost them more answering customer service calls than they would have saved if they had waited three months to properly test the system.

One of the basic systems flaws in companies not tuned in to quality is that they "go to market" with products without involving the support and service units up front. We have seen many cases where applications for a new product are received in the new business department of an insurance company before the department has been told that a new product is being sold. What typically happens is that instead of finding the best and most effective way to support the customer (the independent agent) the new business employees will counter this surprise by letting the applications sit for days. Then the senior manager in support operations will make a political issue out of the lack of communication and involvement. The backlog of new policies is used as a point of conflict and blame, and the unassuming customer is turned off immediately.

The Information/Processing System Gap

When we examine processing systems closely it becomes painfully clear why customers get confused, frustrated, and ultimately disenchanted with the level of service. To explain we will return to the issue of the customer's perception. When a customer is told that his check will be deposited on the first of the month, he expects that to be true. However, banks and thrifts often create customer anxiety and dissatisfaction simply by the way they update their files. Many banks operate in a batch process and update files nightly. When customers with direct deposits (in particular customers receiving Social Security transfers) call to verify the deposit during the day, they find that their account has not been updated. This leads to research of the problem by the bank, and a call back to the customer. It usually results in a follow-up call the next morning to make sure the account was credited overnight. Why does this happen? It happens sometimes because systems are not analyzed and designed with the customer in mind. This can easily be avoided. Many banks run direct deposits in the morning prior to opening. The extra personnel and expense to answer inquiries is not required. It is a matter of cycling the system in the most effective way from the customer's standpoint.

Another example centers on automated teller machines. Deposits and withdrawals submitted through the machines on weekends often are not updated until Monday evening. From the customer's perspective a deposit was made on Saturday, or even Friday night after regular bank hours. When they try to access the money on Monday afternoon, which in the customer's mind should have been in the system since Friday, three days earlier, a message may come up "Exceeds Available Balance" or "Funds Not Available." Again, from the customer's perspective the funds should be available.

Why would the bank give a customer the ability to deposit on day one, and not post the deposit and make it available to him on day three? Does it make sense to you? When banks try to explain to their customers why this has happened, often the discussion becomes technical. "Our cycle runs on weekday nights. Even though the ATM is on-line, it is not real time. Even if it was real time, we have to examine your deposit check to see if we will give you same day availability." The issue is not whether the explanation is accurate or even if it is technically clear. The issue is that systems limitations confuse customers and get in the way of the company being perceived as a quality organization.

Another example of an improperly designed system causing accuracy problems is what we will call the CIF (central information file). In theory a customer need only send his change of address to the bank one time. The change will go directly to the CIF, either key-entered from a terminal in the branch or entered directly from the CIF department.

Again, in theory, every individual product system (savings account, consumer loan account, checking account, charge card account, trust account, etc.) will be updated by the CIF so that individual statements and notices for all the products will be sent to the new address (or better yet, the consolidated statement will be correctly addressed). It saves the bank the time and effort that would be spent individually changing the account information. It should also eliminate the time most companies spend in customer service determining why the statements are continuing to go to the former address when manual systems are not integrated.

Let's think of some customers who have recently purchased a new house and are trying to manage their cash effectively. They depend on their bank to, at the very least, get their statements and bills to them on a timely basis. Their statements are received addressed to the old residence with a forwarding sticker from the Post Office. The customers can now conclude that the U.S. Postal Service is more effective than their trusted bank. How should customers feel about their account accuracy? Should they believe that the bank pays so much attention to financial accuracy that informational accuracy sometimes suffers?

Richard L. Thomas, the president of First Chicago Corporation, while addressing a quality forum, reminded us that "banking is still a business built on credibility, trust, and good faith." He went on to warn that any breach in these areas will invariably lead to long-term damaging effects on the financial institution. We discuss the intelligent planned approach that First Chicago takes to improve quality elsewhere in this book. The point is that trust is easily broken and difficult to earn back. Managing the customer contact points as you can see is much more than concentrating on improving the face-to-face interface. It can often be system-generated contacts that turn our customers into some other company's customers.

Why does the simple updating of customer information continue to haunt many well-meaning institutions? Basically, it is because systems files are organized in different ways, and to tie them all together for a big institution requires a customer link. In one system a customer could be listed as John Doe, while in another he could be John F. Doe. He may also be J. F. Doe, or J. Doe. Some accounts are joint in the names of Joan Doe and John Doe, and other trust accounts may be for Jack Doe although the trust statements are sent to John Doe. Information accuracy will play a major role in determining which companies will emerge as the winners as the financial services industry shakes down in the coming decade.

Third-Party Nightmares

Mortgage banking companies face even greater problems with regard to accuracy. One way they produce income is to buy a block or "pool" of mortgages from a correspondent bank and then service the account for a fee. Servicing involves accepting the payments and keeping the accounting accurate. They also escrow tax and insurance payments and pay the appropriate insurer and municipality for the amount due on time. Tax payment handling is one of the major quality issues for mortgage servicing companies. In simplistic terms, the company must secure a list of taxpayer's bills from the municipality and then remit the proper amounts back to the city or town before being assessed a late payment penalty. The mortgage company acts on behalf of the taxpayer and, in effect, when the company's payment is late, the property owner's (the mortgage company's customer) payment is late.

You can imagine all of the systems complications that arise when dealing with municipalities in multiple states, trying to get tapes or lists of taxpayers. It is not uncommon, especially in New England, for the municipality to ignore the request by the mortgage service company and to send the bill directly to the property owner. The property owner typically disregards the notice, knowing that the mortgage company is holding the escrowed tax money and will pay the bill. The next correspondence the customer receives is a late payment penalty notice. At this point the customer contacts the bank or mortgage company worrying about the penalty. If everything goes right, the customer service person answering the telephone call will take down the proper information, diffuse the customer's anxiety, and set the process in motion to pay the tax and penalty, and follow up with the customer with verification and a letter explaining what went wrong, closing with an apology.

Think about the quality implications and cost. The customer was notified twice that the payment was due. The customer was paying the mortgage company and expected not to have to worry about it. The mortgage company had initially notified the municipality and followed up when the listing was not received. Then the customer contacted a customer service representative who had to contact the appropriate tax clerk. The tax clerk, armed with more facts, contacted the municipality and made a manual payment including the penalty. Then, manually again, the tax clerk or customer service representative using the known facts, constructed a letter of apology and sent it along to the property owner with notification of payment. The additional cost of handling and penalties alone would offset the cost of implementing a quality process in many mortgage companies.

What should have occurred is that the list should have been received and input directly into an automated payment system which would generate one check for all tax payments on the municipality's record serviced by the company. The customer would have been notified by a computer-generated scheduled notice that payment was made.

When Poor Systems Design Overrides Quality

Another common systems problem that causes errors is the automated systems at teller stations designed to control the accuracy of transactions. Most systems have incorporated a function of "stop payments and account holds" that prevents funds from being transacted without proper authorization. Holds are placed on accounts for various reasons. Limits are also placed on tellers by amount of the transaction, as we have previously discussed. The controls are sometimes counterproductive. For example, while we were working at one savings bank we uncovered a situation where a customer was able to place a hold on his account knowing only the amount of the check, not the check number. This forced the savings bank to reject all checks clearing into the account which then had to be reentered manually. The system controls were improperly linked. When the customer came into the bank trying to deposit funds into the account, the teller needed a supervisor to complete the transaction.

Logically, a stop payment on a checking account placed by the customer should not prevent the customer from depositing funds without supervisory override. A supervisory override typically requires the head teller or assistant manager to:

1. Type in a code;
2. Insert and turn a supervisor's key; or
3. Insert an authorization card.

When we visit branches, we always look to see if supervisor's keys or cards are left with the tellers during busy times. Seventy percent of the time the override key is in the teller's machine. The reason is that the controls in place to protect the customer and the bank have not been thoroughly thought out. Without easy key access the customer's transactions would take so long that the service lines would exceed customer's expectations. The correct cure is to make the system conform with handling logic, not to eliminate controls entirely. We have had managers tell us that even though the tellers have the keys, they are still expected to contact the supervisor for certain types of transactions. Our question is always, so why activate the key system at all?

PROCEDURAL ERRORS

Most quality programs concentrate on tracking errors at this level. Quality assurance focuses on error detection, error correction, and error prevention. Error prevention is the key component because this is where quality improvement is planned and executed to eliminate the source of errors. Managers of customer service operations often tell us that they are understaffed for the volume of requests received. They are most often underinformed as to the source of the service requests. In a mutual funds processing company we found that 60 percent of incoming inquiries asked only one question, "What's today's rate for the mutual fund?" A simple taped message on the front end of every call eliminated the need for 60 percent of the human support necessary to properly handle the customer's needs.

Statistical Quality Control

Although this methodology was developed nearly 60 years ago, it is only recently that financial services organizations have attempted to apply the principles. The primary reason for the late adoption of the technique is its apparent complexity of use and interpretation. More often companies use an audit of work after completion. Statistical quality control is a method of evaluating the accuracy of work while it is being performed to determine if quality requirements are being met. The concept is to stop errors from occurring at or prior to the customer contact point, and therefore eliminate the need for an expensive and costly correction process. It is a way to help to do things right the first time.

The primary tool used in the statistical quality control process is a control chart. The development of the concept of control charts is attributed to W. A. Shewhart in the early 1930s. It is a graph that is kept by the person performing the task indicating when and the types of problems that have developed. Correction (in concept) is applied to the basic procedure to eliminate the source of the problem. This prevents errors from recurring. Although the original concept is self-analysis, many organizations use checkers or auditors to randomly review. A proactive posture is essential to make this work.

In our first example we will use a claim coding control chart. The chart in Figure 5.3 gives the inspectors the ability to review the accuracy of items (transmittals, reserve changes, letters of advice), and then documents the result of the inspection. To organize inspection, companies review randomly the output of the entire department, or the individual, or the lines of business. It often depends on the size of the office, the production levels, and the number of people involved in the claim-coding process. For example, some claim departments deal strictly with Worker's Compensation and would more easily use the line of business approach to inspection. Small offices may have very few employees and find it easier to sample the total production. Most often guidelines are established for sampling as shown below.

Figure 5.3
Error Control Chart

Average Production	Number of Items to be Inspected
1–25	5
26–50	8
51–90	13
91–150	20
151–280	32

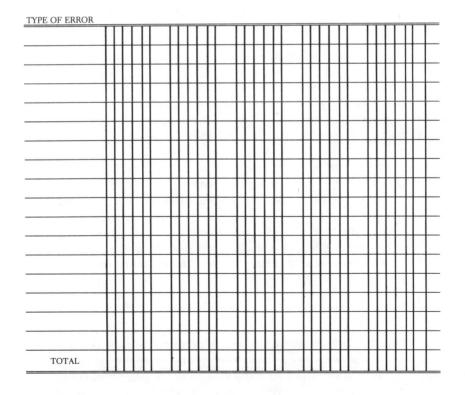

Inspection is an organized daily process. Once the number of items to be inspected has been determined, the quality assurance designer will determine out of the total batch what the frequency is that will be reviewed. For example, using the sample size chart, in a batch of 100 items, 20 would be reviewed; therefore every fifth item would be examined. The inspector could start with one of the first five items and then count five to review the next. The starting point should vary by batch.

The key to prevention is to chart the errors by type and then analyze how to either improve the employee's quality through training, or to redesign the procedure so that the problem will not recur, or to change the forms so that the information used is more clear.

When training inspectors it is imperative that they realize that prevention is the best solution. Identification and classification merely provide data for analysis. Error correction is the short term solution, and should be thought of as a quality Band-Aid. Prevention is the successful operation, to continue the medical analogy, or the long-term solution. Figure 5.4 is a sample of inspection procedures that documents the requirements. Various types of reporting will be explained in Chapter 7 when we discuss consistency.

Another example of an inspection process would be for underwriting in an insurance company. In this function the supervisor often performs the quality inspections. Inspection requires checking policy files for accuracy of: completeness; risk grading; is it within company guidelines; the use of proper authority; and acceptable communications. Expert inspectors will grade the decision-making process to point out potential quality improvement by the underwriter.

One of the fastest growing functions in financial services organizations today is the telephone customer service function. Their ultimate job should be to eliminate the need for their job, not to just respond to the customer's questions.

Many organizations have centralized their customer service to minimize the transferring of clients from one department to another. Some organizations have upscaled the customer service position by training the employees to handle all types of transactions to convey confidence and competence to the customer when solving problems or simply answering routine questions. Accuracy is enhanced when companies forego the urge to use this position as an entry level "low cost" function that they can afford to staff with part-time employees.

Monitoring Service

Checking the CSR's (customer service representative's) work takes two forms. For each unit there is both telephone and correspondence service. The telephone service is monitored by supervisors during the call checking for accuracy of handling, as well as courtesy and knowledge. The feedback

Figure 5.4
Recommended Inspection Procedures

1. Select items for inspection.		Select the items based on instructions from your manager.
2. Inspect items.		Carefully check all coding to ensure the item is complete and accurate. Do not, however, stop the inspection when one error is found. It is necessary to completely inspect the item to identify all errors.

3. Is the item correct?

YES	NO	
4. Complete Documentation.	4. Complete Documentation.	Indicate on inspection record that the item was inspected. Also indicate if the item was in error.
	5. Complete Error Memo.	Identify the item containing the error(s) and give a description of the error(s). Maintain a copy of memo for file.
	6. Return for Correction.	Return the item, with a copy of the Error Memo, to the person responsible for the error for correction.
	7. Verify Corrections.	When item is returned, reinspect the entire document. If item is correct, proceed to Step 8. If item is incorrect, return to Step 5 and repeat the correction process.
5. Release.	8. Release.	Release the item for normal processing.

NOTE: These are recommended procedures. It may be necessary to modify them to fit your individual needs.

can be simultaneous, which tends to be more effective in changing behavior. Have you ever personally called a company for customer service and had the representative say, "Good afternoon. It is possible that this conversation may be monitored by one of our supervisors to ensure accuracy"? Employees typically know they are being monitored or may be monitored. Back to the concept of the control chart for monitoring accuracy.

The objective is to note quality trends or errors while they are occurring so that correction time and cost is limited. Monitoring work live is always favorable to waiting one week or more for the employees to see how well each has performed within the unit.

Recently, companies have begun to experiment with a networked monitor system on departments with employees working predominantly on key entry terminals. (In banking it is proof encoders and lockbox operators, while in insurance it is claims payment, new business, and premium accounting employees.) Live statistical supervision provides a supervisor with a scoreboard to tell where he or she stands with the department's work one hour into the shift when corrections will have the greatest positive impact.

Table 5.1
Control Sampling Chart

Average Production	Normal Inspection	Tightened Inspection	Reduced Inspection
1– 14	5	9	3
15– 65	9	18	4
66– 100	10	20	5
101– 300	30	55	15
301– 500	55	115	30
501– 800	75	150	40
801– 1300	115	225	55
1301– 3200	150	300	75
3201– 8000	225	450	115
8001–22000	300	750	150

Sample sizes can often shift by the complexity of work, the weekly average production, and by past performance of the individual or department. Table 5.1 is an example of an expanded control sampling chart, which could be used for normal variations.

Earlier we had talked about the control chart. An additional form is often used to organize data in such a way that developing patterns of errors may be spotted. This is the quality improvement action worksheet. It is typically an internal chart used to document the accuracy problem, develop an action plan for improvement, and set a time frame for improvement action.

The quality control chart is often displayed by unit on a visible wall using dry pen markers. The accuracy goals are always visible and key ratios can be examined by every visiting employee and manager. The error ratios are sometimes plotted on a graph to depict the trend. The way companies display quality trends largely depends on the image senior management wants their employees to project. Some senior managers are opposed to charts and scoreboards because they personally feel that they clutter the environment or look too clerical. We will discuss this in greater detail in Chapter 8 when we discuss attitude.

SORTING OUT THE ACCURACY EQUATION

What are the accuracy items that are important? Accuracy needs to be defined so that the percent correct is not skewed by an inflated base. Organizations struggle to make the accuracy ratios meaningful. Never mind that the accuracy ratio of the teller function is 98 percent. Ninety-eight percent of what? Do we use keystrokes correctly entered in the teller terminal as a basis? Certainly not. How about transactions handled correctly? Maybe not. The reason is that the count may be calculated on customers properly serviced. Using the customer as the denominator will lower the base and give us a more meaningful picture of accuracy. For example, during an average day a teller may handle two hundred customers, but five hundred and twenty transactions. If the teller completed five transactions incorrectly, the accuracy rate would be calculated as 5/520, or 99 percent correct using transactions as the denominator. When the company correctly uses the number of customers as the denominator the calculation is posted as 5/200, or 97.5 percent correct.

The issue breaks down to the definition of quality. If you believe that it is related to meeting your customer's expectations, then the customers serviced correctly should be used as the ratio basis. If, on the other hand, you are trying to determine the accuracy of all tasks handled by an individual, then you should use the transactions as the basis. Using transactions will ultimately deceive companies into thinking that their accuracy is higher than it is in the customer's eyes.

The accuracy ratio should be discussed at great length with the employees of the unit, and should be tested to get a feel for reasonableness. One commercial bank in their check warehouse function decided to use a ratio of the number of missent/incorrect statements reported by customers and/or branches as the numerator, and the total statements sent as the denominator. What is wrong with this ratio? The customer is used as the barometer as we pointed out as a correct method earlier. The customer is also being used as the inspector, and this is the wrong approach entirely. Remember the concept is *to do it right the first time*.

To carry this example further we have talked with major life insurance companies who use "presidential letters" (customer's complaints directed to the president of the company) as an indicator of overall customer satisfaction. When we asked what was done with the letter we were told that copies were sent to the appropriate department to solve the problem and send a letter of apology. Nothing was done to examine the cause and determine the potential future impact of the problem. In other words, the letters were never used in a systematic way to analyze possible prevention. What happens when presidential letters reach a department for review? In a company where quality is unstructured, often the manager of the department will put a new series of checks or procedures in place to ensure that he or she will never have this problem happen again. The new set of checks have often not been analyzed from the standpoint of "what is the best way to service the customer," but instead from the viewpoint of "how can we prevent this from ever happening again?" As you can begin to see, the accuracy problem may be replaced by a greater problem in timeliness or unit cost by adding additional steps to the procedure.

There are some additional reasons for not using the customer as your inspector. First of all, the majority of customers in our society are not vocal if it means extra work (complaining on the telephone or through a letter) on their part. Many customers will simply let the policy expire (in the case of insurance) and move their business to another company. The independent agent will not oppose, since he or she will receive the first year premium again (agents are generally compensated with a higher percentage for new business than for business that renews). The company will never know the extent of the accuracy problem and will think that their quality is better than it actually is. And the officers will be slow to act on letters since they may represent only one-tenth of one percent of their total customers.

Another good reason for not using customers as inspectors is that you will only find out about a portion of the mistakes. The mistakes you hear about are the ones that do not favor the customer. As an example, in virtually every claims payment department in insurance companies there is a percentage of claims that are overpaid. When pressure is applied to claims payment personnel because of backlog (timeliness measures), clerks tend to guess in favor of the insured to limit extra time checking the coverage or proper procedures. Without an audit of claims paid in place to review accuracy major insurers will pay millions of dollars more than they should. We have seen life insurance companies overpay between three and twenty million dollars annually prior to simplifying procedures and auditing for accuracy. This holds true for all types of unaudited outflows of money.

COMPLETENESS

Accuracy is more than being correct. One of the major accuracy problems for commercial lenders is incomplete data to support a customer's loan application. In the mortgage banking industry whole departments are set up to track down documentation required for the resale of the mortgage not filed by the loan officer when the mortgage originated. The loan officers sometimes feel that the follow-up documentation is a formality, certainly not necessary to serve the customer. In the loan officer's mind the customer is the property owner. Once the loan has been closed, the mortgage company's investments personnel sell the asset of the loan to investors. This is commonly referred to as the secondary market. The investor is a separate customer, just as important to the mortgage company as the property owner.

When the loan officer rushes to close the loan the communications and procedures should be in place to ensure that each of the company's customers is considered and all of the necessary documentation is complete.

What can happen when applications are not complete when the customer initiates a policy or a loan? It can mean contacting the customer again to come to the bank or insurance agent's office to sign a form. This is a tremendous inconvenience to the customer. It also means additional time, materials, telephone usage, and cost.

There are conditions of completeness in every function of every company. One of the more important issues is if the employee has satisfactorily given a customer the information they have requested. When they do not, they require the customer to contact another employee in search of their information. Have you ever contacted a bank using the telephone number listed in newspaper advertisements and asked them to provide a comparison of the advertised certificate of deposit with another product they offer? How often do you hear, "Well, you will have to contact your branch and get the interest information from them and make your own decision." This is incomplete information rarely considered.

Have you ever asked an insurance agent what the cost per month would be if the "face amount" (total coverage) was increased by $100,000, or decreased by a like amount? If you had to wait for them to run another program back at the office, then their sales proposal was incomplete. As you can easily see, accuracy directly affects timeliness in most instances, which leads us into our next chapter.

CHAPTER SUMMARY

The following are the key points made in this chapter.

1. Accuracy occurs at several points within a company:

a) At the *policy level*, where organizations often institutionalize inaccuracy through decisions which later eliminate customers they did not intend to lose.

b) At the *systems level*, where automated and manual systems are not communicating with the customer in the same way.

c) At the *procedural level*, where tasks are performed without definition of quality or training in how accuracy problems cost more to the organization.

2. Statistical control
Control charts are used to give supervisors and employees a way to catch errors before they expand throughout the company. *Do it right the first time.*

3. Accuracy ratios
Make sure that the proper base is used to calculate accuracy. Inflating the denominator with nonessential data leads companies to the false belief that they are better than they actually are.

Don't use the customer as your inspector by using complaints as a barometer of accuracy and overall quality.

4. Completeness

Companies have to think about completeness of information from the customer's viewpoint. Measures of completeness are broader than whether every box is filled in on an application. It focuses on completeness of information since this industry is as much service as product.

NOTES

1. "Error Checklist," Westinghouse Corporation. In Heyel, *Encyclopedia of Management*, p. 1337.

2. Patrick L. Townsend with Joan E. Gebhardt, *Commit To Quality* (New York: John Wiley and Sons, 1986), p. 12.

6   *Timeliness*

INTRODUCTION

We have all been there. You're on your way to an appointment or a night out on the town and your last stop is your bank's ATM machine to get some cash. You fight the traffic. Why is it that when you are in a hurry someone always ends up in front of you who is not? You thank your lucky stars that you can get your money from an efficient machine. There'll be no need to talk with another human being. No need to exchange pleasantries. No need to verify your signature. Just drive up, push the right buttons, and drive away with a fresh supply of cash. Finally your bank branch is in sight. You've only driven a few miles out of your way to get there and amazingly, there's no waiting line to use the machine. You pull up to the machine. You search through your credit cards to locate your bank card. There it is, hidden behind the driver's license you had to give the teller the last time you cashed a check. You pull it out, roll down your window, and just as you prepare to insert the card into the machine you look at the screen and read the message "Temporarily Out of Order, Please Take Your Transaction to Another Machine." You can't believe your bad luck. You are now sure to be late and you still don't have your cash. Your first reaction is anger, but being the rational human being that you are you realize that anger will accomplish nothing and you consider your options. Where is the next closest machine? Your grocery store! Frantically you fight the traffic. As you drive the seconds tick off. There it is! The parking lot is full, but you manage to locate a spot beside an old junk car whose owner will surely put a nice dent in your door with his if he beats you out of the store. You run inside. Where is the machine? Ah, back by the videocassettes and the insurance department that just opened. You run up to the machine and check the screen. You're in luck. This one is working. You insert your card and punch in all the numbers. The machine starts to rumble. It begins to count out your cash and then stops abruptly after dispensing only a few bills. It's out of cash!

Your blood begins to boil. You look at your watch and silently curse the machine. If only you could talk with one of those inefficient tellers right now! Again, you consider the options. You're in luck. The supermarket not only has an ATM but also has a financial services department that allows you to cash a check up to $200. You run up to the window and try to get the attention of the three young tellers who are deep in conversation about their dates last night. Finally one of them sees you and you present your check. "May I have your driver's license number?" she asks. "What is your phone number; how about your office number?" "You were born in 1949? So was my father, perhaps you knew him." "No?" "Well, what is your height and the color of your eyes?" Finally she counts out your cash, less the sixty-five cents the store charges for the privilege of cashing your check. You look at your watch as you run out the door. Your luck must be changing. The junk car next to yours is still there. Unfortunately, so is the shopping cart, right beside the two-inch scratch it put in your door.

Now hopelessly late, you make a mental note to discuss this day's events with your banker with whom you have a appointment tomorrow to discuss refinancing your home now that interest rates have dropped.

The next day you drive to your local branch and sit down with the lending officer. You explain what happened and he is very friendly and interested. In fact, he says that the same thing has happened to him several times and it is about time that someone did something about it. He has complained in the past but, because he's an employee he was not taken seriously. In fact, the operations officer, who was in another division of the bank, felt that he was just trying to make him look bad. The lending officer then asks you to contact the customer service department with your complaint. Of course, customer service is located at the major branch downtown, and that is a forty-minute drive. But, he tells you that you can call them, which you do. You are connected with a very polite representative who explains that the bank has tried and tried to get the machine at your bank fixed, but the vendor's repairman had been unable to fix the problem and the machine breaks down every few days. And, the reason that the ATM at the grocery store ran out of cash was because it was a very busy store and lots of customers need cash at that time of the day.

You return home and open your mail to find a flashy public relations brochure from your bank that is designed to show what high levels of quality and service it offers. As you toss the brochure into the trash you decide to take your account to Sears. They sure did a fine job fixing your lawn mower last summer when it broke down. Now that they offer financial services, perhaps they will be a better alternative than your old bank.

Sound familiar? Most of us could tell a similar story about our dealings with a financial services company. Poor service has become a way of life with many companies across the nation.

What Is Timeliness?

What is timeliness? Does it require an instant response to every customer contact? Does it mean that industry standards must be met? Are there industry standards? Timeliness is a component of quality and therefore, it must be defined within the context of the quality definition discussed in Chapter 3. Hence, timeliness must be defined as "meeting customers' expectations of time service." Time service refers to the time it takes to complete a transaction with the customer.

Someone not familiar with financial services institutions would probably assume that most of them understand their service needs. What could be more important than making sure that the customer is serviced in a timely manner? Knowing what those needs are should be basic to conducting any service-oriented business. Unfortunately, this is not the case. With a few obvious exceptions, companies don't understand what customers really expect, nor would they feel obligated to meet those expectations if they did. Sure, most banks know how long it takes a customer to cash a check, and most personal lines property and casualty insurance companies know how long it takes to respond to an accident claim for a personal auto. But these are the easy examples. And, they represent only a small portion of the total customer contacts any financial services company transacts in any given day. Why is this so?

WHY CUSTOMER EXPECTATIONS ARE NOT MET

You are back in your car after finally getting the cash you need, and so you hurry to make up for lost time, and you have an accident with another motorist who has had an equally bad day. The cars are driveable so you exchange names, driver's license numbers, addresses, and insurance companies. Fortunately you both have up-to-date insurance and you drive away.

The following day you phone your agent. He is very understanding and takes most of the necessary information about the accident over the phone. Then he tells you that you are in luck because there is a regional claims center located right in your city. How fortunate! All you need to do is phone the company and an adjuster will take care of the entire matter.

You phone the office and the operator answers, "Good morning, ABC Company, hold please," and click, your call is placed on hold. When the operator finally gets back on the phone she thanks you for being so patient and asks how she can help you. You think to yourself, "how does she know I was patient, I wasn't given a chance to talk before I was put on hold." But, you decide that fixing your auto is more important than fixing the customer service system and you politely explain that you want to speak with an adjuster. "All our adjusters are out working with customers right now, but if you leave your name, policy number, and phone number, one will get back in touch with you," she replies. "When can I expect to receive the call?" you ask. "We are trying to return all calls by the end of the day, but the adjuster can't do anything for you until your agent enters the claim report into his computer." You provide the necessary callback information and wait for a call from the busy agent.

Let's examine what has happened so far. You called your agent. He patted you on the back and sent you to someone else. You called them and were put on hold. You asked for an adjuster and were told that none was available. But, they did it in a positive manner. Instead of saying that they could not help you right then, they told you that all of their people were out working with customers. Do you really care that they were working with customers? The fact is, they were not available to work with you when you needed them.

Later that afternoon, an adjuster returns your call. He apologizes for not getting back to you sooner but he has really been busy and he asks again for your understanding. You give it and ask him when he can come to the garage that you have selected to see your car. "I can't do anything until I get your claim file off the computer," he replies. You ask why he doesn't already have it, since you called your agent early that morning. He explains that even if the agent had entered the claim into the system right away, it is a batch input system and the adjusters file would not be prepared until the next day, since the updates are run on the computer each night. But, no problem! The adjuster is customer service–oriented. He lets you know that he won't wait for the report before scheduling the visit to examine the damage. He will do it right away. "How about a week from Tuesday?" he asks. You begin cleaning out your ears with your fingers in case you misunderstood what he had just said. "A week from Tuesday?" you ask. "Why so long?" "That's the next day I have open," replies the adjuster. No wonder he was willing to schedule the visit before the claim documentation was complete.

Now you are getting angry again. A week and a half is entirely too much time, especially since you have already been told by the garage that it will take at least two weeks to complete the job. You ask the adjuster if there is any way to speed up the process. He tells you that you could just drive the car by the claims office drive-up department and a resident adjuster could look at it right there. Slowly you count to ten in an attempt to control your temper. You wonder why you weren't told about the drive-up service earlier so all this grief could have been avoided. You ask when you can drive by and you are told that you need to talk with the drive-up department about that. Kindly, he offers to transfer your call, and naturally, it is lost and the phone goes dead in the process.

You redial the office and ask for the drive-up department (after being asked to hold and then thanked for your patience again). Your call finally reaches the proper department and you ask to speak with an adjuster. "Are you calling to make an appointment?" asks the secretary. "An appointment? For a driveup window?" you ask. She doesn't understand your question and you decide that it's easier just to allow her to proceed with her job. "Yes, I want to make an appointment," you respond. "How about a week from today?" she asks. You drop the phone in disbelief. You regain your senses and realize that you'd better get back on the phone or you'll have to call the switchboard again. "Why do I have to wait a week for you to inspect the damage when I'm doing all the work? I'm bringing the car to you and all you have to do is inspect the damage to ensure that the repair shop's estimate is accurate." "I don't make the rules," is the reply. "Besides, you can't expect us to have a staff of adjusters sitting around just waiting for people to drive up. That would cause expenses to us that would result in increased premiums."

Your eyes have now glazed over. Finally, you understand what she said. Translated, it is something like this . . . "In order to keep your costs low and to serve you better, we are making you conform to a schedule that suits us best." Never mind that you are the customer, and that you must drive forty-five minutes to the remote location of the claims center. This is holding your costs down so you should be happy.

You beg for an earlier appointment. You can't imagine being without your car for three weeks. In a moment of weakness the scheduler agrees. If you can get the car to their facility in thirty-five minutes, an adjuster will see you. You thank her, hang up the phone, and race to the facility.

You walk in the front door and identify yourself. The receptionist exchanges glances with her coworker as if to say, "here's the nut who's in such a hurry." She directs you to the claims office. You go in and find two adjusters in a smoke-filled room, drinking a soda and eating potato chips. Must be their break period. One of the men asks if he can help you and you tell him your story. "That's strange, things have been pretty slow around here today," he responds. You clench your fists and the adjuster spends the next five minutes going over the repair shop's estimate and looking at your damaged auto. Finally, he signs the estimate and tells you to have the work completed. He will work out the payment with the shop. Your worries are over.

The entire appraisal took less than ten minutes, even though forty-five minutes had been allocated for it. That is the insurance company's standard for completing an average appraisal. You drive to the repair shop hoping the rest of the day improves.

The above scenario was not fabricated or embellished. It occurred recently with one of the top five largest insurance companies in the United States. Whose fault was it? How could it have been handled better? Let's examine some of the most common reasons why customers' expectations for timeliness are not met.

Acceptance of Normal

Many firms fail or refuse to see the problem. They are so conditioned to the situation that they lose sight of what the customer's needs are. Sometimes, even though the employee empathizes with the customer, he or she is not in a position to do anything about the problem: at least, that is what he thinks. If time service is always bad then it becomes the norm. Customers and employees alike learn to accept the situation and it remains unchanged until some significant event occurs that triggers change. The event could be as simple as a complaint letter to the president that shakes up the branch.

Industry Stagnation

One of the most alarming facts of life in dealing with financial services companies is that they foster what we call "industry stagnation." They are, by nature, conservative. They tend to rely on tried and proven procedures and true innovation is rare. Many creative employees have had good ideas stifled by being asked who else does it that way; as if to say that unless other companies are doing it, it must be a bad idea. But industry stagnation goes deeper than simply stifling good ideas. It is apparent in the matter of industry service guidelines. The competitiveness of financial services companies fosters a tendency to examine service levels in the context of what the rest of the industry is doing rather than to focus on what the customer expects and needs. The implied logic is that there is no reason to do anything any faster than the rest of the industry's doing, even though they could do much better, without any added cost. In fact, many managers have no idea what levels of service they are capable of achieving as long as they are meeting their goals.

Lack of Interest

Some employees simply are not concerned about service. Unless management communicates service-level expectations to employees, it is difficult for most workers to place a high value on them. There are too many other, more important issues to be concerned with. Generally speaking, lack of interest in employees points to the same lack of interest with their managers. An old management adage says that you get what you expect.

Low expectations = low service levels. High expectations = high service levels.

Lack of Empathy with Customer Needs

Many customer contact employees deal with large numbers of customers. Frequently, the employee and the customer don't know one another. The resulting tendency is to forget that the customer is a human being. It's not so much that the employee dislikes the customer as it is that he simply lacks the necessary interest in the customer's welfare. It's often far too easy to remain uninvolved and let the customer suffer his own fate.

Complexity of Systems

Today's systems, both automated and nonautomated, have become very complex. This complexity can result in poorer time service than was formerly possible with far less sophistication and even manual systems. There are times when the employees genuinely want to provide better service, but they are constrained by the system.

For example, years ago before banks and thrift organizations began selling mortgage loans to secondary markets, if a customer had a question the company could simply retrieve the customer's file and answer it. Now, the customer may not even know who to ask because he may not know who holds his loan. But, assuming he does, and he calls his company, there is a good chance that the automated loan servicing system will not be able to provide the needed information, or that the system's response is so slow that the service provided will be inadequate for the customer.

Problems can develop with nonautomated systems as well. As time passes systems tend to become more complex. What was once a straightforward system grows complex as a result of procedural loops that are added to resolve specific situations.

For example, E. F. Hutton Life Insurance Company was one of the first companies to introduce a product known as Universal Life insurance. When the product was first unveiled, many customers switched from their old insurance companies to E. F. Hutton. Most states have regulations against certain sales techniques that are designed to get customers to switch companies without providing additional value to the customer. This new product was so popular that a number of charges were levied against the company claiming that it was using this unfair sales technique to attract customers. To ensure that it was absolutely clean, Hutton formed a replacement unit whose function was simply to ensure that all new sales met the replacement guidelines of the state in which the sale was made. Over the years, other companies copied the Universal Life product and, as they began to realize that there were genuine product differences that had caused them to lose their business they stopped filing complaints. Yet the replacement unit remained at Hutton. It caused a procedural loop in the processing unit that slowed service levels. It continued to exist well after its usefulness had disappeared. However, the situation has been corrected and service levels are now well within industry norms.

Ignorance

A major cause of poor time service is simply ignorance on the part of financial services companies. Often they are unaware of how bad their service really is unless something happens to upset the normal routine. This ignorance will continue well into the future.

Carelessness

Sometimes service problems result from simple carelessness. More than one written transaction has been lost or misplaced by a careless employee and not discovered until the customer calls to complain.

Lack of Defined Procedures

Many service problems can be avoided if adequate procedures are developed and followed. Service delays often occur when employees are left alone to establish how transactions should be completed. There is generally one best way to accomplish a job and the more employees who know what it is and follow it, the higher the level of time service will be achieved.

Too Many Defined Procedures

The opposite effect is sometimes achieved when companies attempt to define too many procedures. All of us can visualize the tough drill sergeant who knows how to make the system work, in spite of the elaborate procedures that have been established. He knows shortcuts that don't adversely affect quality, but that help him accomplish his goal in less time. The same conditions often exist within financial services companies. There is always a better way to accomplish a job. When employees are forced to follow procedures and are not given the opportunity to develop improved methods, time service suffers.

Fragmentation of Job Responsibilities

One of the most common reasons why customer time service expectations are not met is job fragmentation. When companies are small every employee has broad responsibilities. They "wear a bunch of hats." This allows them to be close to the customers, and generally they can see most transactions through from origination to completion. But, as companies grow and staff is increased, new employees do not have the broad background to enable them to handle the same jobs. Hence, jobs are divided into meaningful components, each of which can be learned more quickly and mastered. Eventually, with thorough cross-training programs, these new employees are usually able to master the same tasks as the seasoned employees were once able to do. However, the jobs remain fragmented. Under the old procedures an employee would process a transaction from beginning to end. With the new procedures many employees are required to complete the same cycle. Work is transferred from one employee to another. Each time the document is picked up it must be read before a decision on how to process it can be made. The result is greatly reduced time service, even when the work flow system works. When it doesn't, when there is a problem, the document is sidetracked, which further delays processing. Employees have a tendency to complete the easiest tasks first and set problem tasks aside for later attention. Sometimes this adds days or weeks to service time.

A classic example of this involves a large Blue Cross/Blue Shield plan in the mid-South. Jobs were fragmented. The company had grown substantially over the previous few years, and finding qualified employees was a serious problem. New hires were given the most basic tasks possible, and an assembly-line type of processing system was set up. This philosophy was used throughout the company from the entry room mail operations all the way up to the most senior claims representatives. A claim came through the system that an employee was unable to process. She handed it to a more senior representative who tried to process it. Unable to do so, she passed it to her supervisor, who was also unable to resolve it. That supervisor put it into the box of another supervisor he hoped could process it. Unfortunately, that supervisor had left work because she was pregnant and her baby decided it was time to be born. The claim, which had already been in the company longer than it should have been, sat in the box for several months.

Finally, the subscriber (insured) began receiving threats from the hospital because his bills hadn't been paid. These threats turned into a lawsuit and the insured suffered a heart attack, which he attributed to the pressure he was under because the bill had not been paid. The insurance company couldn't find any record of the claim. It was still in the in-box of the supervisor on maternity leave. Finally, the new mother returned to work and found the old claim. By the time she resolved the problem, a lawsuit had already been filed against the Blue Cross/Blue Shield Plan and they had no legitimate defense. Job fragmentation can have more serious ramifications than just poor service times.

Avoiding the Issues

Many financial services companies recognized the real need to provide good time service years ago, and began tracking service levels of their most critical transactions. Banks tracked teller and platform officer customer wait times. Insurance companies tracked the amount of time required to process claims. When the results of these early measurements were released, many departments reacted predictably, as is human nature. They attempted either to explain why their service was so poor, to attack the measurement system, or to massage the data to make it look better. All these are effective ways to remain complacent with poor time service.

Explaining poor service is easy. People do it every day. We call it "passing the buck." "I couldn't get the work out because the system went down." "I couldn't do it because the file didn't get to me until last Tuesday." "The customer service department told me not to process it until they gave the O.K." The excuses can go on and on, but you get the picture. The point is, no excuse should be acceptable to the customer. What does he care why the service was so poor? The fact remains that it was. Period!

Attacking the measurement system is perhaps the approach that a more polished manager who wants to pass the buck but who realizes the ineffectiveness of that approach would use. If doubt can be cast upon the accuracy of the measurement then no one can be held accountable for poor performance. In fact, no one really even knows whether or not performance is poor. The resulting chaos usually covers up the poor service and gives the offending manager time to take the next step, which is to massage the data to make it appear that things are better than they really are.

Massaging the data is probably the most dangerous way of all to avoid the issue of poor service. We are not suggesting that there is any dishonesty involved, because that is not the case. Managers who massage data do so in an honest attempt to make themselves look better. One example can be found in many financial services companies. Take the case of an insurance company. The scenario would go something like this: Management decides that it wants to measure time service, so a measurement system is installed. Let's say that the service being measured is the time it takes to issue a new policy. The measurement reveals that the average policy is issued in 23 days. Management feels that this is an unacceptable period of time, so an effort is made to improve it. Further study reveals that a majority of the time is lost in the Underwriting Department. Sixteen of the days are consumed underwriting the risk. Management puts pressure on the underwriting manager, who reacts not by looking at better ways to process the work, but by finding a way to massage the measurement system to look better. He first insists that every document entering the system be date stamped. That way, if anyone has a specific complaint about any one policy he can refer to the date stamp to verify whether or not the problem was really caused by his department. Never mind the fact that date stamping each document adds further delay in time service. At least his department will be covered. Next, he learns that a major cause of the delay is applications coming in that are incomplete. They are routinely returned to the agent for completion, or the agent is required to supply the missing information before the risk is underwritten. Since the problem is essentially "out of his hands," there is no reason to hold the department responsible, so the manager decides to change the measurement system to reflect only the amount of time that completed applications take to process. Incomplete ones are not counted. While this may seem fair and logical, the effect is that the true measurement of how long an average application takes from start to finish has been distorted. Only "perfect" applications are counted. The underwriting manager claims that incomplete applications are not his fault. Certainly, no other department claims responsibility for them either. The result is that management develops a false sense that service is good. The only people to suffer are the customers. They realize what the real service levels are.

This points out a major flaw in the way that many financial services companies measure timeliness. Measurement begins when the transaction hits the front door and ends when it leaves the company, completed. For example, if you were to ask a typical insurance company how long it takes them to issue a policy they may be able to tell you. But what you hear will probably be the amount of time that passes from the time it's received in the mail room until the actual policy is mailed out. The company may or may not include time in underwriting, where the application is pending to gather missing information. Rather than look at the total time that passed from start to finish, they add all the pieces and develop a total that is actually less because it doesn't include some of the pieces. Nor does it include time that passes getting the application to the company or the final policy back to the customer.

Looking at this transaction from the customer's perspective we would get a far different picture. To him, the transaction begins when he first contacts his agent. Let's say that occurs on January 1. The agent agrees to meet him at his house the next Thursday, two days later. That evening the application is completed. The agent returns to his office the next day and instructs his assistant to mail the application to the home office for processing. He does so, and the next day it is mailed. Four days later the application is date stamped in the insurance company's mail room and batched with other incoming applications. Since it has a premium attached, some preprocessing is necessary to get the money deposited as quickly as possible. It's then sent to the underwriters. They discover that a Medical Information Bureau report is needed, and the applicant or agent neglected to complete an important part of the application. The report is ordered and the agent is contacted for the missing information. When everything is finally received the underwriter processes the application and updates the computer. The following day, the computer-generated policy pages are assem-

Figure 6.1
Customer Time Line

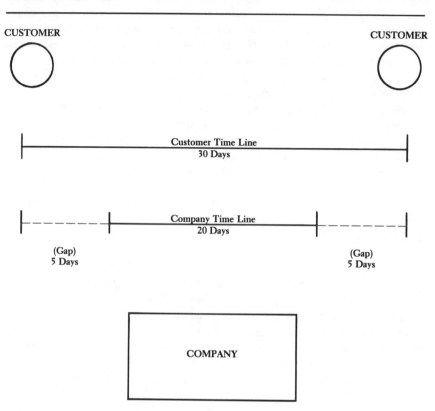

bled with preprinted pages, and the policy is sent to the mail room to be mailed to the customer. It is mailed the next day and four days later it's received by the insured.

The entire transaction took 30 days from the point that the applicant first called the agent to the point that the policy was received by the insured. But, the company's records indicate that the process took only twenty days. The difference can be explained by the lag time involved with the agent and policyholder physically meeting to complete the application, the time that information was in the mail going to the company, possibly the time the application was pending, and the time the policy took to be mailed to the insured.

This is illustrated in Figure 6.1. The customer time line represents the entire time period involved from the first contact through resolution of the problem from the customer's point of view. The company time line represents only the amount of time that the transaction was being processed in-house. The gap between the two can be accounted for by mail time, agent involvement, or any number of reasons. Many companies focus only on their own time line and ignore the customer's.

Hence, the company thinks twenty days. The insured thinks thirty days, 50 percent longer! This is a fairly typical example of a company massaging data to make it appear that its service is better than it actually is. You might come to the defense of the company and say that the delay was beyond its control. The mail can't be controlled. And, an incomplete application is the agent's fault. But the point to remember is that the customer doesn't see it that way. Someone will come along next time with better service and the customer will switch companies. Perhaps their home office will be closer, thus requiring less mail time. Perhaps the application will be submitted over computer lines. Perhaps the policy will be issued in the field rather than the home office. The fact remains that poor service from the customer's perspective caused the loss of business. The company's measurement system failed to reflect the whole picture, and what was reported was massaged to make people within the company look better.

Rework

Another major cause of customer's expectations for service times not being met is rework. Simple reasoning tells us that if a transaction must be processed a second time because it wasn't done correctly the first time, then twice as much time and effort is required. But, this is only part of the problem. Automation often complicates things. Many systems today are categorized as "batch" systems. This means that work is assembled throughout the day into batches that are entered into the computer and processed at night. The following day the computer output is often checked for accuracy to detect errors. The transactions in error are sent back to the originating department for correction. A simple solution would seem to be to correct the error and resubmit the transaction for processing that night, resulting in a one-day loss of service time. However, some major systems require more. They will not accept a correction in this form. What must happen is the in-error transaction must be wiped out one night and the correct one reentered the following day. Employees refer to this as an "undo redo." The result of this type of error is an increase in service time, just for data entry, from one day to three days, three times as long.

As computer technology advances (in fact it already has in some cases) this type of situation will disappear. Many financial services companies have eliminated centralized data input (keypunch) functions, and employees who originate the transactions input data themselves. However, even when this occurs, some computer systems still store transactions throughout the day and update the system at night. Hence, the service problem with rework continues. The optimum system is known as "on-line real time." It eliminates the batch type of input and the employee originating the transaction updates the system when the data is entered. Errors are edited out and corrections can be made much more quickly. However, the fact remains that when an error is made, the error correction requires additional time and effort. Thus, service suffers.

Backlogs

Most financial services companies don't like to talk about backlogs. The name alone implies that the company is behind in its work. But what does it mean in terms of time service?

Perhaps we should not lump all financial services companies together when we discuss backlogs. For example, many bankers would rightly claim that their business requires them to be current. If a customer's deposit is not processed on the day it is received, then someone, either the customer or the bank loses interest on the money. The same is true with withdrawals, except in the opposite. In contrast to the banks would be the Blue Cross/Blue Shield and other health insurance companies. To them, backlogs are a way of life. In fact, many measure their productivity on the basis of the size of their backlog.

Even though the nature of work in the lobby of a bank and the claims department of a health insurance company may be different, the gap between the two is narrowing, along with the expanding scope of services each offers. For example, banks may not have backlogs in branch offices (although we question this on a payday Friday afternoon, for example), but how about in their mortgage lending operation? Have you ever bought a home and gone to a bank to fill out the paperwork?

Insurance companies are under some of the same strains today as banks are in terms of their depository cash at the end of each day. It is rare indeed to find an insurance company today that has not analyzed its cash handling procedures in an attempt to deposit all money the same day it is received by the company. Insurance companies used to keep the customer's premium check with the application until the policy was issued, often 20 to 30 days. Finally, someone realized that they were losing a great deal of interest on those funds and more attention was placed on getting money deposited into the bank sooner. It is routine today for insurance companies to deposit all money into a bank on the same day that it is received.

Hence, as banks have expanded their services beyond accepting simple deposits and withdrawals, and insurance companies have gained sophistication in handling money more effectively, we find that the similarities between the actual work being performed are obvious.

The truth is that all financial services companies have backlogs. Let's look at how they can affect service. Imagine a processing department without a backlog. Work enters the department and goes to a distribution clerk, who logs it in and sends it to a processor. The processor completes the transaction and returns it to the distribution clerk, who batches it for the daily computer update. The system has flaws, but it is fairly simple and it has worked well for years. Then, without warning a surge of increased volume hits. Work begins to pile up. Employees work overtime, but they continue to fall behind. Customers begin to complain about poor service. Management turns on the heat and applies pressure to get the work out faster. This results in increased errors. The errors result in the undo redo's described earlier. Service slips further. Finally, management decides to change the way work is processed in an attempt to push work through. A new position is created just to log in new work received and to keep track of what's being processed in case customers call in about the transaction's status. Then, a second position is created to deal with irate customers who phone for status. Some customers don't phone in but write instead, so the backlog of correspondence increases further. Customer service positions are created to handle written correspondence, just as the telephone customer service representatives handle phone calls. Next, management decides that the customer service representatives have problems locating customer files, so they decide to hire some systems analysts to design an automated customer service system to assist the service representatives. The backlog continues to grow. A preprocessing position is created to assemble all the customer information for the processors. The new function also opens the automated file for the processors. The work gets so far behind that some customers cancel transactions. They write a letter to do so. Now, some customers have their initial transaction documents, calls and letters asking what is going on, and cancellation documents, all in the backlog at the same time. Chances are that their work will be processed in the order it was received when it really didn't need to be processed at all, because the customer ultimately canceled it.

The backlog has caused job fragmentation, a classic cause of poor service, the creation of what should be unnecessary work for the systems analyst, preprocessors, customer service representatives, and control clerks, and still the problem has not been solved. Eventually the system begins to work and the backlog is under control. Unfortunately, service has suffered and costs have risen dramatically. The backlog becomes routine and life goes on.

Lack of Clearly Defined Goals

Poor service time also results when management doesn't make it clear to all employees what the company's service goals are. Many managers manage service levels by monitoring backlogs. If backlogs don't start, where there are none, or if they don't increase from week to week, the managers assume that service goals are being met. In reality, employees could be simply processing easy transactions, and putting off processing more difficult ones. The result would be that the backlog would remain constant, but some of the work would not be processed in a timely fashion. Management must monitor service levels more effectively than by simply relying on backlog controls.

Lack of Employee Feedback on Service Goals

Just as bad as not having clearly defined goals is the problem of managers who do not provide direct feedback to employees about results of their efforts. Even the best measurement system will fail if employees are not kept informed as to how well they are doing.

Summary

All of the situations described above can result in customer expectations on service times not being met. The list is admittedly incomplete. The reasons are endless, but these stand out as some of the most prominent. Almost all financial services companies suffer from at least some of the conditions. The problems are not confined to any particular industry. Nor are they found in any single region of the country. They exist universally, and the organizations that will survive to the end of the century and beyond will be the ones that learn to identify and manage them effectively.

HOW TIMELY SHOULD FINANCIAL SERVICES COMPANIES BE?

Changing Attitudes

Much has changed in the past ten to fifteen years. The MBA gained prominence, and companies began to "manage by the numbers." A common philosophy on time service with the new breed of MBAs in the early 1970s was that financial services companies should provide as poor a level of service as the customer would accept without switching to a competitor. The theory was that providing high quality customer service was expensive, and profitability could be increased by cutting back on service as long as the customer didn't get so upset that he would leave. Actually, the issue of attempting to strike a balance between quantity and quality has been around for years. A recent issue of *Mortgage Banking* was devoted to the subject. As it said about its cover story:

Quantity and quality—so frequently mentioned in the same breath—are less often found in the same package. There are things about each one of them that are incompatible with one another. The achievement of the balance between the two has been the bane of production lines since man came up with the idea that it might be profitable for other people.[1]

In recent years we have been bombarded with recitations of a "new" philosophy, one in which the customer is king. Attitudes within many financial services companies have shifted from the "numbers orientation" of the 1970s to the "customer orientation" of the 1980s. Management's focus is now squarely set on the customer and his needs.

Changing Customer Expectations

Much of this shift was necessary because customers' expectations changed. Today's consumers are more educated and more interested in business news than ever before. In fact, most media sources devote a substantial part of their efforts to reporting business news. Take a look at tonight's evening newscast, or the newspaper, or this week's *Time* or *Newsweek* magazine. You can be fairly sure that they all contain some discussion of a business event. Along with this coverage generally comes an experienced commentator's explanation of the situation. He makes what formerly seemed to be complex issues seem to be simple.

As a result, consumers today are becoming more and more confident. They realize they are better informed and they often are willing to go to great lengths to prove their point. They have become more demanding and they have learned to use the "power of the press" to make their feelings known. If they don't like the service level they are getting from their financial services company, then they will quickly take their business elsewhere.

Educating Customers

While the increased education and sophistication of customers is generally positive, it creates some unique problems. We have all heard the old adage that a little knowledge is a dangerous thing. Well, this couldn't be more true in describing the customers of financial services companies. For example, customers are much more informed today about mortgage banking than they were several years ago. They understand the various types of financing available and are able to calculate the value of, say a loan with 9.5 percent interest and 3 points versus a loan with 9.75 percent interest and 2 points. But, along with this knowledge sometimes comes unrealistic expectations for service. Many customers enter the process expecting it to be completed much faster than is possible. They understand the result of the application process, but are unaware of the details involved in the documentation requests and other necessary steps. Consequently, educated customers who are ignorant of the details will become frustrated with the process and may consider switching companies. Of course when they do, they will run into the same situation there, but they will be more prepared for it at the expense of the first company.

The same situation exists with all types of financial services companies. Consequently, they can no longer afford to remain passive while trying to educate the customer to establish realistic expectations. The companies and their respective trade associations need to do a better job of educating the customer. If customers' service goals cannot be met, you must explain why not.

Unfortunately, this approach can lead to complacency. Earlier we discussed industry stagnation. Some companies look at industry averages for service times and, as long as they are in line, they assume that they are doing a good job. The use of industry comparative data is an interesting study in psychology. Most companies look at it. Some manage by it. They actually make changes based on how well the data tells them they stack up. However, by and large, most companies look at the data, and if it makes them look good they believe it. If it makes them look bad, they find reasons to explain why it is inaccurate for their situation. They rationalize that other companies don't have the same computer system, they don't have the same type of agency system, they are a direct response company, their branches are in better locations, they have more ATMs, and so on. The excuses are endless but, unfortunately, the success of their company is not. As long as they are willing to accept results that are higher than the industry average they will lose customers to the better companies. No excuse is valid.

Once more, competition is coming from all directions. Not only must you compete with your normal competitors, but foreign corporations are increasing their market share in many industries and other nontraditional competitors are entering new industries. For example, if insurance companies continue to compete only with other insurance companies, it will only be a matter of time before a bank, that may or may not be aware of industry standards, enters the market and gains a large share.

CONTROL SYSTEMS

What Are They?

Control systems are the devices that companies use to monitor service, quality, and productivity. They can be targeted in many different directions. One company might be most concerned with individual employees and, hence, would focus their efforts there. Another company might be more concerned with groups of employees. Sometimes the system focuses on service; sometimes it focuses on productivity or quality. Often the company tries to measure all of them.

How Do They Work?

Again, this varies from company to company and industry to industry. Generally, the more customer contact involved, the more sophisticated the measuring device. This is not only because companies want to control their customer contact points, but also because these are often high volume areas that lend themselves to measurement. For example, in retail banks, the area with the highest volume of customer contacts is typically the branch. In this context, the word branch refers to the location where tellers and platform employees greet the customers. Some states do not allow branch banking, but there are still "branches" using this broad definition. There are many ways to measure service in a branch. The simplest are probably basic transaction logs kept by the employees themselves. This approach has obvious limitations, such as the extra time it takes away from working with customers, the possibility of incorrect reporting and even cheating, and the large effort that is required to summarize the information reported, but it can be useful. From there the possibilities grow in complexity and cost. Many banks have developed internal departments that perform industrial engineering functions. These trained experts often conduct studies over several weeks or months to monitor service levels. Another approach is to install pressure sensitive floor mats to count incoming customers. Door counters are almost as effective. Some branches even use laser beams to gather the counts. Again, these typically are placed on or near the entry doors. Finally, some branches rely on computer reports to track transaction volumes. These reports are generally fairly sophisticated and contain a record of all transactions, broken down by the employees who processed them, the specific type of transaction involved, the time of day, and so forth.

Another classic area where control systems are being used effectively is in telephone-oriented departments. Most up-do-date equipment routinely produces reports showing the number of incoming and outgoing calls, broken down by individual operator, time of day, and length of call. The reports may even show the amount of time operators are not using the phones, as well as the number of calls that are lost because all phones are busy and the customer hangs up after being put on hold for several minutes.

Unfortunately, as the complexity of the job increases, the effectiveness of current control systems decreases proportionately. Jobs that have the greatest amount of responsibility associated with them typically have the least effective controls. Also, the broader the task being measured, the more difficult it is to measure. For example, in an insurance company, measuring a customer service telephone representative or a data entry operator is relatively simple. But measuring the cumulative amount of time and effort needed to underwrite an application and issue a policy is much more difficult.

Benefits of Control Systems

The benefits appear to be obvious. The system provides statistics that can be used to enhance productivity, maintain standards, determine staffing needs, monitor quality levels, evaluate equipment, and observe employee customer contact (manage the contact points). Service can be improved along with quality, and productivity can be increased. To take a position against control systems would be akin to being against God, mom, and apple pie.

Problems That Must Be Overcome

Unfortunately, control systems are not as simple as they appear to be, and numerous problems occur which must be dealt with effectively if the benefits of the systems are to be fully achieved. The following are a few of the usual problems that must be overcome:

Excessive Recordkeeping. Perhaps the biggest complaint about control systems in general is that they require excessive amounts of recordkeeping. Often the complaints are exaggerated, but they occur so frequently that they must have some basis in fact. Some automated functions are ideal areas for control. Data entry and telephone customer service are two such examples. But they comprise a small portion of all positions found in a typical financial services company. The remaining functions require some type of manual recordkeeping, and these are the areas where the problem is greatest. Exploring the solutions to this problem is an exercise that goes well beyond the scope of this book, but we will address some of the possibilities later when we look at the future of control systems.

Privacy. Often when employees complain of excessive recordkeeping, their real concern is that of privacy, or more specifically, the company's invasion of it. There is a fine line between monitoring productivity levels and customer contacts, and invading the employee's privacy. Few rational people would contend that management doesn't have the right to manage the business but some management techniques can be seen as assaults on autonomy and personal dignity.

Difficulty of Monitoring Nonclerical Work. As discussed above, recordkeeping is much easier with functions that are routine and clerical. As the level of technical and managerial work increases, so does the degree of difficulty in measuring it. By definition, clerical work is routine and repetitive. The same steps are taken time after time. But, as the level of the job increases, the work performed becomes less defined. And, completion of a task can take days instead of minutes. There are effective techniques for monitoring nonclerical work, but again this subject exceeds the scope of this book.

Internal Politics. Even where control systems are accurate and effective the problem of internal politics still exists. We would like to think of a financial services company as one big team of employees, all working together to achieve a common purpose. Unfortunately this is not always the case. Control systems "tell the score." Poor players don't want to see the score published. Poor performers will use every weapon available to discredit the data and destroy its credibility.

Accuracy. Any control system must be accurate to be effective. Again, in highly automated situations this is not a problem. But where manual input is required, accuracy is often suspect. Poor performers sometimes supply false data, and even good employees sometimes make errors. When the data is used by senior management to evaluate performance, employers expect extremely high levels of accuracy.

Timeliness. Timeliness, or lack of it, can be a problem. To be effective, control systems must report results that reflect the current situation. Management must then determine what actions are appropriate to take, based on the control reports. Because nonautomated reporting is still quite common, and because a fair amount of effort is required to assemble reports and compile them into meaningful management data, timeliness is a major concern. Often the data is a week or more old before it is presented to senior management. This may not be a problem, depending on the condition being reported. If the data is being reported so that management can provide feedback to employees on the results of their efforts, a week may be too long a period. Some employees simply would not react to data that old. For others it might be quite sufficient. For example, an experienced teller in a bank might be very familiar with her normal job performance. She has little need for immediate feedback. However, a teller trainee is in a different situation. She might need feedback at the end of each day so adjustments can be made the following day. For the trainee to be given data that is a week or more old would be a waste. We must use state-of-the-art approaches to gather data so that it can be summarized and reported on a timely basis.

Cost. Another significant hurdle to overcome in using control systems is their cost. Costs can range from very low for basic information to hundreds of thousands of dollars for large companies or for companies that choose to report sophisticated information. One large West Coast insurance company spent over $3 million quantifying the amount of money it wasted each year because of poor quality. Cost is a major issue, and most companies will not accept control systems that do not provide benefits that are at least equal to the costs of developing and maintaining them.

Maintenance. Perhaps the most significant problem to overcome in any ongoing process of control is that of maintaining the system. Regardless of what is being controlled, be it time service, productivity, quality, or something else, if the system is not maintained adequately, it will eventually fall into a state of disuse and it will die. By nature, control systems are perceived negatively by many users. They find lots of ways to criticize even the best systems, but many of their arguments against the systems are philosophical in nature. They have little basis in fact. However, when systems are permitted to get out of date then opponents can rightly claim that the data is nearly useless. Who would like to base important management decisions on old data that might be inaccurate? If the maintenance problem is allowed to persist too long, executives sometimes decide that the system must be redesigned from scratch. And, since the cost of developing new systems is often substantial, a decision to do without them entirely is sometimes made.

The Future of Control Systems. The future holds both good news and bad news for control systems. The good news is that automation in general can eliminate almost all of the problems discussed above. The bad news is that automation opens up a whole new set of circumstances that must be examined.

Office automation is one of the fastest growing industries in the United States today. As few as ten years ago you could have walked into any financial services company and the only evidence of computerization you might have seen would have been computer printouts piled on someone's desk or a stack of punch cards sitting beside them. Today, the situation is much different. The punch cards have all but disappeared, to be replaced by much more effective devices. Gone are the word processing pools and the data entry departments. They became obsolete when computer terminals became commonplace at workstations. No longer do employees manually create computer input forms, they input and update themselves, directly into their terminals.

It used to be rare to see a CRT screen anywhere but within the Data Processing Department. Even there, it was common for programmers and analysts to have to share them. Some companies went so far as to restrict the data processing employees from using terminals during normal working hours. They were required instead to come in during the evening hours when they were less likely to slow down the system.

Today, every programmer and analyst usually has a terminal of his own. What's more, it's becoming commonplace for all employees to have their own terminals. Data processing is no longer the domain of systems analysts. It belongs to everyone. Much of this new trend has been the result of technological improvements, especially the development and refinement of the personal computer. Personal computers today often offer the power of yesterday's mainframe computers. Employees who previously were computer illiterates are increasingly buying home computers for use in their personal lives for everything from playing games with their children to performing sophisticated financial planning functions.

In the past, if non–data processing employees wanted a problem to be fixed through additional automation they had to complete a request for assistance form for the data processing department. The forms would be analyzed and prioritized by the data processing staff. Often, if a project was too large or complex it would simply not get done, or users were told that it would be at least six months before it could be started and it would take another six months to complete.

While this situation still exists in some companies, the advent of the personal computer is rapidly changing things. Non–data processing professionals have found that they can often purchase basic software for a few hundred dollars at their local computer store that will perform many of the functions they want automated. They are finding that it is often much cheaper and easier and faster to do it themselves on a personal computer than it is to do it through their company's mainframe system.

Naturally, some data processing professionals are concerned about all this. They point out, and rightly so, that their companies are losing control. Information is being developed and stored in computers throughout the organization. Many of the new data processing experts are able to run their programs, but have no knowledge of basic safeguards like backing up important data and off-site storage of important files in the case of fire or other disasters. Additionally, since the information is stored in so many different, separate locations it may be impossible to use it in any type of data base or other shared manner. Yet, once again technology is not far behind the need. Local area networks (LANs) are becoming more and more common. They effectively link personal computers together so knowledge can be shared. Programs are now available to up-load data off the personal computer to the company's mainframe and vice versa (downloading).

Automation, however, extends well beyond personal computers. PBX (private branch exchanges) telephone equipment has become very sophisticated. There are a number of vendors that offer hardware and software to monitor all calls, and track the destination, cost, duration, and other useful statistics.

Word processing equipment manufacturers have not sat idly by while all this was going on. They developed more sophisticated equipment that extends the definition of word processing well beyond where it was a few years ago. In fact, much of their equipment is now fully IBM-compatible and can be linked to personal computers and mainframe alike.

Finally, the trusty old data processing people have also responded by making their services and products more attractive. Companies often find that they can buy huge computer capacity at a fraction of what it used to cost and once it has the capacity, terminals can be placed on everyone's desk much less expensively than the cost of purchasing large numbers of personal computers. What's more, their networking capacity gives them the ability to offer services such as electronic mail. Memos may become extinct. The paperless office may not be far away.

How does all this affect the issue of timeliness? The answer is that financial services companies are finding it easier and easier to rely on technology to solve their control system problems. Increasingly, data and transaction information will be captured directly by computers, with or without the knowledge of the employees. Information will be available to mangers immediately, rather than having to wait for days or weeks for it. Employee recordkeeping will become a thing of the past. The computers will do it automatically. Accuracy will be improved. There will be little room for human error. In fact, more and more transactions will actually be made directly by the customer, without the need for an employee to be involved.

Perhaps there will always be some degree of manual effort involved. But new technology is currently developed and being perfected to deal with that possibility as well. For example, all of us have probably seen bar graph equipment in use in grocery store check out lines. A similar type of equipment is now in use in a number of financial services companies to monitor service levels and perform a list of other functions. Each piece of correspondence is tagged with its own unique bar graph, then as it passes through the company from location to location, employees simply pass an electronic "wand" over it and its movement is automatically recorded. Technology is making great progress in simplifying today's control systems and monitoring and improving financial services companies' time service levels.

Work Measurement

One of the oldest and most effective ways of monitoring and improving time service has been through the use of work measurement. This subject is discussed in detail in Chapter 9.

CHAPTER SUMMARY

The following are the key points made in this chapter.

1. Timeliness is defined as "meeting customers' expectations of time service." Time service refers to the time it takes to complete a transaction with the customer.

2. There are many reasons why customers' expectations for time service are not met. They include, but are not limited to: acceptance of normal, industry stagnation, lack of interest, lack of empathy with customer needs, complexity of systems, ignorance, carelessness, lack of procedures, too many procedures, job fragmentation, issue avoidance, rework, backlogs, lack of clearly defined goals, lack of employee feedback, changing attitudes, and changing customer expectations.

3. Customers are becoming better informed, but "a little knowledge can be a dangerous thing." Financial services companies need to better educate customers as to why things are as they are.

4. Looking at comparative industry data is not an effective way to evaluate service

levels. The entire industry can be providing poor quality and service and new entrants into the market who are unaware of industry standards are beginning to gain major footholds.

5. Control systems monitor service, quality, and productivity. They provide valuable data for use in managing financial services companies. In the past they have been plagued with problems such as excessive recordkeeping, lack of privacy, difficulty in using them in non-clerical functions, internal politics, accuracy, timeliness, cost, and maintenance. However, as companies become more and more automated many of these former obstacles will disappear.

NOTE

1. Richard W. Helgerson, "About the Cover," *Mortgage Banking*, February 1987, p. 5.

7   *Consistency*

WHAT IS IT?

> Next to profitability, the most important goal a company should strive
> for is consistency.
> —Mark H. McCormack, author of *What They Don't Teach You At Harvard Business School*[1]

It is Friday night. You and your spouse have deposited the kids with a baby sitter and have headed out to try the new French restaurant that opened a few weeks ago in your neighborhood. You arrive at the crowded parking lot. There are no empty spaces, but a polite uniformed valet offers to put your car in a safe place for a nominal charge. You are hesitant to turn over the keys because you remember the last time you did so at another popular restaurant. The valet could have given racing pointers to A. J. Foyt. He gunned the engine, threw your car into gear and squealed the tires on his way to the narrowest spot available—one that was sure to provide a ding in your door. But you are surprised! The valet asks you if it is OK to park your car out in front of the restaurant where it is safer. This is turning out to be a great evening. You walk to the front door and the hostess quickly locates your reservations and escorts you to a large table right by the window, close enough to the pianist that you can enjoy her rendition of "Moonlight Sonata," but far enough away that it doesn't sound like the "1812 Overture." The view is superb. Next, the wine steward delivers a wine menu and you open it to find an outstanding selection of vintages priced only about 30 percent above liquor store prices. The food menu is equally good. A prix fixe includes everything but the wine; a price that defies belief. The very entertaining waiter steers you toward tonight's specials which turn out to be perfect in every regard. The vegetables are colorful and crisp; the meat is cooked to perfection; the salad is crisp and light; and the dessert is the type that dreams are made of—a souffle so light that it seems to defy gravity. After the meal, the check arrives at just the right moment, following the rich aromatic coffee served piping hot. You leave a generous tip and head for the door. Outside, your car's waiting with the motor running and without any scratches. You drive away, proud of your new "find." A great restaurant with outstanding food, a nice wine list at reasonable prices, and a staff of waiters who are eager to serve.

You and your spouse decide to take your new boss there the following week when he arrives from his home in another state. You call the restaurant and make the reservations. No problem. Table for four at 7:30 P.M. Great! Perhaps this will be the night that he gives you that big promotion you have been working so hard for these past months.

The eventful night arrives. You dress in your best clothes and head to the airport to meet your guests. Their plane arrives on schedule. Everything is going like clockwork. Wait until they see the restaurant. You drive up to the valet parking area and see the attendant you used last week help another couple with their car. Again, he is very careful and polite. The other attendant walks up to your car. You glance at his face and your body goes limp with fear. A. J.'s brother has found a new employer. Doubtless, he damaged one too many cars in his last job. You pray that he has turned over a new leaf. As you enter the restaurant you hear your car screech around the corner while another angry motorist honks his horn at the attendant after a near-miss collision. Your knees begin to shake. Your luck might be changing. You hope not.

The restaurant is much more crowded and noisy. The head waiter escorts you past your prime table over to the one located next to the kitchen. You know the one. It has the trays of dirty dishes stacked up just outside the door. After twenty minutes or so a waiter finally shows up and apologizes for being so slow. It seems that he is usually the bartender, but a wedding party is being held in one of the rear dining rooms and all the usual waiters are busy with it. You place your orders as the bartender-turned-waiter painstakingly records every word. "The service was much better the last time we were here," you explain. "Just wait until the food arrives. It is fantastic!" Finally, after 40 minutes it does arrive, and it is not fantastic. You take a bite of the pale green-grey asparagus and it reminds you of slightly overcooked pasta. The meat is cold and just a bit tougher than water buffalo hide. Finally the dessert arrives and your boss compliments you on the pound cake. You debate whether or not you should tell him that it is really angel food. The coffee doesn't arrive until everyone has finished their dessert, and when it does, it is tepid, not hot. You wait another twenty minutes for the bill to come and you pay it and head for the racetrack outside. There you overhear the parking attendants discussing which of the cars they parked that night handles the best on corners. You interrupt them and ask for your car which arrives without a scratch. Relieved, you leave a large tip and get inside and start the engine. It's difficult to tell when it has started because the radio is operating at full volume, turned to a station that only parking lot attendants listen to, and you couldn't see the engine gauges because of the blue haze of cigarette smoke. Maybe your boss will discuss the promotion next time.

The following week your local newspaper highlights the restaurant as one of the finest new offerings in the city. The night the critic dined there everything was as flawless as your first visit. You will never know if it just had a bad night or not because you will never return for a third time; or if you do, you will be sure that all the "kinks" have been worked out first.

Restaurant critics worldwide have long recognized that consistency in food, attitude, and atmosphere is essential in a great restaurant. What is acceptable poor quality? Is one bad meal out of ten OK? How about one out of five? The simple fact is that if you are the poor soul who happens to get the bad meal, then your view of the restaurant is that it is no good.

This analogy can easily be applied to financial services companies as well as restaurants. Customers expect consistency. Just as they don't want a dry overcooked steak in the restaurant, they also don't want slow service at the teller window or busy signals in the customer service department.

Consistency in financial services companies must be viewed from at least two dimensions. First of all, customers expect good quality at each contact. Hence, companies must manage each contact point now and forever into the future to ensure that the customer is treated with the same level of service each time. It is useless to exceed expectations on one occasion if expectations are not met on a subsequent contact. The second dimension is that every employee within the company who has customer contacts must be managed in this fashion. Once again, it is useless for the marketing or sales representatives to be consistent if the customer service employees are not. How many times have we seen a sales person promise the world and then the employees down the line fail to deliver it? That's frustrating to the customer and often leads to a negative perception of institutional quality.

Michael and Timothy Mescon perhaps summed it up best in an article entitled, "It's Not Over Till It's Over."

Good or bad, right or wrong, customers are most likely to recall the last, not the first, experience. Customers will remember the end of the story, not the beginning. Unfortunately, sales and management energies are expanded as if companies were running sprints rather than marathons. What the consuming public wants (and demands) is consistent service, start to finish. Yet, most deals end with a whimper, not a bang.[2]

Good customer service means providing consistent high levels where the customer's expectations are met. Providing bursts or short-term spurts of high quality service is not enough. Nor is it enough for some employees to provide good quality and service while others do not. The key to consistency is that the customer receives the same high level of quality and service regardless of when he has contact with an employee and regardless with whom he has contact.

Observations on Consistency

Difficult to Explain. The issue of consistency is one that is difficult to explain. This chapter is devoted to it but in a way, so is the entire book. Consistency is actually a measure of the achievement of quality. It is different from the other key elements of accuracy, timeliness, and cost in that its measures are not so much measures of consistency, but rather they are measures of how well all of the others are achieved and how well you are able to maintain your gains. For example, if you wanted to measure the consistency of a customer service function, the major question you would have to answer would be what portion of the time was your organization able to meet their goals, such as service, quality, and cost. It would not be whether or not these goals were met. Consistency deals with measures of the percent of time that goals for other measures are met. If this issue still does not make sense, then it proves our point. It is difficult to explain and define. Perhaps the rest of this chapter will make it easier.

The Larger and More Diverse the Company, the More Difficult It Is to Achieve It. If your company had just two employees, yourself plus one other, consistency would be easy to achieve. You could work in the same area and communicate with each other throughout the day. When a customer contact point arose you could listen to each other's response or, if it was a written type of contact, you could read the other's response. But, as your company increases in size, so does the difficulty of maintaining consistency. What if two customers phoned in at the same moment in time? How could you listen to both your employee's responses? As the size grows, so does the complexity. At some point in time, if the growth continues, you would have to split your company into two sections. This could mean using two different rooms, and the complexity would increase further. Continued growth would lead to even more departments. Different products would be introduced, and the complexity would become even greater. Now you must be concerned not only with how your old employees manage the contact points, but you need to know how your new contact points are managed as well.

Further complicating the issue is the fact that some products have different quality goals than others. For example, customers may be willing to accept poorer levels of quality in the building grounds maintenance department than they will in the billing department. If the grass is allowed to grow for ten days without being cut when it is usually cut every three days, the chances are your customers will not mind. But, if their bill is one penny over what it should be on a $300 charge they will be concerned. Hence, size and diversity of products and functions are both factors that increase the difficulty in achieving high consistency.

The Faster the Company Grows, the More Difficult It Is to Achieve It. Just as size and diversity increase complexity, so does the rate of growth. Companies that grow quickly find it very difficult to ensure consistency. New employees are hired and trained quickly—frequently more quickly than is normal. Their inexperience often causes them to deal with customers in a manner that is inconsistent with the company norm. Not because they want to, but because they don't know any better.

Maintaining Consistency Is Just as Difficult as Achieving It. Unfortunately, maintaining consistency can be likened to rowing a boat upstream. You can't stop. If you do, you drift backward. If your company doesn't pay constant attention to the issue of consistency it will erode to its previous levels, whatever they were.

HOW TO GET STARTED

Much of the remainder of this chapter will be devoted to measurement. Measurement is the yardstick by which to gauge the success of any quality effort. Consistency is but one element that is measured, but the techniques used to measure it are the same as those used to measure other elements such as timeliness, accuracy, and productivity. Hence, we will discuss the measurement techniques here even though they could have been discussed in earlier chapters.

Two types of measures are necessary. One measures the customer's perception of quality. The other measures the time level of quality defined in the organization's terms. This issue of "fact versus perception" was discussed in some level of detail back in Chapter 3. The vehicle for measuring perception is a customer perception survey. The vehicle for measuring quality in fact is a quality matrix. We will discuss each of these in more detail later in this chapter.

Lay the Groundwork

The first step in starting any type of measurement is to lay the groundwork for it. Measurement often causes fear among employees who will be affected by it, and unless they understand how it might impact them, they will be less than cooperative. Actually, it is a matter of basic human rights. Anytime anyone institutes a measure that might have a large influence on employees' jobs, a thorough explanation of it is in order.

Rather than attempt to tell all employees about every aspect of the measurement systems at one time, it's best to introduce the concepts slowly, over a period of time. The first communication should be rather general, and should include a philosophical statement about why quality is important to the organization as a whole and why it is important to each employee. The first of the two measurement systems introduced is the perception survey, and many employees won't see a direct relationship between it and their jobs. This bridge must be built, and the initial communication with employees is the place to do it.

Most companies accomplish this by explaining the reason why financial services companies exist—to serve the customer. This seems like a simple concept to understand, but it is amazing how few employees really do. Even when they understand it, it is difficult for them to appreciate it. If they don't, the second form of measurement, the quality matrix, will probably be met with suspicion and mistrust.

John Guaspari uses an interesting explanation of quality to drive home this point. He says that, "Quality is value viewed from the inside out."[3] He says that when companies initiate quality programs there is a strong tendency to focus on internal matters, because they must be improved in order for quality to improve. This can be dangerous because, by focusing inward it is very easy to lose sight of the reason that the quality concerns were of any relevance in the first place. Guaspari feels that there is an immense gap between one mindset that says that "quality targets must be met because management established them," and the mindset that believes that "quality targets must be met because they offer the most reasonable way that the company can meet its customer's expectations, and thus, continue to remain profitable, allowing for all employees to be compensated for their efforts."

Once this "corporate" view of why quality (and measurement of it) is important is understood by all employees, then a second communication should be prepared and distributed. It should provide the details of the quality matrix including what it is, how it is used, and what will happen with the data it generates. As you will learn later in this chapter when we discuss the matrix, if the employees understand the corporate philosophy and appreciate it for its concern for the customer, the matrix will be perceived as a logical and necessary part of the overall quality process.

Establish a Baseline

The first step in beginning any improvement effort is to measure the current situation. What is the customer's perception of quality? How well is your company meeting his expectations? The customer perception survey is an excellent vehicle to use in establishing the baseline of quality levels.

The Customer Perception/Expectation Survey

A customer perception/expectation survey is basically a questionnaire which is prepared and distributed to a company's customers. Its purpose is to define their attitudes toward current quality and service levels. Typically two separate survey forms are prepared, one for the company's external customers and one for internal customers. Although the purpose of the two survey forms is similar, the surveys themselves are quite different. The biggest difference is that the internal surveys are usually far more detailed than the external ones. Since internal surveys are sent to employees of the company involved, they can be expected to spend more time and supply far more detail. It requires a commitment of time to complete a survey, and outside customers should be inconvenienced as little as possible. Naturally, this is also true of inside customers, but they are employees and that means that they are being paid for their efforts.

Benefits of the Survey

The surveys provide a number of important benefits:

Measures Quality. Most important, this is done from the customer's viewpoint. Professional managers often become so involved with the burden of getting the work out that they lose their perspective of what the customer actually expects. Rather than ask the customer, these managers look at the internal effort to service the customer and then predict what they feel is a "reasonable" level of quality and service. As long as customers don't complain about these service levels everything runs smoothly, at least from the manager's viewpoint. These quality and service level goals are further justified in the manger's mind when he attends industry conferences and talks with managers from other companies who have gone through the same exercise. They develop a type of "mutual admiration society" in which they all pat themselves on the back for achieving goals that they established without consulting the customer.

The customer perception surveys help to bring the customer's goals back into focus. They balance the manager's views with the reality of what the customer expects and what the customer believes he is getting.

Identifies Where Improvement Is Needed. If properly structured, the surveys will zero in on areas that need attention. This is good news because it helps management isolate problem areas so they can be corrected. However, the negative side of this is that the survey becomes a sort of "report card." Insecure managers who do not have a good understanding of their customer's perceptions will be threatened by it. Management needs to pay careful attention to this problem and address it in a positive way.

Helps Clarify Roles and Responsibilities between Departments. When customers zero in on problem areas, managers can more clearly define departmental responsibilities for addressing them. One of the major causes of customer's expectations not being met is the lack of organizational responsibility for them. When managers understand customer needs they usually are willing to take the responsibility for meeting those needs. The problems arise when the needs are unclear and the problems "fall through the cracks" of an individual manager's duties.

Helps Establish a Baseline to Measure Improvement. It is difficult to measure improvement without knowing where you started. Which manager has done the better job, one who improved his department's quality and service by 40 percent in one year or a manager who improved it 8 percent? Of course, it is impossible to determine unless you know where each manager started. The manager who improved quality by 40 percent could have started out achieving only 30 percent of his customers' objectives. Even with the improvement, he is still just slightly above 40 percent. On the other hand, the manger who improved just 8 percent may have started at 90 percent. His 8 percent improvement brings him much closer to his customer's goals.

Survey Helps Involve Supervisor and Employee in Business. Many employees and supervisors are so specialized that it is difficult for them to relate to the customer and even to the products offered by the company. Their involvement with the survey allows them to get closer to the customer and the products, thereby instilling a greater sense of belonging to the corporate team. In fact, since the survey is developed and administered by a team of employees the entire effort encourages teamwork and group participation.

Survey Sends Message to Customer That Company Cares. Customers often treat companies in a like manner to the way in which they are treated. Thus, if they are treated with apathy by the employees, they in turn develop an apathetic posture in dealing with the company. They don't care to improve things because they feel that the company doesn't care to do so. The survey sends a very positive message to the customer that someone cares. Often that is all it takes to unlock negative customer apathy and turn it into positive constructive criticism. Of course, with this comes a responsibility to make the necessary adjustments to improve quality and service. If the customer thinks that his voice will be listened to but then he finds that no improvements were made, he will probably never again get involved. In fact, he may choose to move his business to another competitor who is more interested in his welfare. Even if the company can't correct the customer's problems or reach his quality and service goals, every effort must be made to communicate that you have heard his comments and that you are working on an acceptable solution.

Survey Data Helps Identify "Doing Things Right." Most important, it does so from the customer's perspective. Managers attempt to be as professional as possible. This often involves their attending industry and functional conferences. In the functional conferences they are exposed to people who do the same kind of work as themselves but in different industries. This is both good and bad. The good comes from exposure to new ideas and broadening their scope of vision. The bad comes when ideas that work in one industry are implemented outside that industry. While this cross-pollination can be helpful, in many cases the concepts are not interchangeable. An excellent example of this involves the purchasing function. Purchasing managers in financial services industries often have responsibilities centering on the purchase of office furniture, supplies and forms, and so forth. However, purchasing managers in steel companies, for example, have much more responsibility. They are responsible for purchasing most of the raw materials and sometimes even get involved with scheduling production. When purchasing mangers from different industries get together they talk about how the purchasing function can be improved and/or expanded. Doing so often results in adding unnecessary costs and processes. The customers' needs are often not considered when these functions are added. Over time these functions grow and become ingrained into the corporation. The perception survey helps to identify those functions that don't provide value to the customer. It also highlights those functions that do provide value so management can devote the necessary resources to them.

Problems of the Survey

The customer perception surveys also have some negative elements that should be understood. Whether or not they are truly negative depends on how the surveys are developed and administered. These negatives can frequently be turned into positives with the proper management attention. But, in order to accomplish this, it is necessary to understand the risks.

Surveys Create Expectations. One of the major problems with surveys is that they create expectations that might be difficult to satisfy or that you might not want to satisfy. If a company tells its customers that it is interested in learning their thoughts about quality and that it wants to identify areas that need improvement, the customer may feel flattered that he was asked. The act of asking creates an expectation that the problems will be addressed. But, there are times when it is better not to act on the customer's input. Perhaps the customer has a viewpoint that is not shared by a majority of other customers. Or, perhaps the customer demands a level of service that would not be profitable to provide. In these cases it is best to let a sleeping dog lie.

Conversely, sometimes it is a good idea to create expectations. Let's assume that your bank knows that service at one of its branches is poor. The reason is because there simply are not enough teller windows to accommodate all the customers. Rather than drive them away with poor service, a survey can be a useful device to use to inform the customer that he is important. Later, when the expansion is approved the customer will feel, and rightly so, that his input was heard.

Surveys Require Commitments of Time. Not only are perception surveys a nuisance for the customer to complete, but they require a substantial amount of time to create. For example, someone must decide how they will be structured, departmentally, functionally, or otherwise. Someone must decide what questions to ask, and how to ask them. A routing system must be developed, a sample size decision on how much of the customer base to include must be made, and someone must decide whether the survey should measure all products and services or just selected ones. Lastly, but very important, someone must be prepared to summarize the data from the returned surveys, no small task.

Fear of Report Card. One of the most common fears many employees develop over the use of customer perception surveys is that they serve as a type of report card. Departments that know beforehand that their service is poor will often resist them because they fear that management will find out how bad things really are. Interestingly enough, sometimes even good employees who offer high levels of quality and service will be fearful that they or their department will not "look good" in the survey results. Their fear is often unfounded, but it exists nevertheless.

They Can Be Expensive. We have already discussed the amount of time that is required to develop the surveys and compile their results. But another cost involved can be that of postage. Four or five thousand surveys might represent a small sample of your entire customer base, yet each survey involves postage expense both for mailing to the customer and the return postage. Paper and printing costs must also be considered.

They Require a Data Collection System. It is nearly impossible to compile the results of thousands of questionnaires without the use of some automated data collection system. Some are available for microcomputers with just a little customization, and they are fairly inexpensive. Still, a system is required, and someone must enter the data received on each survey form.

Pre-Survey Activities

A number of details must be dealt with before the survey can be used. Perhaps the most important of them is to determine what the coverage and/or limitations of the survey will be. Asking customers what they think of Bank XYZ is a nice global question that may give you some insight into customer's overall opinion of the company, but the answer will be heavily biased.

For example, what if the customer uses the bank for his checking account only? Day in and day out he conducts his business without any real problems. If he responds to a customer perception survey, he will do so in reference to his checking account. Should that input be used to evaluate the mortgage servicing function? How about the platform function? Obviously not!

It is important to know in advance what departments and functions are to be measured by the survey. The questions must be carefully designed so that the company is certain that it gets input on all of the departments and functions. Otherwise, another survey must be distributed. It is not a disaster if a second survey has to be sent out, because it would go to customers other than the ones who participated in the first survey. However, it is much easier to gather all the input at one time. And, the survey is designed to measure quality. Wouldn't it be ironic to have to send out a second survey because the first one was not prepared correctly?

Another major presurvey activity to consider is how to structure and organize the survey. It is commonly done along departmental lines, product lines, functional lines, or cost center lines. Any form of organization can be equally as successful as the others. There doesn't seem to be a single best way to do it for all companies. The key is to organize it around a system that fits the company using it.

If your company plans to use quality workshops to improve quality, it is often helpful to organize the surveys along the same lines as the workshops so that the data obtained from the survey can be easily applied to the workshops.

Another consideration that is part of the presurvey activities is to decide what additional input may be required on the surveys of internal customers. Remember, these customers are internal departments of the company that use the services of other departments. For example, all departments use the Human Resources Department. Most departments use the Information Services Department. Hence, these departments have many internal customers.

Since the internal customers are employees of the company it is fair to assume that they will be willing to spend a little more time completing the questionnaire forms. Therefore, you can include more questions and receive more input. Of course, remember that these people are still customers and treat them accordingly.

Prepare Documentation

Different forms of documentation are required for internal and external surveys. For internal surveys, typically the president or another highly placed individual signs a letter to all survey participants, explaining why the survey is necessary and asking for everyone's support. The letter should stress that the survey is not to be used as a report card on the departments included, but rather to establish a baseline of information which will be used to monitor future performance and quality improvements.

External surveys also need a letter from the president or another highly placed official, but the contents should be much more general. There is no need to stress the issue of the report card; in fact, customers who are not satisfied with the quality and service that they receive would probably prefer to see the results used as such. The most important point to make in the outside customer's letter is that the company values their input and, without it, it will be more difficult to meet their needs.

Both the internal and external customer perception surveys should include a simple set of instructions as to how to complete them. Companies often find that including a set of definitions of terms used in the surveys is helpful. We often forget that industry terms that are familiar to those of us who work in the company every day are not always understood by laypeople who do not work within the industry.

Prepare Survey

One of the first things that must be done when preparing the survey is to decide on the attributes or factors which are to be used to measure the performance and quality. Some attributes that are commonly used include: accuracy, timeliness, competence and experience, courtesy and cooperation, sensitivity to customer needs, availability of service, and availability of information. Naturally, these attributes should be different for internal and external customer surveys, and additional attributes should be used where they are relevant to the areas under study. Once again, providing each recipient with a consolidated listing of factor definitions will help guarantee that every respondent interprets the factors the same way. This will enhance the accuracy of the data which is obtained.

An important part of preparing the survey is to determine the scope of the customer base that will receive the survey (both internal and external surveys). Every company will have a different view of the degree of statistical accuracy that is acceptable, and once this decision is made it is a simple matter to determine the sample size through the use of common statistical sampling formulas.

As explained earlier, someone must decide how to organize the survey. Once this has been decided it is generally a good idea to insert a paragraph that explains the nature of the subject the customer is being asked to comment on. For example, if the subject is the customer service department, then the paragraph should explain the general purpose of the department and how the customer interacts with it.

Another issue to decide is whether to have just two versions of the survey, one for inside customers and one for outside customers, or whether to have multiple versions of each. The problem is that some of the recipients may not interact with some of the subjects being addressed by the survey. For example, a policyholder of a term life insurance policy may not also own a mortgage policy offered by the insurance company. If the survey is not customized for each situation and sent only to customers to whom it applies, then some of the questions on it will be meaningless. Rather than go through the considerable effort to design customized surveys, most companies simply provide a way for the customers to indicate that they have no knowledge of the subject addressed by that particular question.

Another necessary step in preparing the survey is to determine which performance and or quality factors (or attributes) are appropriate for each subject listed on the survey. The best way to determine this is to meet with the management team that is responsible for the subject being addressed in the survey and let them define the factors. These people usually have the most insight as to what is important and what is not.

Deciding on the rating scale is a relatively simple step. Many companies choose to use a rating scale from one to ten. This allows customers a lot of flexibility in deciding how they want to score. The opposite approach is to use a much smaller scale of perhaps one to three. With the small scale approach a "one" means poor, a "two" is average, and a "three" is superior. The customer must make a forced decision among those three choices. The larger system can be viewed as a continuum with "one" being the lowest and "ten" being the highest. The customer isn't forced to choose between poor, average, and superior and is free to choose a response that fits in between one of those three choices.

It is possible to get even more sophisticated by asking the customer to rate the value of each subject to him as well as rating just the performance. For example, the customer might be asked to rate the value of service to cost, or to rate the relative importance of accuracy to helpfulness.

Tabulate Results

After all the survey forms are returned someone must tabulate the results. In most cases it is necessary to use some type of computer support in this effort. Typically, companies rely on the use of microcomputers and some type of simple data base software. Regardless of the brand of software used, it is important to ensure that the system has the capability to sort results by various categories. For example, you might want to sort by division number or by product number.

The system should also have the ability to add columns of numbers and to provide averages and summary information.

Use the Data

The data provide measures of the gap between the measures of actual service levels and the customers' perception of the service levels. The best quality companies are those that have the narrowest gaps. The number one priority of companies that want to improve their quality must be to narrow their gap.

Also, the data obtained in the surveys should be used to provide a baseline which will enable future quality improvements to be monitored and measured. The same survey should be sent out at some point in the future when measurable improvements have been made in quality and performance.

The survey data also provide excellent guidance as to where to focus quality improvement efforts. It is rare to find that all functions and departments have equal needs for improvement, and the survey helps companies to direct their improvement efforts to places needing them most.

HOW TO IMPROVE

Develop and Use Quality Matrix

The performance matrix is a way to measure and control quality within a company on an ongoing basis. The true value to the organization of outputs from individuals and units can rarely be measured on any single dimension. Usually some combination of accuracy, timeliness, productivity, cost, and courtesy is necessary. This is where the matrix nature of this system comes into play. Where applicable each of these dimensions of an individual and unit output is measured. The system also addresses the real-world fact that each dimension is not of equal importance to the organization, and thus allows the dimensions to be weighted accordingly.

How It Works

An example of a quality matrix can be seen in Figure 7.1. The top part of the form describes the dimensions of the individual output that is being measured. In most cases there will be at least three dimensions—accuracy, timeliness, and productivity. In addition, each employee who has frequent contact with outside customers has measures for courtesy and helpfulness, and any other customer-oriented measures that the company decides are important. Above the individual, the dimension of cost is often included.

Under the heading of each dimension is a brief description of how it is quantified for that particular function. Note that some descriptions are stated as percentages or averages. This is done to ensure that the figures will be true measures of performance that have meaning over extended periods of time.

Beneath each heading are ten boxes with numbers in them. They are numbered from 10 to 1 on the left side of the form and labeled as "Performance Rating." The number in the "10" box at the top of each column is the performance that management has determined to be the best possible performance that can be expected. The number in the "1" box of each column represents the least possible performance that will be accepted. The numbers in boxes "2" through "9" represent varying degrees of acceptable performance.

The third row from the bottom, labeled "Earned Rating," is where the

Figure 7.1
Sample Quality Output Matrix

		ACCURACY Percent of errors from Processors	TIMELINESS Average hours from receipt to Processor	PRODUCTION No. of claims prepared	MEASUREMENT RATIOS
P	10	100.00%	24.0	10000	
E					
R	9	99.89%	25.3	9667	
F					
O	8	99.78%	26.7	9333	
R					
M	7	99.67%	28.0	9000	
A					
N	6	99.56%	29.3	8667	
C					
E	5	99.44%	30.7	8333	
	4	99.33%	32.0	8000	
R					
A	3	99.22%	33.3	7667	
T					
I	2	99.11%	34.7	7333	
N					
G	1	99.00%	36.0	7000	
EARNED RATING					
Weights = 100		0%	0%	0%	TOTAL PERFORMANCE

actual results for the reporting period are recorded along with the "Performance Rating" that those results earned (i.e., 1 to 10).

The row labeled "Weights" is where senior management communicates the relative importance of each dimension of output. In the example shown in Figure 7.1 management has communicated that ACCURACY (45 percent) and PRODUCTIVITY (30 percent) are more important than TIMELINESS (25 percent). At the Unit level all three may be more important than COST.

The figures in the bottom row are obtained by multiplying the "Earned Rating" for each dimension by its weight. The figures are then added across to obtain a "Total Performance" number for the Individual, Unit, or Department for that reporting period.

Advantages of Matrix

Use of the matrix has a number of advantages:

It provides ongoing quality measures, including indicators of performance, accuracy, timeliness, and others that are determined to be important. The customer perception survey that was discussed earlier in this chapter provides a vehicle to measure perceptions of a company's quality levels. Once those perceptions are known and understood, then the next thing that must be done is to find out what the true quality levels are. Frequently, the customer's perception of quality and the actual levels of quality are not the same. If the the customer is ever to be truly satisfied the company must meet his expectations.

Defining the actual quality level is the first step to take following the definition of the customer's expectations. Once actual quality levels are known, management can take the steps that are necessary to improve it to meet the level of expectations. Without the quality matrix, management would have little information on which to take action.

Quality matrices are a vehicle to recognize good employees. Few managers today are very good at recognizing and rewarding good employees. By recognizing we do not mean simply identifying them. The issue is one of public recognition, before their fellow employees.

A recent study reviewed 42 case histories and found that in every case employees performed better when they were given an objective to meet and some quantitative feedback about their own performance.

The study suggested that feedback works as well as it does because it serves both to motivate and teach employees. When people are given what they believe is objective feedback they can compare what they actually did to what they thought they did and also to what they were expected to do. In many cases this feedback can correct misconceptions and inaccurate perceptions about what they have been doing.[4]

The quality matrix sets standards of good performance. Quality matrices can be used to establish standards of performance in all quality areas: productivity, accuracy, timeliness, and so forth. Without clear standards management is unable to function effectively. They have little control over work. The old adage applies as much today as it did years ago, "You can't manage what you can't measure."

The quality matrix increases supervisor involvement. All too often standards are established by a group of industrial engineers without a great deal of supervisory involvement. As a result, when the standards show that performance goals are not being met, the first thing that usually happens is that the employee and the supervisor question the validity of the measurement.

Of course, the more modern engineers today recognize the need for supervisory participation in standard setting, and many of the measurement systems include a great deal of supervisory involvement.

Quality matrices are very participative. Typically, this is how they are developed:

1. A kickoff meeting is held with all employees in a particular area. Its purpose is to explain the matrix and to solicit input for defining the measurement factors that need to be tracked. Again, these usually focus on quality, productivity, and timeliness at the employee level, and often include cost information as well at the unit level.

2. Management decides which measurement factors are appropriate and decides how to gather information that can be used as input in the measurement process. For example, if timeliness is the factor to be measured in an application process, then management might decide that the computer contains a log-in date and a completion date and that the difference between the two dates should be the measure.

3. Another meeting is held with the employees to inform them of progress on the matrix and to solicit input on the "best level of performance that can be achieved" and the "least level of performance that is acceptable."

4. Management then agrees or modifies the employee's input and informs employees of any changes. Next, management assigns importance "weights" for each of the factors.

5. Management reviews the entire matrix with senior management to ensure that everything has been considered and that senior management accepts the matrix as it has been designed.

This participative approach helps to assure ownership of the matrix within the unit, and it helps to ensure that senior management is on board.

Matrices can be used to spot needs for management attention. Any one of the dimensions may need attention for an infinite number of reasons. Perhaps the matrix begins to show that accuracy is slipping. Management can investigate the cause and correct it before it becomes a large enough problem that the customer notices it. Perhaps timeliness slips. The problem may be caused by a number of reasons. Perhaps volume has increased and employees simply are not capable of getting the work processed with the current staff.

Unfortunately, the matrices will only show that a problem exists. They will not explain why the problem began, nor will they explain how to deal with it. But, if the dimensions being measured are properly defined, management should never be surprised with an "out of control" situation. Corrective action can be taken in a timely manner, and disaster can be avoided.

The quality matrices are designed to focus on outputs and not activities. One problem with measurement systems over the years has been that they are often keyed into some type of unit count. Take the case of an underwriting department. Traditional measurement systems have focused on unit counts such as applications handled. The measurement should have focused on cases completed. This may seem like a minor difference, but what often has happened is that an application comes into the underwriting department incomplete. The underwriter must get the missing information before the case can be completed and there are a number of different ways to accomplish this. He can call the applicant. He might refer it to a clerical support person. He might even return it to the applicant for completion.

If the measurement system is based on unit counts, then the underwriter receives credit for each time he handles the document, and thus can actually maximize his performance by handling the same document over and over. Of course, the customer suffers because of the increased amount of time wasted in getting the application processed.

The way the matrix is designed, the unit of count is the completed case. It is unimportant how much handling goes into completing the application, because it can not be counted until it is complete.

Use of the matrix fosters communication between employees and management. Management should receive the matrix results on a regular basis and should pass them on to the employees who are being measured. This sets up many opportunities for them to communicate, and results in a better work environment all around.

Disadvantages of Matrix

The matrix is not a cure-all. It has several inherent problems that must be considered. If it is well designed and implemented these problems can be overcome, but it is important to anticipate them and plan an effective course of action to overcome them.

Resistance to Measurement. As we have discussed earlier, most of us have a tendency to resist measurement. Some experts contend that "It's only the poor players who don't want the score published," but we doubt that this is the case. Even top performers will often be hesitant to begin reporting on a measurement system.

For years we thought that measurement was okay for clerical employees but not for technical ones. Hence, we focused all of our attention on them. But, as the ratio of clerical employees to technical and managerial employees decreased it became painfully obvious that measurement of all employees was necessary.

Interestingly enough, studies have shown that some technical employees want to be measured. For example, a mid-sized property and casualty insurance company located in the Southwest had a telephone claims unit. Its purpose was to try to process simple claims such as vandalism and windshield breakage over the phone without the assistance of an outside adjuster.

The telephone unit was staffed with recent college graduates who were just starting out in the insurance industry. For the most part they were bright, eager employees who wanted desperately to advance their careers into management and higher level technical positions. The unit had about fifty employees in it and they were all at the same job level. Supervision was difficult because they spent such a large portion of their day on the telephone, and advancement seemed to be less dependent on their doing a good job than it was on their appearance and their popularity.

A measurement system was introduced and, for the first time, they had a way to prove their value to the company. This allowed management to use objective data in evaluating salaries and prospects for promotion to higher level positions.

The lesson that was learned was that even though people in general might fear and distrust measurement, if it is done properly, and the benefits are explained to everyone involved, then it can become a very positive experience.

Lessons from Video Games. Video games have experienced a tremendous popularity. But some psychologists fear that they teach us unhealthy thinking. Most of them are designed to be a challenge of our skills. We work and work to beat the system. When we do, what happens? Another board or screen appears that is far more challenging than the previous one.

No matter how successful we are at meeting the obstacles, there always seems to be another one standing in our way. Finally, either out of boredom or frustration, we simply give up and cease to try to win and accept a challenge in simply playing the game.

How does this video game phenomenon relate to the issue of measurement? The answer lies in the problem of the moving target. Just as the video games have what appears to be a moving target goal, with new screens appearing every time that we accomplish a goal, the same thing happens with a quality matrix measurement system. Employees and management meet and jointly define the "best level of performance that is acceptable." When this happens, they are confident that performance cannot exceed the "best possible level." Unfortunately, or fortunately, depending on your point of view, this simply is not the case. Improvements are made to the system that speed processing. Edits are added that increase accuracy levels and eliminate time-consuming rework. Improvements are made that eliminate or combine tasks.

As a result, over a period of time what was once considered to be the "best possible performance" becomes simply average. The only alternative, as far as the quality matrix is concerned, is to go back to management and employees and ask them to redefine the ranges. While this may seem logical to an outsider, to the employees who are trying desperately to meet performance goals, it appears to be grossly unfair. "You have been telling us all along that our goals are "XX" and now that we have improved to the point where we consistently meet those goals, you change them," they say. They have a point.

The best way to handle this problem is to talk about it up front. Explain that the company constantly looks for ways to do things better and when such ways are found, the standards must be updated. While this will not make the problem go away, it will lessen its impact.

Matrices Involve Recordkeeping. As we discussed earlier, one of the major complaints that management and employees share about the use of measurement systems is the amount of recordkeeping that they require. No one likes to keep "tic marks." Professional people complain that it is demeaning, and clerical people complain that they spend more time counting and recording what they do than they do working.

While the quality matrices do not eliminate this problem, they go a long way toward it. One of the major differences between the modern matrix and the old system of "tic marks" is that the matrix measures major outputs.

The "tic mark" systems usually measured activities (this concept was discussed earlier). Because of this most of the counts can be obtained through the computer systems, and little manual counting and recording is needed. For example, in the case of the telephone claims examiners discussed earlier, no manual recordkeeping was required at all. The computer tracked completed work volumes, accuracy, and timeliness, and automatically generated summary reports at predetermined regular intervals.

With the state of technology being what it is today, and the future of office automation being as hot a market as it is, we have little doubt that manual recordkeeping will no longer be required in even the most manual situations for very much longer.

Decentralized Ownership of Results

In addition to the use of the quality matrix measurement system, perhaps the best way to improve consistency is to decentralize ownership of the results of the improvement process. What this means is that even if your company has a "quality guru," someone who is responsible for coordinating corporate quality on a full-time basis, it is essential for improvement results to be credited to the lowest possible denominator. This means that the quality guru should praise the vice-president over the area that was responsible for the changes. The vice-president should refuse the praise and give it to the director. That person should pass it on to the manager, who should give it to the supervisor, who should proudly hand it over to the employees.

From the corporate standpoint, it is irrelevant who is responsible. The main concern should be that it is accomplished. The customer is the beneficiary of the improvement, whether it be in the form of lower product costs, higher levels of accuracy, better time service, or anything else. However, everyone involved should feel that they had a role in the improvement, and the employees should take the lion's share of the praise.

Promote It

The final way to improve consistency is to promote it. Everyone likes to see their name in "print," and promoting it can be fun. This is the easy part. All the hard work went into accomplishing the good results. Now that they have been realized it is time to talk about it.

Promoting it can be done in many ways. Some companies publish good results in their internal newspapers. Some mention good quality results in their annual statements and board of director meetings. Some mention them in their sales literature. Some write books about them. In fact, a quality program at the Paul Revere Insurance Company was so successful that a book, entitled "Commit to Quality," was written about it.[5] The book has been enormously successful and even nonfinancial services companies are using it as a guide in developing their quality improvement processes.

The ways of promoting good results are limited only by your imagination.

CHAPTER SUMMARY

The following are the key points made in this chapter.

1. Next to profitability, the most important goal a company should strive for is consistency.
2. The concept of consistency is difficult to define and explain. Essentially, it is a measure of overall quality. It is required in all elements of a quality program, including accuracy, timeliness, productivity, and cost.
3. Measurement is essential in achieving consistency. This includes both measurement of the customer's perception of quality and measurement of actual quality.
4. Measurement of customer perception is accomplished through the customer perception survey, sent to internal as well as external customers.

5. Measurement of actual quality is accomplished through the use of the quality matrix.

6. Other than the use of the two measurement tools, the best way to improve quality is by decentralizing the ownership of results and by promoting it.

NOTES

1. Mark H. McCormack, *What They Don't Teach You at Harvard Business School: Notes from a Street-Smart Executive* (New York: Bantam Books, 1985), p. 191.

2. Michael Mescon and Timothy Mescon, "It's Not Over Till It's Over," *Sky*, February 1987, p. 52.

3. John Guaspari, "Selling Quality Improvements to Employees," *Management Review*, March 1987, p. 5.

4. Richard E. Kopelman, *Managing Productivity in Organizations: A Practical, People-Oriented Approach* (New York: McGraw-Hill, 1986), pp. 163–87.

5. Patrick L. Townsend with Joan E. Gebhardt, *Commit To Quality* (New York: John Wiley and Sons, 1986).

8   *Attitudes*

Improving attitudes is like improving the air. It is often difficult to see the change, but you can smell it right away.

—Grasing and Hessick

THE NEED FOR CHANGE

Attitudes are the feelings individuals have about a situation, formed by their experiences and values, and expressed by their behavior and general mood. In financial services organizations the customers' experiences with the representatives of the company form their opinion of the organization's commitment toward customers. It can be influenced by what transpires, but too often how the contact transpires forms the basis of the customer's experience.

Let's examine the case of a customer applying for a home equity loan at the local branch office of the customer's bank. The customer service representative (CSR) takes the application willingly and as much as promises the customer that there will be no problem with getting the loan approved. "It will take about one week to get the paperwork processed, but I will call as soon as you can have the money."

How confident would you feel about getting the money to finish your basement? The customer didn't think of trying to make contacts elsewhere because of the confidence of the CSR. What the CSR didn't say was that, based on a short-term strategy to balance their long- and short-term assets and liabilities, the lending committee had temporarily put a hold on this category of loan.

Two weeks later the customer called and was informed that it is out of the CSR's hands and the head office has not approved it yet. Several days later the CSR called to explain that the bank would not be able to approve the loan at this time. He assured the customer that the loan would surely be approved by another bank in town and asked him to call again when in need of service.

This scenario and the attitude of the CSR is all too familiar in today's market. The customer was deceived by the CSR who was afraid to state outright that the chances were slim that the loan application would be approved because of a short-term corporate asset management decision. He blamed the head office for the problem. He wasted the customer's time, raised his hopes (in order to pass blame later), and asked him to come back when he was turned away nearly three weeks later. This attitude shows a lack of self-esteem on the part of the CSR, and a total lack of sensitivity to the customer.

How do we go about changing attitudes in a business world where employees are busy making quotas? We start by developing a sense of respect for the customer. But, even before that, many employees have to start by identifying just who the customer is.

THE CUSTOMER

The customer is often misunderstood. We discussed in other chapters that the customer may be another internal or external company department. It may also be an independent agent or a broker. It is often the ultimate consumer. A good starting point is for employees to identify who their customer is. Often we hear, "I don't have a customer really. I just encode dollar amounts on checks so they can be processed by another department." Employees in some departments feel that the customer is the ultimate consumer and, therefore, downplay the people they really service on a day-to-day basis.

If you are setting out to improve attitudes toward customers throughout the company, then your employees have to understand who the customer is. The customer is their patron by definition. The manager of the print shop may tell you that his customer is the ultimate consumer, but that consumer is not requesting service daily. Don't get us wrong, the print shop should be conscious of the ultimate consumer while being responsive to the departments requesting printing. It is not as easy to determine who the customer is as some people think. Who is the customer of the general accounting department? Is it the departments that want an accurate accounting of their income and expenses? Is it the senior management of the company who are accountable to the board of directors? How about the audit function or the human resources department? What we can say is that the discussion of who the customer is can often be as revealing as any aspect of the quality improvement process to change direction. When the management of a function determines that the agent is their customer and is not just some "pain in the neck who interrupts my staff's work," attitudes will shift overnight.

Many books discuss the key to success as being keeping in mind that the customer is king, but they fail to identify that customer. In Karl Albrecht and Ron Zemke's book *Service America*, they put structure to the service organization in order to make it easier for management to identify how the customer is served by each component of workers. They classify people in service organizations into three categories:

1. The primary service people—those who have direct planned contact with the customer.
2. The secondary service people—those who usually serve the customer unseen, but do have incidental contact with customers.
3. The service support people—everyone else.[1]

The key in their service scenario is that everyone can focus on knowing whom to serve. We believe that classification may help to get employees to focus on their customer. The important first step is to get them to agree upon who the customer is, and then they can start to work on serving them better. Attitudes form the basis for behavior and, with an improper focus on the customer, attitudes would naturally be directed at satisfying something other than the real customer's expectations. The process actually gives a new meaning to work for employees who have not been focused properly. Think of how you would feel if you determined that your antagonist is really your reason to exist. It could eliminate negative feelings you have been harboring about other employees entirely and pump new life into your career.

CORPORATE VALUES

What does a corporate value system have to do with the way individual employees relate to customers? Are stated values that important to an overall quality process? We believe stated values are important to establish consistent behavior in employees. In the absence of such a corporate position, employees develop their own understanding of acceptable corporate behavior largely from first-hand experience with their peers. Of course, this leaves a lot to chance. It also leads to inconsistency in the way service is marketed and ultimately delivered.

When organizational or operational changes take place in companies where value systems are in place, the employees know where they stand with management. This knowledge leads to trust and imbues employees and middle management with the confidence that the new operation is in the best interest of the customer and the employees.

An article in the June 1986 issue of *Management Review* on white-collar effectiveness discussed alternative approaches to productivity improvement in professional and technical functions.[2] In the author's concluding statements he professed that he believes there are principles associated with success regardless of the improvement techniques employed. His research led to the basic principle that "management must trust and involve employees" in the improvement process. Although trust is essential, it is not a one-way street. More important, employees must trust management. The greater the degree of trust, the more open and creative the employees will be in finding and implementing solutions. Trust is developed over time through experience, but new employees should have a basic understanding of corporate behavior from their first day of employment.

Stated corporate values give employees a way to evaluate what will be successful within their own organization's environment. Larry Miller, in his popular book *American Spirit*, argues that stated values are the basis for changing the corporate culture in emerging business in the United States.[3] Miller believes that corporate integrity inspires confidence; confidence that the corporation will make decisions based on what is right rather than expediency. We agree, and so do many of the more progressive financial services organizations.

Sears Mortgage Corporation is one of the nation's top companies in this specialized market. Their growth has been astounding over the 1984 to 1987 period, and the prospects of continued growth look bright. Their growth success has not blinded them to the belief that quality and service will determine the outcome of the outstanding mortgage companies in the next ten years. They also recognize that with growth comes new employees, and all the more reason to publicize their *values* in the form of a mission statement and supporting *philosophies*. We think that in combination it says a lot about their values.

Mission

To become America's premier provider of residential mortgage products and services by satisfying customer needs for high quality and value while maintaining the highest levels of professionalism and integrity and earning profits in excess of industry averages.

Philosophies

- Our most valuable asset is the consumer's trust.
- Our goal is to identify and satisfy our customer's true needs.
- We will provide our customers with the best combination of product, price, and service.
- We will encourage, value, and be responsive to our employees' ideas.
- We will attract superior employees through above-average compensation, and retain them by providing advancement in recognition of quality performance.
- We will provide our employees with opportunities to develop their skills and talents.

- We will forsake short-term gains in favor of long-term benefits for our parent and ourselves.
- We will achieve success through teamwork, cooperation, and communication.
- We will strive for simplicity and professionalism in all that we do.
- We will remember that it is okay to make a mistake.[4]

It is interesting to review the mission and philosophies of a company to determine how customers and employees are treated. Does Sears Mortgage Corporation believe that they need to identify and meet customer expectations? Indeed they do. The mission statement identifies satisfying their customer's needs for high quality and value as the primary motivator if they are to become America's premier provider of residential mortgage products and services.

In their stated philosophies, one important goal is to identify and satisfy their customer's true needs. New and existing employees get impressions from reading the mission statement and philosophies: Sears recognizes quality performance; Sears provides career opportunities; teamwork is expected and encouraged; professionalism and integrity are essential; Sears strives for simplicity; and satisfied customers are the reason for their existence.

The last statement in the Philosophies is a plea for openness and fairness and is not intended as a sign of lower expectations. It is an effort to let people who are striving to achieve the overall goals know that with innovation comes risk, and as long as the risk is directed at the good of the company, keeping the principles of integrity and professionalism squarely in front of them, an error or calculated risk will not be met punitively.

Wayne Minnick in his 1966 book *The Art of Persuasion* said that "Values are the general yardsticks by which we decide what goals we will pursue and what means we will allow ourselves to use attaining them."[5] Sears has given their employees and managers a framework to grow within and expectations of behavior which define the "means" described by Minnick.

Society Bank in Ohio is another rapidly growing, progressive financial services organization that believes in stating values and defining behavior. Six shared values are primary at Society:

1. An unwavering commitment to quality.
2. An emphasis on initiative and innovation.
3. A dedication to providing superior service to the customer.
4. A commitment to the well-being and growth of employees.
5. An active concern for the well-being of our communities.
6. A dedication to providing a consistently high rate of return to shareholders.[6]

Society explains what it means by quality:

Quality. At Society Corporation, we believe that quality should pervade all our activities and endeavors.

Quality must be reflected first and foremost in the people we employ. Quality people value the achievement of excellence by striving to do their best and conducting themselves with honesty and integrity.

We seek quality relationships with our customers and believe that strong customer relationships built through professionalism and candor support a quality asset portfolio and a sound balance sheet. We believe customers equate quality with institutional stability.

We want our products and services, and the way we deal with customers to earn us the reputation as the quality bank in the markets we serve.

Society's explanation of service to the customer follows:

Service to the Customer. Society Corporation has a commitment to providing superior service to the customer. Customer service is rooted in the delivery of value to customers. While value can take many forms, e.g., providing responsive service or high quality products and expertise, it must always be based on a deep, underlying knowledge of customer's needs, and a persistent desire to exceed our customer's expectations and our competitors' abilities.

To that end we believe in:

• Delegating decision-making as far as possible to the point of contact with the customer and to managers resident in the local marketplace.

• Looking to every employee—not just those routinely in contact with the customer—to think about ways to sustain and improve customer service.

If you were an employee or manager in Society Bank Corporation, would you expect the overriding decisions to be based on return on investment if the customer might perceive some slippage in service level? Probably not. When a customer calls for information, would you expect the service representative to say that this is the wrong department and please call another telephone number? I would not expect this to be the norm either. Society states the belief that decision making should be positioned as close to the customer as possible. They also restate Albrecht and Zemke's message in *Service America*: "If you're not serving the customer, you'd better be serving someone who is."[7]

This statement and belief is difficult for many individuals to comprehend. In a major life insurance company we found that corporate values were not stated. The behavior management stressed and rewarded both in pay and recognition was production. With individual production goals as their focus, new business processors viewed agent inquiries as an interruption of their most valued work. We heard over and over again that, "If I didn't have to answer these telephone calls, my production would be up 20 percent." Certainly the new business representatives did not know who the customer was, what their role with the customer was, and how to fill the customer's needs. Stated corporate values would help to shape behavior at the management level as well as the employee level. If managers pressured employees outside the stated guidelines, it would provide an opportunity and basis for discussion.

Terrence Deal and Allan Kennedy discuss values in their book *Corporate Cultures* as "the basic concepts and beliefs of an organization."[8] They go on to say that values define success in concrete terms for employees; "If you do this, you will be a success." Deal and Kennedy feel that values are the basis for standards of achievement within the organization and take the form of the heart of the corporate culture. Our past example of the new business department of the life insurance company is important, because senior management in that organization is concerned with quality and has plans in place to improve, but to date has not communicated effectively their beliefs or followed through to ensure consistency in management thinking. By stating their values and beliefs the company would start patterning their behavior after what is expected. Deal and Kennedy discuss a company with a strong culture as one with informal rules that spell out how people are to behave most of the time. "By knowing what exactly is expected of them employees will waste little time in deciding how to act in a given situation."[9]

How would a company start to organize their beliefs? The strategic planning process is an excellent starting place, since quality and the necessary corporate actions are linked to supporting successful differentiation by this strategic element. We are not saying that interested companies should wait for the next scheduled planning session to get going, but simply that the senior executives should all be involved in shaping and clearly stating the beliefs as they relate to quality.

Once the mission and values are stated in a form that is easy to understand, then the management team is forced to follow through. At Sears the managers distributed credit card-sized plastic cards stating the mission and philosophies so that employees could easily refer to the principles. Once the communication and distribution takes place actions will start to be critically evaluated.

A religious organization has an excellent television ad currently running that shows a parent lecturing his child about the virtue of honesty. The parent tells the child what he expects and why. The conversation is interrupted by a telephone call, which the child answers. When the child learns that the caller wants to talk to the parent and tries to hand the telephone to him, the father asks his son to say that he is "not at home." It turns out to be a simple example of the importance of follow-through. The child is learning a double standard. It's the old "do as I say, not as I do" routine.

In the case of management teams it points out the need for getting participation and concurrence on the quality values and principles early in the

process. Without good communication, understanding, and belief the in-
evitable failures will lead to a lack of trust by middle management and all
who follow.

In an August 1986 article on the quality process, J. M. Juran stated his
belief that companies will have to go into strategic quality planning in a
way similar to financial planning in order to be successful in the near future.
He envisions the responsibility to be assigned to a quality manager much
like that of the controller for finances.[10]

The quality manager's new role will involve assisting the company managers to prepare the strategic quality goals—as Juran sees it, the quality
equivalent of the financial budget. In addition, the quality manager will help
evaluate competitive quality trends in the marketplace. Training will be
directed at assisting company personnel to carry out changes necessary to
successfully compete without sacrificing long-term quality goals.

Juran points out that for many quality managers the new role will involve
a dramatic shift in emphasis: from technology to business management; from
quality control and assurance to strategic quality planning. This added dimension in the planning process of stating corporate values lays a foundation
for employees that they can make judgments from and build upon.

Albrecht and Zemke feel that unless the shared values, norms, beliefs,
and ideologies of the organization—the organization's culture—are clearly
and consciously focused on serving the customer, there is virtually no
chance that the organization will be able to deliver a consistent quality of
service and develop a sustained reputation for service.[11]

We believe that unless these shared values, norms, beliefs, and ideologies
are put into a written format and unless steps are taken to back it up with
actions developed in the planning process, the first step will never be taken
on the journey to optimizing the customer's experience and satisfaction.

SHATTER THE CRYSTAL PALACE

Employees' attitudes are influenced by other characteristics in the work
environment. The attitude often exists that senior management is unap-
proachable. Frequently when this occurs senior management collectively
is referred to by the location of the executive offices. It doesn't matter if it
is the twenty-eighth floor or the fourth floor; the secluded location establishes an elitist pocket of the company. When employees refer to management in this way, they might as well be located in a crystal palace. The
psychology would be the same.

How does the executive team break the elitist stigma? Employees often
view attempts as phony, because trappings are linked to the individual goals
of some executives and change can be incomplete. What makes executives
stand out in your organization? Executive parking spaces are an obvious
trapping. One of the less obvious is the telephone extension. Where a

supervisor's telephone extension number might be 4204, an executive's would likely be 4200. Executive dining rooms used every day and not just for guests is another indicator of status. The office and desk size and type are elitist indicators, and in some offices the art and rugs often tell the tale.

Is it really necessary to eliminate rank entirely from the company? No, we are simply pointing out how many trappings do exist which create the crystal palace effect. Teamwork and customer focus are essential to a quality process, and companies can go a long way to make their executives approachable by changing the environment. The point would be to indicate to all employees that the customer is the truly important human component of the business and all employees, including executive management, are there to serve the customer.

Some companies have attempted to accomplish this breakdown of elitism by eliminating offices entirely and making executives work in cubicles. Other companies have placed their executives on the floor of the functions they manage. We have seen companies insist that the executives sit with employees of other divisions at lunch periodically. When the employees feel that they can talk openly with executive management, then they begin to trust that they are all on the same team working for the customer.

COURTESY

Have you as a customer ever gone to your neighborhood teller machine only to find that the machine has been removed and there isn't a trace of where it was in the wall of the building? What was your first thought? My initial thought was a memory of how the bank had aggressively marketed the location and benefits of using this machine. I remember the day that they replaced random ten-dollar bills with twenties, and a few twenties with one-hundred-dollar bills. Of course the intention was to increase customer usage and, over time, comfort with the machine. How did I know that they were going to offer this cash promotion? I was notified by several mailings from their marketing department. So, now that a decision has been made by the bank that the machine location is not cost effective, how did I find out that the service will no longer be offered? I found out by walking up to the spot in the wall where service was once rendered. I wasn't angry that they removed it; I was upset about the inconvenience of going up to a blank wall in a building to find out. The unstated message to customers is, "You aren't important enough *now* to spend the money or time to inform," or "We don't value you or your time." How many customers have left their bank as a result of such an incident? I know one who did.

We will get back to this question later. It is another example of the old sales mentality (making a sale and then courting prospects while ignoring paying customers). Customers should be treated like friends. Friends are loyal, ready to aid, cordial, and courteous. If you truly want a customer for life, treat him like a friend.

Like in true friendships, courtesy toward customers is always tested when a problem occurs. A good example can be made of an overdrawn checkbook. How are you (or your customers) treated when your account is overdrawn? Let's paint the scene. Jim and Mamie are a hard-working couple with a starter house and a young family. Their credit is impeccable. They have a savings account with the bank as well as their mortgage and checking account. They are never late with their mortgage or consumer loan payments. This month Jim forgot to deposit his paycheck into the checking account. He entered the deposit into the checkbook, but placed the deposit envelope in a little used drawer in his desk at work during a hectic day. Bills were paid on time, as was the norm. Two weeks into the month a "Muggsy Malone" letter was received in the mail. "Your account is overdrawn by $375, and the following six checks have been returned for insufficient funds. We demand immediate payment of the funds to cover the checks, and have assessed a penalty of $150 ($25 per item). Any further delay will result in additional penalties." Jim and Mamie were upset. They felt like criminals awaiting prosecution. The communication and the communication vehicle were designed to get action. The action often results in good customers, with an otherwise flawless relationship, feeling first intimidated and then enraged.

Imagine the same scene, with the exception that a branch manager calls Jim and Mamie to notify them that there may be a problem. At this time the branch manager tells them that the account is overdrawn and they can either transfer funds from their savings account or come down today with funds to cover the amount. The branch manager reassures Jim and Mamie that the bank considers them excellent customers. In fact, the manager explains how they might be interested in overdraft protection (a line of credit tied to their checking account) so that an oversight in the future won't cost them penalties or the inconvenience of making a special trip to make a deposit.

Now think about it. Does your bank treat you like a friend or like a wanted criminal when a simple problem occurs? If you or your customers feel like Muggsy Malone, then your bank has failed to realize the impact of each customer contact.

Yes, a story is told when problems occur. No one likes to deliver bad news. It is interesting to review communications of denied new business. In property and casualty insurance companies the applicant can be made to feel like the fringe of society if they were involved in accidents recently.

We talked to an insured couple who had been involved in two accidents in the past three years. They were in their fifties and, prior to the recent accidents, had not submitted a claim to the insurance company in the previous twenty years. They received a notice at renewal time which explained that their recent record was poor and if another claim was filed they would be considered a poor risk, and subject to losing coverage. Furthermore, because of the increased risk they would find that their rates were being raised significantly. The customers' perception was that the insurance company was looking for any excuse to drop their coverage and was merely documenting the plan to drop this "poor risk" at the slightest provocation. The innuendo was "don't be a minute late with your payment and make sure that no one hits your car while you are shopping, or 'you're history.'" The amusing part of the story is that, after the latest accident, the insureds had purchased a larger car that was considered safer by insurance rating standards and, in fact, their premium payments had not increased at all. The payment amount was lower by $50.

When you consider the communication to the customer the message is clear: *We will take your premium, but we don't consider you a good customer. Don't mess up or you will be someone else's problem.* This company does not have any idea about common courtesy or customer orientation.

Earlier we talked about ATMs (automated teller machines). Have you looked at surveys of why the younger customers use them? Convenience usually heads the list, of course, depending on how the survey questions were asked. Not far behind in many surveys is, "I don't get hassled by the machine," as a response. When we follow up with customers they tell us that they don't want a twenty-year-old kid who has worked for the bank for three weeks asking them for additional identification and then asking them to sign the withdrawal slip in front of them. "No one teaches tellers how to be courteous." "Even when they smile it's obvious by their voice that they are checking to make sure I'm okay."

The problem with many surveys is that the company doesn't take proper corrective action to such a response. We have actually seen banks respond to this situation "positively" by thinking that the ATMs are great because of the little hassle and ease of use, over time the usage will go up and unit cost on transactions will go down. In fact, many banks purposely strategize deflection (deflecting customers away from tellers) as a method of attaining low cost in their branch operations. This strategy, taken to an extreme, is like placing manure at the entrance of the teller line to encourage higher usage of ATMs. The customer's desires and experiences are never considered in the strategy, only the result. This policy of considering the "bottom line today" instead of considering the customer could easily be called the *manure strategy*. It stinks for your customers and, in the long run, for you.

How do you think customers feel about looking at the name plate or name tag on the employee serving them and reading "Trainee"? Should knowing the reason for your lower level of service also lower your expectations? Most customers will tell you that it aggravates them to be told in advance that service will be below standard. It also slows down the service because customers feel compelled to check everything the trainee does, because they are apprehensive about accuracy. If the employee cannot meet the customer's standards for service, then the employee should be watching or learning in a structured environment until he or she is considered fully trained. It is amazing to see how many companies place newly hired and trained employees into a customer service department. When you have problems with your food in a restaurant do you ask for the busboy or dishwasher who was just hired two weeks ago at minimum wage? Of course not.

Some companies feel compelled to just answer the phones, and that *never* results in lowering the incoming phone calls by actually solving quality problems. It merely gives the customer a message taker to talk to. The point is that to be courteous to the customer goes beyond teaching employees to smile and be polite. It involves structuring the customer service function and contact points in a way that limits the time the customer needs to spend to get a problem resolved, and staffing the positions with qualified, knowledgeable, and well-trained employees.

Employee selection, training, and retention gets a lot of attention in some companies, while others merely give it lip service. "What can be so difficult about recruiting employees?" "Sure, we train employees in our introductory training, and the rest is on the job like all of our competitors." We will talk about recruitment and how this affects the "customer's experience" later in this chapter.

"Disclosure" is often abused by organizations in setting the tone for a customer relationship. The definition of disclosure is to reveal. Some companies have taken disclosure to the point that they threaten rather than reveal. Earlier we talked about the insurance company that threatened to drop their customers' coverage if they were to file another claim. The objective is ostensibly disclosure. The reality of presentation was a threat.

Banks are compelled by law to disclose that there is a penalty for early withdrawal of funds in certain fixed-period, interest bearing deposit accounts. How do they communicate this to the customer? "Early withdrawal will be assessed a substantial penalty." Or, does the bank say, "In accordance with regulations customers will pay a fee if early withdrawal is required?" The first disclosure is a statement of power over the customer. The second simply explains facts to the customer about the transaction. It merely *reveals* the facts. Companies that use intimidation and power statements will ultimately be the losers when customers realize that there is a difference between financial *products* organizations and financial *services* organizations.

Disclosure impacts the customer in several ways. First, the customer is informed. The second aspect is how the customer is informed, which impacts their attitudes. Then there is the aspect of how long it takes to inform the customer. Some business development types feel that they are responsible for reading every word to the customer. The reality is that today's financial service customer has opened, closed, and transferred far more accounts than the customer's disclosure was established for years ago. For many customers the time taken to go over the fine points is a nuisance. The new business person can simply ask if they are fully aware of the terms and conditions, and would they like a copy of the disclosure? Many new business employees "read the customer their rights." For all good companies, the policy should provide flexibility to fit the conditions of each customer. They should fully inform the new or infrequent customer, and efficiently service the experienced customer. Compliance officers will argue that organizations are so tightly regulated that there is very little room to change wording. It gets back to how you say things, not so much what you say.

One important aspect of being courteous to customers is to respect their intelligence. If it becomes necessary to tighten controls and the customers will be required to spend more time identifying themselves, that should be presented for what it is. It infuriates customers to receive an "in order to serve you better" letter. It usually reads something like this: "In order to serve you better we are lowering the total amount of cash any one customer may take from an Automated Teller Machine to two hundred dollars per visit."

The implication here is that customers who withdraw more than $200 per visit are the cause of the machine running out of cash on the weekend. The bank's solution is to make those customers travel to two or three machines in order to get the level of cash they require. After all, it would be expensive for the bank to send service staff to refill cash at highly used machines on weekends. It is also hard to get employees to reliably staff this function on weekends.

Banks should fully examine what they are telling customers in their communications. Some bank officers will actually say privately that they have to "train the customers" to get their cash prior to the weekend.

"In order to serve you better" letters are found in every financial services industry. In Chapter 3 we told the story of how the property and casualty company centrally located their adjusters in a remote (lower cost) claims office all designed to "serve us better."

The point here is that we have to be sensitive in our communications with customers. If we have bad news to convey, we should be careful not to attack them with it and also not to sugarcoat it, either. I haven't found a customer yet who enjoys being attacked or insulted.

ASK THE SILENT MAJORITY

Are attitudes that important to an ongoing business relationship? With your customers, we think so. A recent study conducted for the White House Office of Consumer Affairs revealed that the average business never hears from 96 percent of its unhappy customers. Nearly 50 percent of the customers who register a complaint will take their business elsewhere. The interesting component is that the study reveals that, of those customers filing a complaint who get rapid satisfaction, the business retention goes up to 95 percent. That is great news for those companies that are trying to retain a better portion of that 4 percent of customers who complain. The silent majority, 96 percent to be exact, will never let you know until they move their business.

John Guaspari has a great line in his modern fable about quality, *I Know It When I See It*, that can be applied to the silent majority. The advice of a character in the book, "the boss," when discussing how to improve quality was to "listen to the sound of your piece of the market share pie shrinking. That's the sound of your customers telling you about quality. Listen to the sound of your stock price falling because your earnings aren't what you'd hoped they would be. That is the sound of your customers telling you about quality."[12]

One mistake a company can make is to think that by analyzing customer complaints they have tapped a positive source for developing successful marketing strategies. This strategy spends time and resources to:

- Document, track and report all complaints.
- Document and track all reasons for "closed accounts."
- Establish "complaint-handling" performance standards for customer contact personnel (formalize procedures).
- Review the nature of complaints in order to sell additional services.
- Send quarterly "complaint response" cards to customers.
- Solicit feedback from customers upon resolution of the problem.

This last item really should be placed in the quality hall of infamy. Think about it. The customer has been forced to contact the company with a problem due to an error by the company employees. As if the customer's time to bring the problem to the company's attention is not enough of an inconvenience, now, a few days after resolution, the company is asking, "Well how did we do?" As a customer this would be enough to make me part of the silent majority. It is a telling tale of the company's attitude toward the customer's valuable time. The silent majority is alive and busy moving their business until they find a company that will satisfy their needs. If companies would spend as much time, cost, and energy preventing problems, they would most certainly be better off and their customers would not be pushed to move their business.

JOB DESIGN

"One face to the customer" is a standard that many organizations are rallying behind incorrectly. The basic concept calls for attitudes, information, and knowledge to be equal at the key customer contact points. Some group health insurance organizations have devised a strategy of hiring and training each employee at a level where they do all jobs for one major customer (new business, billing, payment processing, claims payment, and file maintenance). The "how" to get one face to the customer in this case is ideally correct, but impractical. It would take years for employees to master all of these functions and with changes in product, policy, and automation, it is impossible to maintain effective knowledge. It is also difficult to support normal increases in business due to the long tail on training. Don't be fooled by the "whole job" allure some experts propose.

Good employees become frustrated in functions where they are underemployed or overemployed. Employees who cannot master all the functions become frustrated and turnover is the result. Making each employee a "minicompany" has some advantages. Job levels are generally higher since the scope of work is so broad. The company can thereby justify higher salary ranges and can "cherry pick" the good employees from other companies. There is also the attraction of a learning curve for employees unequaled in other organizations.

The problems are also exaggerated. In a "whole job" environment when the employee is out (lunch, break, illness, or vacation) it is as if the company shut down. Backup employees merely take messages, much like an answering service. Priorities are also left up to the employee on processing. When they come in each morning there may be claims, enrollment cards, payments, and service letters. Employees tend to work on what they like to do first. Some work may wait days artificially.

"One face to the customer" is a valid goal, but it should be accomplished by designing intelligence, information, and knowledge into the key customer contact points and not by trying to turn all employees into companies. It is akin to a football team making each player learn every play and every position on both offense and defense in order to have proper backup at each position and to give them more options. What you would end up with is a smart team which didn't have sufficient practice to be proficient at any position.

MAKING THE CUSTOMER ATTITUDE HAPPEN

Hiring People Who Fit the Job

When we talk to companies in a similar employee marketplace we are always interested in finding out what their employee turnover is. It is amazing to see competitors where one has a turnover rate of 40 percent, while the other's may be 8 percent. The problem often starts at the point of hire. Recruiting and hiring employees is not what should be expected of the human resources department. It should be recruiting and hiring the *right* people. Each job has requirements of technical, communications, experience, and behavioral ability.

Many service organizations have had an outside psychologist develop testing that helps to identify characteristics of a function designed to add value to the hiring decision. People in service functions will not be successful if they do not like human interaction. Even without testing, human resources departments should be made accountable for their hires in every customer sensitive function. Human resources' customer is the department manager they service, and one thing that we have found is that it is much easier to hire people with a good attitude than to try to change after they hire people who are ambivalent.

Training the Customer Focus

Once a good employee is hired there should be orientation as to what the company is, who the customer is, and why the customer is important. Many organizations use films to help them get the quality message across. The orientation should be conceptual. When an employee has completed it, he should walk away knowing that he joined a company with a common purpose... to meet customers' expectations.

Too often the next aspect of training is that all too familiar OJT (on-the-job training). Based on the original orientation, the new employee should ask, "Who is the customer of this department?", "What are the service standards our customers expect?", and "What are the key measures of accuracy for our department?" If the OJT has not been structured to answer these questions and the orientation didn't plant the questions in the mind of the new employee, then the quality orientation has been ineffective. The orientation and training should be geared around building confidence and self-esteem in each new employee. The new hire should be confident that he and every other employee will be trained to be the most effective, customer service–oriented person in the industry. Departmental training should be designed to make them identify how their individual effort is important.

The old saw, "the chain is only as strong as its weakest link," has a direct application in the service business. Too often employees are rewarded only for successfully completing their own job and not for attempting to attain the corporate good. In those environments where quality is not strategically implemented it pays to be better than your peers. In fact, by not helping his peers an employee may be in a better position for promotion because of the failure of others. In a quality organization the system will be designed to reward the team player and customer-focused employee more than the individual performer.

Feedback That Reinforces

The One Minute Manager, a best-selling business book by Kenneth Blanchard and Spencer Johnson, was successful because of its simple yet effective message. One of the concepts directed at positive reinforcement was to "catch people doing something right."[13] Several organizations have formalized this theme with the feedback in their quality process. Paul Revere issues wooden coins to their executives for distribution to employees who exemplify "above the call of duty attitude and actions." The executives must go and find such employees and report who they are to the next quality steering committee meeting. If the executive does not find three such people, it is presumed that he/she did not have three such people working at excellent quality levels during the period.

The coins are in fact gift certificates for a meal, which can be turned in any time the employee would like. Pat Townsend, director of Quality Team Control at Paul Revere, explained recently that many people (approximately half) prefer to hold onto the wooden coin for what it represents rather than trade it in for the meal. This simple way of recognizing people is effective at supporting and reinforcing attitudes that win for customers.

Recently a senior vice-president of a property and casualty firm in the Midwest told us that he is embarrassed about how he and his peers in the industry have stressed production volume as the critical management element for the past twenty years. He said, "It's so obvious that quality is what we should have been reinforcing all along." Now, he and the senior managers of other progressive companies have nothing to be ashamed of . . . if they follow through by defining, measuring, training, and reinforcing quality. It will be interesting to see if the weight shifts on performance evaluation forms toward excellence on those activities that focus on meeting the customer's expectations.

Some financial services organizations have been using "shoppers" to request business and service through various means in order to determine how their employees (the company) rate from time to time and in comparison to other financial services organizations. The shoppers look for attitude (courtesy and friendliness), as well as incidence of cross-selling, product knowledge, timeliness, and efficiency. The data is normally collected subjectively through a series of ratings of telephone calls or direct observations.

The major weakness in the process is that the ratings of performance are subjective. The comparison to like institutions only tells a company their quality performance relative to their competition. There is a false sense of security in being the best of a bad lot. Companies should be most interested in how *their* customers view them and not how a professional shopper views them.

Attitudes are contagious in both directions. If an employee has a bad attitude and finds fault with every customer or manager with whom they come in contact, it will inevitably influence the surrounding employees to some degree. Hence the old saying, "one bad apple will spoil the whole lot."

Positive attitudes and actions that go above and beyond the call of duty will also influence every surrounding employee in a positive way. It is common to see pockets of both super- and sub-par workers in any company. The more we reinforce the super customer service employees with meaningful recognition, the more they will want to continue behaving in this way, as will their coworkers. Good attitudes can be nurtured. It takes thoughtfulness on the part of management and open-mindedness on the part of executives who were previously geared to production and audited numbers. If you think about it, the shopper system is a carry-over from the old way of management. The shopper information is independent, but the comparative measurement is still focused on errors. Employees don't think of the shoppers as people looking for people doing things right, they often consider them henchmen and spies. Customer attitudes can be reinforced to bond a company. Skepticism will be difficult to change. In some people it may never change.

Of all the components of quality a company will have difficulty validating, attitudes will head the list. Of all the components of quality a management team will have difficulty planning for, changing attitudes will head the list. Attitudes are the least tangible yet potentially the most influential aspects of becoming a quality organization that can be worked on. Don't feel discouraged if your evidence of attitude improvement is examples of behavior that you wouldn't expect in years gone by. Your ability to measure the change will come by watching your market share go up along with your dividends. Remember, you don't have to measure the improvement in attitudes to know that it is there. It is more advisable to identify that great behavior and reinforce it.

CHAPTER SUMMARY

The following are the key points made in this chapter.

1. Employee attitudes are difficult to measure and determine the status of. It is often the resulting behavior and moods that express how the employee feels about the company and the customer. It is the most difficult element of quality to change, yet potentially the most influential.

2. A good starting point for employees is to identify *the customer*. Many employees may have other employees or outside brokers as customers.

3. Companies can establish a basis of employee behavior by publishing and supporting a statement of corporate values. This will set the stage for trust of management by employees. In progressive companies it is a natural outgrowth of the

mission statement. You will see more and more chief quality officers in companies as the quality strategy becomes key to differentiation.

4. Courtesy is more than smiling and saying, "Please come again" or "Have a nice day." It is a reflection of all decisions made that impact a customer. Customers treated as friends are more apt to stay. The true test comes when there is a problem to resolve. Customers are just as often attacked as they are informed.

5. Ninety-six percent of dissatisfied customers never contact the company to voice their displeasure. They simply take their business elsewhere. It is important to devise a way to prevent the failures, and a key is how we communicate with them regularly.

6. Some hints for getting attitudes focused properly are to: (1) hire people with generally good attitudes to begin with; (2) properly train and orient customer service employees; and (3) reinforce behavior which evidences excellent attitudes toward customers.

NOTES

1. Karl Albrecht and Ron Zemke, *Service America—Doing Business in the New Economy* (Homewood, Ill.: Dow Jones-Irwin, 1985), p. 106.

2. Jac Fitz-enz, "White-Collar Effectiveness," *Management Review* (June 1986), p. 52.

3. Lawrence M. Miller, *American Spirit: Views of a New Corporate Culture* (New York: Warner Books, 1984), p. 157.

4. Sears Mortgage Corporation, "Corporate Mission Statement and Philosophies." Lincolnshire, Ill.: Sears Mortgage Corporation.

5. Wayne Minnick, *The Art of Persuasion* (Boston: Houghton Mifflin Co., 1968).

6. Society Bank, "A Statement of Mission and Corporate Culture" (Cleveland: Society Bank, November 1985).

7. Ibid.

8. Terrence E. Deal and Allan A. Kennedy, *Corporate Cultures: The Rites and Rituals of Corporate Life* (Reading, Mass.: Addison-Wesley, 1982), p. 21.

9. Ibid., p. 36.

10. J. M. Juran, "A Universal Approach to Managing for Quality," *Quality Progress* (August 1986), p. 24.

11. Karl Albrecht and Ron Zemke, *Service America*, p. 190.

12. John Guaspari, *I Know It When I See It: A Modern Fable about Quality* (New York: AMACOM, 1985), p. 77.

13. Kenneth Blanchard and Spencer Johnson, *The One Minute Manager*, ed. Pat Golbitz (New York: William Morrow, 1982), p. 38.

9   *Success*

WHAT IS SUCCESS?

How do you know when you have achieved what you set out to accomplish when you began your quest for quality? If your objectives were specific enough, then you should have some basic measures that could help you decide. On a very general level you could ask yourself, "Are we meeting our customers' expectations?" Unfortunately, it is very difficult to answer this question, because there are so many different types of customers and so many different expectations.

Perhaps Harold Geneen had the answer. Think back to our discussion in Chapter 3. Geneen said,

> When all is said and done, a company, its chief executive, and his whole management team are judged by one criterion alone—performance. Lost and lay forgotten are the speeches, the lunches, dinners, conventions and conferences; the public causes endorsed and supported: all those supposedly key contacts with important people. What remains is the record of the company and its performance.[1]

Geneen is absolutely correct. Your customers eventually decide whether you are meeting their expectations. They vote with their wallets. If they are unhappy they simply switch to one of your competitors who is usually more than willing to accept them into the fold. Unhappy customers translate into lower income and, more often than not, reduced profitability and ultimately, forced merger or complete failure.

The message seems to be clear. You must meet your customers' expectations. The measurement of how well you do this appears to be equally clear. You must achieve and maintain good profitability.

Why It Is So Difficult to Succeed

How can something so simple be so difficult? The whole "master plan" of quality sounds so simple. "Please the customers and they will reward you with their business." We consultants sometimes like to oversimply the issue, but the issue is really very basic. You must meet the customers' expectations if you hope to be regarded as a quality company. Quality zealots often act out a role that is designed to make anyone who disagrees with them, or even anyone who is not actively supporting their concepts, seem to be blithering idiots. Actually, there are a number of reasons why today's financial services companies find it difficult both to please the customer and to manage to the bottom line.

Retooling. We have all heard the nation's leading industrialists say that our factories are hopelessly obsolete. We use machinery that was developed at the turn of the century and we are competing with Japan, whose factories are much newer. Their old ones were destroyed in World War II and they were replaced with modern ones when they were rebuilt. This appears to be a terrible disadvantage and many people believe, and rightly so, that our factories must be modernized if we are ever to be able to regain our superior position as the world's leading and most respected industrial nation.

But how does this apply to financial services companies? It may be true for factories, but what about offices? The answer is that the same, or at least a very similar condition exists. Many of today's offices are also obsolete. Sure they have made great strides. Ten years ago new product introductions were somewhat rare. When a vendor developed a new machine, word of its virtues spread quickly. Many managers felt that they were "up to date" with office technology. Today all that has changed. Products are being introduced at an amazing rate and even consultants are unable to stay abreast of new developments. But, in spite of the great strides in automation, most financial services companies can still be regarded as near obsolete. The new equipment is generally very focused and is aimed at specific applications. Today's financial services companies are so complex that any one of these fixes barely makes a dent in overall processing.

Modernization of a financial services company requires more than the installation of a few pieces of new machinery. In fact, there is some question as to whether new labor-saving machines actually save labor. Take phone systems as an example. New PBX systems allow their users to do things that just a few years ago would have been considered "star wars" type technology. Calls can be forwarded to other numbers; employees can be automatically alerted when someone else is attempting to call them while they are already on the line; recorded messages can be left when the person you are trying to call is not at his or her office; conference calls between several people can be arranged; when you attempt to call a number that is busy the phone automatically redials the number when the line opens up and then also calls you to let you know the other party is being recalled. The features go on and on. But how has this new sophistication affected companies' profit and loss statements? How many banks do you know of that reduced their staff because of the installation of new phone equipment? Even though the vendor probably promised productivity improvement, it is questionable whether it's ever actually realized. People simply find other activities to fill their excess time. And, in some cases, the new equipment actually increased the workload.

Consider the advent of personal computers. When they were first introduced and managers learned that they were no longer dependent on non-responsive corporate information systems departments for automation, predictions of vastly improved productivity were common. Many computer purchases were justified on the basis that they would make the manager's work easier and they would require less time and effort to accomplish the same or better results than could be achieved manually. But what has happened? How many functions have been eliminated through personal computer automation? Not many. In fact, in a number of cases the opposite has happened. People who formerly could not even spell the word computer have become hopelessly addicted to them. They attempt to automate everything they do. We have all witnessed these computer addicts attempting to automate simple tasks that are better off processed manually because they are performed infrequently or because they require a very minor manual effort. Automation of each of these activities might take days to complete. These addicts lose sight of their real job responsibilities and focus instead on their new toys. Their primary goal is to make their computer programs work. In the meantime their old responsibilities go unmet and effectiveness suffers. Even where employees have used computers effectively it is rare to see bottom-line results increase because of the personal computer. Since the work being automated is often considered managerial or technical, staff reduction is rare. These people are so valuable to their companies that they simply find other work to do to keep busy. The net effect of most personal computer purchases is simply the increased cost involved in purchasing the computer and a shifting of costs away from the corporate information systems departments to the user areas.

Another form of automation that often is considered to be a breakthrough is electronic mail. Consider a typical scenario. You are working on an important project. An outside customer is expecting to hear from you before the end of the day and it is already two o'clock. You are under the gun. Suddenly you reach a roadblock. You need to talk with someone else in your company to obtain a vital piece of missing information. You pick up your phone and call his office. There is no answer. Then after the fourth ring you hear the all too familiar "click" that tells you that his phone calls have been forwarded to someone else's phone. You hope that he will be at the new location but your luck runs out. His coworker answers for him and says that he is tied up in a meeting. You look at your watch. You must have that piece of missing information! The customer is waiting for your call. You decide to walk (or run) to his office to possibly catch him as soon as he returns or to write him a message. You waste ten minutes getting there, and of course, he is still in the meeting and no one knows where it is being held or when he will return. You decide to leave a message. Frantically you scour the area to find a pen and paper. Then you write it out. You walk over to his desk to leave it where he will see it and you find the desk covered with papers, spread out in all directions. You doubt that he would be able to find your message before quitting time, much less get back to you with the needed information in time for you to solve the problem and return the call to your customer. Once more, in addition to the messy desk you find dozens of other notes from people who want him to call them as soon as he returns. Several of them are even written on the adhesive memo pads that are so popular and they are stuck all over his office in places where he is sure to see them—on the telephone, on the shelf hanging over his desk, on his lamp, on the nameplate of his outside office wall, etc....

Along comes electronic mail. Advocates would have us believe that it will solve these types of problems. All we need to do is enter our message into the computer terminal located on our desk and the message will instantly be sent to the computer terminal sitting on his desk. The instant he walks into his office he will look at his computer screen to check his messages. They will be neatly displayed in prioritized order for him to handle quickly and efficiently. Of course, each sender of messages will be honest and fair in assigning their messages lower priority numbers because they understand that other people have more urgent needs of his time than their own. Sure they will.... Let's look at what really happens. You develop the same urgent need for information. You have the same customer waiting for your phone call by the end of the day. You make the same call to your coworker. The phone is still faster than the computer, if he is in his office. He is not, so your call is transferred to the other employee who still cannot help you. Or, if the company is automating, perhaps you leave a message on the phone's voice mail system. Anyway, you continue to worry about your customer so you decide to use the computer to send an electronic mail message. You spend fifteen minutes composing a message and then send it to his terminal where it is mixed with ten other, equally urgent messages. After several more minutes you decide you still should run to his office anyway. Perhaps he didn't get your message. Perhaps his terminal is not turned on. In any event, you go to meet him. You get there and wait for an hour or so and his next door office neighbor asks why you are standing in his office. You explain that you need to speak with him as soon as possible and the neighbor says that you will have to wait until the following Monday because he is out on vacation, and has been out all week. Obviously the other coworker was misinformed.

What was the productivity gain of the new automation? The net effect is that instead of the old way where you have had three attempts, the phone, the memo, and the visit, you now have four attempts, the phone, the memo, the visit, and the automated electronic mail. We hope we aren't blessed with many more of these labor-saving devices!

Seriously, automation of financial services companies is extremely important. Today's customers are more sophisticated and better educated and they have higher expectations than ever before. They may temporarily accept many of today's poor service and quality levels because few other companies in their industries are doing any better. But as soon as some new entrant joins the field who is ignorant of industry standards and who offers vastly superior service, customers will beat a path to its door.

Some companies will incorrectly maintain that they have already spent millions and millions of dollars on automation and therefore they do not need to be as concerned. Let's discuss what we mean when we relate automation to retooling in factories. Factories also constantly look for better ways to product their products. Techniques like Just In Time, Statistical Process Control, and Quality Assurance have been introduced to speed processing, reduce costs, and improve quality. The concept of robotics has made giant inroads in most plants. But retooling, as we define it, refers to the massive redesign similar to what the major auto makers go through when they introduce a new body style. The distinction between this retooling effort and the normal maintenance-type improvements is similar to the difference between introducing a new body style one year and improving it each year for the next four or five years or more. Each year a "new" model is improved. Perhaps the brakes are strengthened, the engine horsepower is increased or it is turbocharged, the tail lights are fitted with brighter lights. But the basic body style remains the same.

Such has been the case with financial services companies. The current "body style" was introduced years ago. It was updated with product changes and new subsystems, but few companies have started from "scratch" and designed processing systems, quality systems, and customer service systems that are thoroughly integrated and effective. Take the case of an insurance company located in the Midwest. They used a nonindustry standard computer manufacturer (assuming there is such a thing as an industry standard computer manufacturer).

Since they had equipment different from 90 percent of the rest of their industry, all of the software that ran on the system had to be purchased from the lesser-known software vendors or developed in-house. They usually chose to develop in-house. As a result, they started with less than they would have had, had they followed the main line of the rest of the industry, and each new system was designed to interface with that inferior initial system. As these new systems aged and were replaced or enhanced, the improved versions were designed to run like the old systems they replaced.

This vicious cycle continued for years and years until it got to the point where all the systems were hopelessly inadequate and a major effort and amount of expense was needed to turn things around.

Essentially, this turnaround effort is the retooling that we feel is required. Not that all companies need to change their equipment or all of their systems, but someone needs to challenge the conventional wisdom within most companies and ask whether the systems are truly capable of providing the levels of service that are necessary in tomorrow's competitive environment. New entrants into the field do not have the burden of old systems to carry. They are building from the ground up, and if financial services companies are not careful the same thing might happen to them that happened to U.S. automobile and steel companies.

Shifting Economy. Another reason that it is so difficult to manage like Geneen asks us to is that today's financial services companies are in a state of flux. We have talked about the merging of financial services companies where banks, insurance companies, brokerage firms, thrift companies, mortgage servicing companies, and others have come together under one roof. Sears is a great example. You can walk in to most of their stores and buy an insurance policy, refinance your home, open a credit card account that gives you access to nationwide bank-like services, buy stocks, and even purchase a lawnmower. But in reality, if you were able to look deeper, you would find that the "financial services center" within the store is really still a shell. The chances are that you would have to talk with a different sales person for each of the transactions, because the center is really just a grouping of services under one roof. This is not so bad as it might seem, however. In fact, it is somewhat naive to think that thousands of sales people can be cross-trained to sell all the various financial products available today. Even if this were possible, the smartest investors would still probably go to someone who specializes in one area that was of particular interest.

Looking deeper you would find that not only are the sales people a grouping of similar industries, but the products they represent are relatively homogeneous. Sears insurance is really Allstate Insurance. Sears' brokerage people are with Coldwell Banker. Sears' mortgage representatives work for Sears Mortgage Company. For the most part, each company was an established company in its own industry before it became part of the Sears family of financial services companies. Each one operates somewhat autonomously, with common very senior management, but with its own unique management team.

The point of all this is that some companies have made great strides on a marketing level of promoting a financial supermarket image, but in reality they are still not that dissimilar to a farmers market, where independent farmers come into town to sell their produce along with other farmers with other types of produce. Few of these supermarkets are fully merged at an operating level. This next step may or may not happen. Companies are still experimenting. Banks are offering insurance services in their branch offices. In most instances, these insurance services are sold through insurance agents who either have set up shop in the branch or who call on the bank's customers at their homes. The logical step is full integration where the somewhat obsolete agency system of distribution of insurance products is replaced with bank tellers or platform agents. The distribution cost of selling insurance is very high, as is the bank branch office staff cost. As each of these functions becomes more and more automated, financial services companies may begin to develop branch people who can work with customers on more technical matters such as selling insurance products, opening loans, and selling investments, instead of the rather simple and mundane tasks like cashing checks, selling personal lines automobile and homeowners insurance, and others.

This vision is not shared by all people. Many companies will continue to rely on tried and true distribution systems and methods of operating. That's why the financial services industry is currently in a state of flux. And that's why it is so difficult to follow Geneen's advice and evaluate management based on the bottom line. The scenario discussed above is just one of many different scenarios. Some are less revolutionary and more evolutionary. Some are the opposite. But all of them require a commitment to dramatic change and a major expense. Until this whole subject settles down it is doubtful that the Geneen style of management will be too effective.

Price Versus Service. Almost since the beginning of time, or at least since the beginning of business, a debate has raged over which is the best way to compete. Should companies emphasize low cost to customers, or should they emphasize quality and service? Right now, America is reevaluating this subject as never before.

Most companies have avoided the issue and attempted to take a middle-of-the-road approach by balancing the two. They contend that price is important to their customers, but no more so than service. If your customers are treated poorly they will switch to a competitor, regardless of the price. And, sometimes the customers actually find that your price was not all that great, either.

Other companies have shifted more to one side or the other with mixed success. Right now it is popular to believe that Americans want high quality, and they are willing to pay for it. Don't confuse luxury with quality. Remember quality is defined simply as "meeting customer expectations." Luxury means exceeding their expectations, and is not necessary in delivering quality. A few years ago the conventional wisdom was that cost was most important and service simply had to be adequate in order to keep the customer coming back. We can probably assume that, as long as a basic balance exists things will remain the same, but if either one gains too much emphasis it will only be a matter of time before consumers revolt and companies shift back to the other.

One way that very successful companies will compete effectively will be to offer differing levels of service and quality and cost, depending on the product being sold and depending on who the product is sold to. For example, anyone who has ever bought a house is aware of the horrendously antiquated and bureaucratic procedures involved in closing on it. By anyone's estimate, service stinks! Four weeks is considered good, and eight or more weeks is common. Yet this terrible service is happening at a time of extreme stress in most customers. The purchase of a house is one of the most important transactions they will make in their entire lifetime, and the chances are that they are on edge and more sensitive to problems than normal. Some companies may decide that service must be improved. They will probably increase their costs to do so, and in most instances their business will go down. Why? Because customers who are making what is perhaps the largest investment of their lives are very concerned with cost. They look at their closing papers and realize that they will pay as much in interest over 30 years as they will pay for the house itself. A loan at 9 percent is much less expensive over the 30-year period than a loan at 9.5 or 10 percent interest. Hence, they will "put up" with poor service to get a lower price. Companies may have little incentive to improve service if it causes them to increase their prices. Because consumers don't frequently buy houses, they are willing to deal with poor quality for the limited period of time it takes to complete the purchase. Price becomes more important than quality.

Conversely, other types of transactions occur more frequently and are less price sensitive and more service sensitive. Take a typical checking account. The customer may write an average of ten to fifteen checks per month. Each is a potential contact with the financial services company. At the end of the month before payday the customer may make a bookkeeping error and accidentally overdraw his account. Banks that have swung too far to the cost emphasis side of balance will immediately hit the customer with a service fee for the overdraft. Because of the sophistication of today's cost accounting systems, the numbers they generate might tell the bank that the special handling required on the overdraft has a fully loaded expense of $25 to $35. They pass this charge on to the customer. The customer is faced with what he considers to be an excessive fee, as well as the problem caused when the merchant gets the check returned for nonsufficient funds. One customer bookkeeping error can result in four or five overdrafts, and penalty fees of over $100. Let's ask ourselves a few commonsense questions.

1. Are customers honest people who sometimes make mistakes, or are they dishonest people who try to pass bad checks off on their banks? Most studies show that a huge majority of customers seldom have overdrafts, and the problem is caused primarily by a few poor customers.

2. Are fees of $25–$35 and above fair? Few companies actually spend that much

money in special handling. The "unit cost" figures are misleading and theoretical in nature.

3. Wouldn't it be best for a service-oriented company to offer some form of overdraft protection that would "cover" bad checks? Many banks do so by opening a small line of credit, and overdrafts turn into automatic loans and thus are never returned.

4. Would people be willing to pay a little more for this extra service? Most would. When customers perceive a value for a service enhancement they are willing to pay for it.

Hence, this is an example of a transaction that is more service-oriented than cost-oriented. So, ultimately the answer on the price/service issue may be to offer differing levels of service for different products and people. Until these are better defined though, it will be difficult to follow Geneen's advice.

Focus on Short-Term Profit. Much has been written about America's tendency to focus on short-term profit instead of looking at the long run. The old adage, "It's hard to think about draining the swamp when you are waist deep in alligators," seems to apply. Most executives pride themselves on their vision. They like to think that they can look past immediate problems and focus on long-term solutions. But the financial services industries are no different than any other. Merger mania is the rule. Weak companies, those with depressed stock prices, and even mutual companies are fair game. Five years ago it was extremely rare for a mutual insurance company to be purchased by a stock company, or even for a mutual savings bank or savings and loan to convert to a stock company. Today these are common events.

This constant threat of takeover forces executives to focus on short-term profits. Of course, there are many other reasons as well. For example, when the insurance industry was more stable, owners were often satisfied with industry average earnings. Today, many of these same companies are owned by parent companies who are not other insurance companies. Many are owned by foreign investors. These new owners have a different set of corporate profitability goals. They often expect a return on their investment that is equal to or greater than the returns that they could achieve through other sources. They might be willing to accept a bad year or two, but if poor earnings continue over an extended period then the chances are that the companies will be put up for sale. Few executives cherish the instability of a sale without a strategy in place that offers them some protection. Hence, key executives begin to leave. So do strong managers. Only the weak employees, those who are locked into their current position for one reason or another, remain. It is very difficult to turn around earnings in a poorly performing company that has lost its key employees.

This tendency for executives to focus on short-term profit makes it very difficult to follow Geneen's strategy, although it would appear that this was not the case. Actually, Geneen would probably not advise focusing on the short-term, because this discourages making the capital expenditures that are necessary to remain competitive over a long period of time. "Retooling" a financial services company is not inexpensive and we have already discussed the need for many companies to do so.

Fear. Many companies find it difficult to manage to the bottom line because of simple fear. Poor profitability can cause fear but it is not nearly as strong as other fears, including fear that people will lose their jobs, fear that service will suffer if cutbacks are made, fear of being the first to attempt something that few others in the industry have attempted, fear that the company's image will be tarnished with agents or investors or customers, and so many others that we could not possibly list them all.

Financial services companies used to be relatively easy to run. The industries were stable and there were definite rules to follow. Stick to the established rules and it was actually difficult to fail. People went to work for them for various reasons, but one of the strongest was that they provided a "safe haven," a place with high levels of job security. In fact, they were not that dissimilar from Japanese companies in that they often had a family atmosphere and provided lifetime security. Dissension was not tolerated. Advancement was possible only after you paid your dues and those dues required years of dedicated work. The pay was never great but it was never bad, either. Regardless of how poor or how good your performance was you could expect to receive an average raise. The better employees received a percent or two more than average; the poorer employees, a percent or two less. By the time taxes and other deductions were taken from your paychecks it seemed that the raises were about enough to take you and your family to the movies.

WHAT HAS WORKED IN THE PAST?

Large Clerical Staffs

In the past most financial services companies were much more clerical than they are today. The vast majority of employees worked in nontechnical and nonmanagerial jobs. Much of the automation that we take for granted today was nonexistent then. Large information services departments were unheard of. The computer was in its infancy. One of the first successful control programs was called work measurement.

Work Measurement

Work measurement was fathered by Frederick Taylor. His is considered to be the first scientific approach to the subject. He was an engineer at the Midvale Steel Company near Philadelphia, Pennsylvania, and he started the popular negative image of the efficiency expert and the stopwatch method of setting time standards. Taylor felt that employees in his plant were not producing a fair day's work for the pay they received. He studied what was then the collective wisdom in the field of work management and developed a principle that the greatest production results when each worker is given a definite task to be performed in a definite time and in a definite manner. He then worked with the employees to establish time standards based on past performance, and later he introduced the stopwatch method of standard setting. Taylor's concepts became popular and many companies (primarily manufacturing) adopted his philosophy.

As more and more companies began using these new "scientific management" techniques, they began to uncover weaknesses. There were too many variables to consider. The raw stopwatch timings had to undergo a process known as "leveling" in which the person using the watch had to evaluate the person performing the task in terms of his proficiency. This introduced an element of judgment and it was difficult to determine when an engineer had enough training to evaluate proficiency. Another variable concerned the clarity of the instructions given the worker. Another focused on which workers would be timed, the good ones or the poor ones. Other questions centered on how to determine the correct number of workers to time before a correct standard could be established. All this uncertainty and experimentation fueled the negative image people developed of the efficiency expert.

Soon after that the Gilbreths, Frank and Lillian, entered the field. They were also very interested in productivity and are credited with developing a technique called "methods study." Frank Gilbreth was involved in the construction industry. As a bricklayer apprentice he learned that there were many different ways to lay bricks. This simple finding led him to attempt to define the "one best way" of doing it. He became convinced that the greatest productivity levels would be accomplished when workers were given specific instructions on the "proper" method to accomplish work. His interest intensified, and he and his wife opened a laboratory where they could study productivity. Their research eventually led to the development of "micromotion" study, in which real-world procedures were duplicated in the laboratory. They broke down methods of getting work completed into small elements called "Therbligs," a word that when spelled backward is almost "Gilbreth."

Both Taylor and the Gilbreths gained many followers. They were the real pioneers of modern control systems. Each camp felt that they had the secret to achieving high productivity. Taylor felt that the dominant factor was time control, and the Gilbreths believed that controlling the methods was the key.

Eventually, the two schools of thought came together. They realized that both time and motion (methods) should be considered whenever productivity is to be maximized. The key to bringing them together was that they concluded that variations in the amount of time that it takes workers to complete the same motion are essentially small, as long as the workers have adequate opportunities to practice the motions.

This merging of the two camps led to the development of predetermined time systems. The first widely recognized system was developed by A. G. Segur. It was called Motion Time Analysis, and was based on the theory that within practical limits the time required for experts to perform true fundamental motions is constant. Other systems followed. Joseph Quick developed a system known as Work Factor; General Electric Company developed a number of systems including Get and Place, Motion Time Standards, and Dimensional Motion Times.

But, by far, the most widely known system is Methods-Time Measurement, better known as MTM. It was developed by the Methods Engineering Council in Pittsburgh, Pennsylvania, after preliminary work on it was performed at the Westinghouse Electric Company around 1946. Today it is still the most widely used predetermined time system in the world. Over 50,000 companies use it. It is the only predetermined time system for which both data and research are available to the public. The authors of the system, Harold B. Maynard, Gustave J. Stegmerten, and John L. Schwab, helped develop an organization known as the MTM Association for Standards and Research. All of their data and development rights were given to the association, and it still functions today, helping businesses further develop the field of scientific management through its training and research programs.

MTM is effective because it provides time values for virtually every body motion possible in a work environment. It was developed by gathering people of average age, size, and physical characteristics together in a room with average environmental conditions (lighting, heat, ventilation, etc.). They were asked to perform a series of motions which were filmed using high-speed, constant-speed cameras. Then, well-trained experienced industrial engineers pace-rated their performances using constant-speed projectors. The result of their efforts were validated standards for all of the basic motions performed.

While these time values enabled engineers to establish very accurate standards to within plus or minus 5 percent, they were very cumbersome to use because they dealt with extremely small units of time. For example, the time that is required to release an object is .072 seconds. This type of system worked well in factory situations, where simple motions were performed over and over. But, imagine how difficult it was to apply MTM data in the office. Even the most simple clerical jobs changed regularly and lacked the repeatability found in the factory. Still, a number of companies used MTM then, and, in fact, continue to use it.

Early Application of Work Measurement in Offices

A number of firms recognized the problems caused by the level of detail with basic MTM, and developed higher level data systems incorporating MTM that were designed specifically for the office environment. These include:

- UOC: Universal Office Controls, developed by the H.B. Maynard Company.
- MTM-C: Methods Time Measurement-Clerical, developed by a consortium of MTM Association members.
- MTV: Motion Time Values, developed in the 1960s by Booz Allen and Hamilton.
- MODAPTS: Modular Arrangement of Predetermined Time Standards, developed in the late 1960s by Chris Heyde at the Unilever Company in Australia.
- MCD: Master Clerical Data, developed by the Serge A. Birn Company in 1958.
- CSD: Clerical Standard Data, developed in 1960 by Bruce Payne Associates.
- AOC: Advanced Office Controls, developed in 1973 by the Robert E. Nolan Company.

All of these systems offer vast improvements over basic MTM when applied in an office environment. One of them, AOC (Advanced Office Controls), was developed specifically for use by financial services companies and thus is more easily applied and maintained than the other systems.[2]

Regardless of the measurement system used, the value of any work management system lies in the use of the data it provides. People have a need to know how they are doing in their jobs. Data from work management can supply much of the information needed in these evaluations.

HOW IS TODAY DIFFERENT?

Is the present day any different? The answer is yes, and no. Do employees still have an interest in knowing how well they are doing? Of course they do. Do supervisors still need data to help them distribute work, evaluate various processes, and give feedback to employees? Sure they do. Then how is it different? How have things changed?

As we have already discussed, there have been massive changes in the customer and the products offered. But perhaps the biggest change within the company has been the shifting in staff from clerical to technical and managerial. This shift is illustrated in Figures 9.1 and 9.2. The former illustrates the historical shape of a company. In past years the clerical employees constituted the largest percentage. Managerial employees were next, followed by technical and professional people. This makeup constituted a pyramid, as seen in Figure 9.1. However, in recent years this shape has

Figure 9.1
Historical Organization Shape

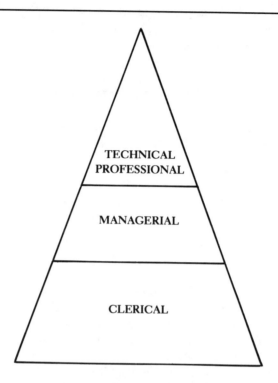

changed, as seen in Figure 9.2. Note how the proportion of clerical employees has shrunk while the other two layers have grown.

Most of what were once considered to be the routine clerical jobs have now been automated. Some of them still remain, but even those positions that were once the most entry level now have a degree of technical skill associated with them. For example, mail rooms used to involve the classic entry-level jobs. People with no experience and little formal education would start their careers there. The hardest workers and those who showed the most initiative would eventually be promoted to more demanding positions and begin their slow climb up the corporate ladder.

But today, mail rooms have become pretty sophisticated places. Automated sorting machines have replaced the old sorting bins, and computer terminals are used to access various customer files. Many financial services companies separate money from correspondence in the mail room, and some even apply it to the correct account before the correspondence is forwarded to the line department.

Even mail distribution has become automated. Robots are becoming common. They are not the walking, talking type that we saw on the old Flash

Figure 9.2
Present-Day Organization Shape

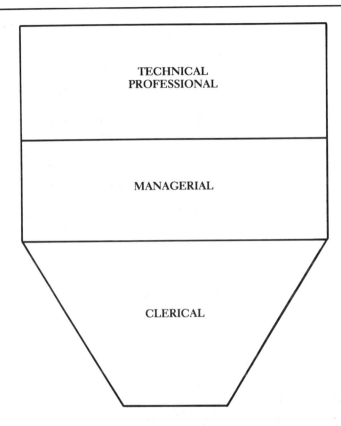

Gordon television show years ago. Instead, they usually are rather boxy looking carts on motorized wheels with electronic sensors that follow pre-defined paths throughout the buildings. They are even programmed to stop at various mail drop points where they make some sort of noise (bell, buzz, etc.) to inform employees that it is time to remove mail from the carts or insert mail into them. Around special occasions such as Easter and Christmas it is not uncommon for employees to personify them by dressing them up with hats and wool scarves, or by painting faces onto them.

This type of automation has occurred throughout financial services companies. Many of the traditional clerical jobs have been replaced, and the skill level for all employees has increased dramatically.

One might think with all this automation that the number of employees working for the companies would have dropped substantially. This could explain the personification of the robots. Employees need companionship, and when the number of employees is reduced by automation they befriend the robots. While this has happened in some instances, unfortunately, it is rare. Automation often does not lead to fewer employees. In fact, it frequently leads to more.

How to Ensure Success

There are a number of techniques that good financial services companies use to ensure success in both their improvement efforts and their entire operation.

Evolve and Maintain Work Management Systems. Work management systems are based on the premise that supervisors and managers need objective data on which to make good decisions, and all employees need to know how well they are doing in terms of the quantity of work they produce, its quality, and the service levels achieved. In the past, work management systems were very detail-oriented, involved a great deal of manual record-keeping, and focused on clerical-level employees. Technicians and managers were not required to participate with them. This was acceptable as long as companies were so heavily clerically oriented.

Now that the situation has changed and the percentage of technical and managerial employees has increased so dramatically, it is unwise for these people not to report on a work management system. Modern versions such as Advanced Office Controls and the use of techniques such as key output analysis and micro measurement have made work management acceptable to most employees, and the information provided is absolutely essential to manage effectively. The best companies recognize this and maintain work management systems of some type.

Develop a "More for Less" Attitude. Successful financial services companies share an attitude in which they constantly attempt to achieve "more for less." In other words, they try to produce more output with less input. Some equate running a company with rowing a boat upstream on a river. You can't stop. If you do, you will drift backwards. You must either move forward or slip backward.

Productivity can be defined as input divided by output (see Figure 9.3). The only ways to increase it are to produce more output with the same or less input, or to produce the same amount of output with less input. Period. There are no other ways.

Make the Tough Decisions. If a company is growing, the decisions that must be made to improve productivity and quality are easier to make. Since the output side of the productivity equation is growing, productivity can be increased by either freezing or retarding the input to a growth rate that is less than that of the output. Although management must become more demanding, no satisfactory employees need to lose their jobs.

However, when the output side of the equation is not growing, management must make some tougher decisions. The only way to improve is to

Figure 9.3
Productivity Equation

$$\text{Productivity} = \frac{\text{Input}}{\text{Output}}$$

To increase it:

- Increase output with the same or less input; or

- Maintain output and decrease input.

---

decrease the input side of the equation, and this means that some people will have to lose their jobs.

A similar condition occurs almost every time that a company successfully completes any improvement process. The studies invariably eliminate some work, thus "freeing up" employees. If the company is in a growth mode then the employees can be reassigned to other positions. But, if the company is not growing, management must come to grips with the fact that some people must lose their jobs.

To date, financial services companies have been very weak on this point. They have not been willing to make the tough decision to reduce staff if it means using any form of a layoff. No manager, in any industry, enjoys this aspect of management. But some industries handle it better than others. Financial services companies are to be applauded for their compassionate treatment of displaced employees, but at the same time they should be chastised for their unwillingness to make the tough decisions required.

There is a middle-of-the-ground position that we hesitate to mention because too many managers rely on it already and it often is not effective. If turnover is sufficiently large enough to handle the excess staff identified, then a hiring freeze may be a solution. In the past, when companies had a larger percentage of clerical employees, this was an effective technique. Since many clerical jobs were considered to be dead end jobs, or since they offered the employees little stimulation, turnover in them was often high.

Unfortunately, the same rate of turnover does not occur in technical and managerial positions, except in certain areas such as data processing, where the skills can be used in many different industries and where there are shortages of skilled people looking for employment. Since today's companies have become more technical and managerial, normal attrition is seldom a satisfactory solution to an overstaffed situation. Turnover rates are simply not high enough in the technical and managerial levels to be of much help.

There are other problems with using normal attrition to handle excess staffing situations. If the turnover does not occur quickly enough then the excess employees will naturally find other "work" to keep busy with. Most employees want to put in a fair day's work and they naturally seek ways to keep busy. In fact, how many times have we as managers said to our employees, "There is always something for you to work on. I don't want anyone to sit idle with nothing to do. If you don't have any work then come and see me and I will find something." While this approach may seem like a good idea, what it actually tells employees to do is to stretch out their work or find "busy work" to occupy their time.

In the case where improvement efforts have resulted in a reduced workload and the company has relied on normal attrition to take care of the excess staff, the employees with nothing to do actually invent work to keep busy. They may rationalize to themselves that the new work is necessary, but it seldom is. While management is waiting for attrition to occur, the work performed by "idle" employees becomes legitimized. Then, when the turnover actually occurs, the employees are too busy with new work and the vacated positions must be filled. The result is that the savings are never realized.

The other major problem with using normal attrition to handle excess staff is that, since companies have become so technical, it often is not possible just to reassign someone to a new job without a great deal of retraining. Training has always been an issue, even when we dealt with turnover at the clerical level. But it has become much more difficult now that more technical skills are required. Many jobs require a specialized degree or advanced training. For example, it would be difficult to retrain a branch manager in a bank to become an investment officer, or it would be difficult to retrain a customer service representative in an insurance company to become an actuary.

Focus on Improvements That Can be Implemented Quickly. Another technique that successful companies rely on is developing implementation timeliness that focuses on ideas that can be implemented quickly. All too often, companies rely on long-term solutions. Somewhere between the time that the improvements are recommended and the time at which they are to be implemented, priorities change and the improvements are never made. We are not suggesting that companies focus on short-term profits, or that they ignore solutions that require more time to implement. Rather, we have found that companies that act quickly and capture as much as possible when the issues are "hot," generally are the most successful in their improvement efforts.

Budget for Improvement. Another technique that is often successful is to budget for improvement. One of the biggest problems with introducing any new process into a financial services company is that of getting people to shift their priorities and support the new effort. We have yet to see a company where managers are just sitting idle, waiting for someone who wants to try something new. Can you picture this situation? A superior would walk by and ask why the manager was not busy and he would reply that he was waiting for someone to introduce a new quality process. Unlikely!

The real situation is that most managers are very busy. They come to work early and they are the last to leave. Some are even reluctant to support new processes that require a time commitment because they feel their superiors might think that they weren't busy enough before. What all of this means is that getting people to commit their time is a difficult task, regardless of the value of the new process being introduced.

Yet, some of these new processes have the blessing of senior management, and not supporting them can be equally dangerous. Some of the middle-of-the-road and weaker managers feel that they can "beat the system" by simply paying "lip service" to new processes. "After all," they reason, "these new programs come and go all the time. All I have to do is act like I support them and the probability is that I can put off spending any real time on them until their newness wears off and they go away like all the others have done. These new processes never seem to last." In all fairness to those managers, they are partly right. Most progressive financial services companies constantly try new processes that are aimed to improve some aspect of their business. Many of these fail, as a result of a number of factors, of which commitment, or lack of it, is but one of many.

How then can senior management convince its middle managers that quality is a serious issue and a new quality process is more than just a "flash in the pan" type of program that is introduced with great fanfare, slowly loses support, and then withers and dies? The answer is to budget for improvement. One thing that most managers take seriously is their budget.

How can the budget be tied to a quality process? Quality improvement will eventually lead to increased profitability, but can prudent management expect it to translate directly into detailed budgets? You bet it can! If it can't, then we should forget the whole concept of quality improvement. Like Geneen says, if it isn't reflected in the bottom line then it isn't really important.

This means that managers must project the impact that the new quality process will have on their expense budget. If their volume is increasing, then their expenses should increase at a rate that is retarded because of quality improvements. If their volume is static or shrinking then their expenses must be reduced because of both the volume decreases *and* the anticipated quality improvements.

How does a manager know the amount of quality improvements that will be realized until the process is completed? This is a difficult question, because normally some departments achieve a greater percentage improvement than others. This might be because the departments were in worse shape to begin with, or because the managers tried harder to achieve results because the work performed lent itself more to quality improvements, or a host of other possible explanations. But it is common for some areas to achieve more than other areas.

This is where senior management must be firm in their conviction that improvements will be made and that all managers can make them. Normally, a well-designed quality process will include a documented proposal for senior management to review. Part of that proposal should be an estimate of how much improvement will be possible. Although this estimate is seldom broken down department by department, it can be expressed in a percentage form. For example, "costs will be reduced by 25 percent." This rate can become the gaol for all managers, and individual budgets can be compiled accordingly.

Doubtless, some managers will not agree with this approach. Even some senior managers will not agree with it. After all, this technique seems to penalize the better managers who, in the past "ran a tighter ship." It appears to favor managers who managed poorly and who thus have more room for improvement. While this may be true, we have found that well-managed departments often achieve even greater results than poorly managed departments. This could result from many reasons. Perhaps the management team is better organized. Perhaps they are more committed. Perhaps they are simply better managers who are more creative in their improvement ideas. The reason is not important. The common goal for all departments is.

Without this budget commitment, managers never really have to support the improvement process. Many of the more political ones will even go so far as to support the process on a corporate level but not at the level of their departments. They will agree with a corporate goal but say to themselves and their employees that all the other departments need to improve more than their own. On the outside they will say, "This is a great process. Just what this company needs." Inside they will be thinking, "In the customer service department, the accounting department, and the mail room, but not in my area. We are already very customer-oriented and we probably have less of a need for improvement than the other areas."

Share the Wealth. An important concept that better companies have is to reward people for their accomplishments. On the surface this would seem to be a plea for bonuses and incentives. But this is actually a much broader issue than those alone. It is a way of correcting a flaw found in most financial services companies. Overall compensation is low. It's not nearly as high as it is in other industries such as utilities or general manufacturing. As we discussed in a previous chapter, this poor pay has hurt financial services companies. Generally speaking the "best and the brightest" new people seldom consider careers in them unless they are with the more "glamorous" side such as investment banking. The idea of working for a bank at 25 to 35 percent less than they could earn at a manufacturing company simply is not very appealing. Granted, some of these new employees will look to the future and realize that the United States is becoming more service-oriented while manufacturing is on the decline. This might lead the more risk-oriented people to forego the higher pay for the increased opportunities that are generally offered in growth industries. But, the current conditions found in most financial services companies would cause them to question their decision after just a short while.

One could even argue that attracting the best and the brightest is not important. That after five or so years of working in the real world the gap between average and superior intellect diminishes in value. In fact, some of us believe that average people have a better chance of success than the brightest people do, because they have always had to work harder to achieve their goals. Whether or not this is true is a discussion that extends well beyond the parameters of this book.

Other than the effect that low compensation has on being able to hire the best and the brightest, how is it important? The answer is with documented studies that people who are well paid simply act in a more professional and responsible manner, and they usually have a higher self-image.

Forget the issue of attracting the best and the brightest. Do you think that managers in higher paying industries are any more intelligent or capable human beings than those in financial services companies? Very few people would say so. As consultants to a number of industries we certainly have seen no difference. But, do managers in higher paying companies behave differently? Yes, they do. They are almost always more dedicated to their companies and they seldom lose sight of corporate goals.

It is always interesting to talk with someone who has spent his entire career working for a financial services company and who then switches and goes to work in a higher paying industry. For example, our firm trained a new college graduate in some work analysis techniques. She worked for a mid-sized property and casualty insurance company located in the eastern United States. Her starting salary was about average for someone with a degree and no business experience who is just entering the insurance industry. After working for several years as an analyst, she used her new skill to get a job in a utility company in the same city. Her new salary was 80 percent higher and she was performing essentially the same type of work. She was paid for her analyst skills and not her industry knowledge. We talked with her just prior to her move and she was very nervous about her ability. She wasn't sure that she could do the "new" job as effectively as she had done in the insurance company. "After all," she said, "why would they be willing to pay me so much more if the work isn't harder?" We talked with her about six months after the change and she was a new person. She had no doubts about her abilities and, in fact, within the following year she was promoted to manager of the department. She found that the work was no harder, the people were no more intelligent, and there were few instances where her lack of utility industry experience hurt her. The only major difference between the two companies was her pay level. When she began working with the utility company she decided that anyone earning that much money should be confident of her abilities, and thus she became so.

This is only one example, but we have found many others that are very similar. Our experience has shown us that the issue is not that any particular industry attracts better people than any other. The real determinant is pay level. Be it insurance, banking, manufacturing, or utilities, those companies that pay the best seem to expect and get more from their employees.

Financial services companies could counter this argument by explaining that their expenses are already as high as they can stand. They could not be increased any more without jeopardizing their competitive posture. Higher salaries would lead to higher costs and higher costs would drive away customers. While this would be the case if salaries were simply increased without making additional improvements, it would not happen if some of the cost improvements generated in a quality process were redirected to increased salaries. Ultimately companies would be leaner and managers would be better paid. There would be fewer of them, but those remaining would be much more productive. They would have a greater self-image, and because of the simple fact that there were fewer employees, management would be less complicated.

Pay for Performance. Another excellent technique for ensuring success is to pay for performance. For as far back as most of us would care to remember, financial services companies have developed their pay scales through the use of what is loosely known as "point factor" systems. These could be considered to be scientific, engineered ways of establishing job values. They are typically based on a number of core dimensions such as the number of people supervised (in the case of a management job), the total budget amount managed, the amount of direct contact with outside customers, the potential impact the position could have on profits and losses, and so forth. The factors vary, depending on which system is being discussed, but they all work pretty much the same way.

Each of the factors is assigned a weighting. For example, the total amount of budget managed might be one-half as important as the amount of impact the job has on profitability. Or the number of employees managed might be more or less important than the number of contacts with outside customers.

Following the weighting, each of the factors is assigned a range of "points." Again the size of the range depends on whatever characteristics the company wants to emphasize. Then each job being evaluated is measured against the factors. The job scores for each factor are added together to develop a total point value for the job, and then the total point value is slotted into a salary level, with each level made up of a range of points. For example, a programmer might score a value of 345 points. That might qualify for an entry-level technical salary level. A manager of customer service might score 750 points, qualifying him for a much higher level. Ultimately, this technique allows human resource professionals to compare dissimilar jobs and slot them into their company's pay ranges.

Point factor systems gained a great deal of prominence during the early 1970s when companies feared discrimination charges from disgruntled employees. They provided a way to help ensure that pay was directly related to the value of the position being analyzed and not to some racial or sexual bias. They were very effective, and they can still be found in modified forms in most financial services companies.

Unfortunately, or fortunately, depending on your point of view, they have recently come under increasing criticism. The major charges against them are twofold. The first is that they encourage bureaucracy and overstaffing by rewarding managers for having large numbers of employees reporting to them and for controlling large budgets. Naturally, the systems are not designed to do this, but this is the effect they have. Second, and perhaps even more damning is the charge that they define too precisely what a person's responsibilities are. While you might think that this is an asset and not a liability, consider this. Traditional financial services companies are organized in an assembly-line manner. The jobs are very fragmented, as we discussed in an earlier chapter. In this environment, point factor systems can be very effective. Perhaps this is a major reason for their success in the past.

However, the more progressive companies today are attempting to organize in a much less structured format, where employees are not tied to any one particular job. In fact, any employee may perform any job that he is qualified for. This is especially important when employees are attempting to resolve customer problems. The worst thing that can happen is for an irate customer to be passed back and forth between employees because none of them is qualified to handle the entire transaction.

These progressive companies are attempting to compensate their employees more on the basis of what they accomplish than on how they fill their days. The new job descriptions are very broad, and compensation is composed of a combination of salary and a performance bonus. The salary is relatively low. In fact, in theory it should provide no more than one-half of an employee's total income. The rest is provided through a performance bonus. When performance is low, so is the income. When it is high, so is the income.

Bonuses have been around for a long time, but they have been used mostly at the senior executive level. This is because the senior people could be held accountable for overall corporate performance, whereas lower level employees could not. With today's improved reporting and tracking systems the bonus technique can be pushed down to almost any level of job.

Shift to Profit Centers. The final technique makes it easier to administer the bonus system mentioned above and accomplishes a number of other benefits as well, including increasing the accountability of the people within the centers and narrowing the gap between the company and its customers.

Oversimplified, the profit center form of organization makes big companies into smaller ones. Instead of one large organization there evolve a number of different organizations, each one operating somewhat autonomously. Each is operated as if it were the only company, and is responsible for profit and loss results. Naturally, some "corporate" services are maintained in a centralized manner—the most common being accounting, information services, and human resources. But in some of the larger companies even these are decentralized.

Since each profit center must be profitable in order to survive, their accountability is increased. No longer can some centers claim they are simply going through a downcycle and with contributions from their parent corporation they can survive without making the real adjustments that they would have to make if they truly were a separate entity.

The centers also narrow the gap between the company and its customers. Small companies very seldom have problems staying in touch with customers. Employees wear a number of hats and they recognize the value of each individual customer. Unfortunately, the same cannot always be said about larger companies. Many of them grow to the point where customers lose their identity. They simply become numbers. Customer contacts are viewed as extra work and they are dealt with impersonally. Employees just don't have the appreciation for how hard it is to develop a customer and why it is so important to maintain a good relationship with him.

CHAPTER SUMMARY

The following are the key points made in this chapter.

1. Success is measured through monitoring profitability. There are many other indicators that can be used to present different aspects of success and to report interim progress, but the bottom line is profitability. Companies that achieve high levels of quality will be successful. The customers will ensure it.

2. There are many factors that can prevent companies from being successful. Most of these can divert management's attention from the key issue of quality. Companies that allow this dimension to occur may fail.

3. In the past, most financial services companies' staffs were composed primarily of clerical employees. Today that has changed. Companies have become increasingly automated and complex. Managers and technicians now make up a majority

of the work force.

Work management has been an effective type of control technique. It evolved from industrial settings and was reshaped for the office. It can still be very effective as long as the measurement technique is state-of-the-art, the recordkeeping is automated and simple, and the program is sensitive to the needs of professionals.

4. Financial services companies should follow a few basic techniques to help ensure their success when introducing quality processes. While the techniques are simple to understand on a conceptual level, they may be difficult to implement because they challenge managers to question some of their most basic beliefs and values. Some of the techniques are tried and true. Others are controversial and will require breaking out of industry molds.

NOTES

1. Harold Geneen and Alvin Moscow, *Managing* (New York: Doubleday, 1984), p. 33.

2. Robert E. Nolan, Ben DiSylvester, and Richard T. Young, *Improving Productivity through Advanced Office Controls* (New York: AMACOM, 1980), pp. 138–141.

10

Quality Expectations: How to Get Started

Quality is more a journey than a destination.
—John J. Creedon, President and Chief Executive Officer,
Metropolitan Life Insurance Company.

Understanding that every journey starts with but one step, we offer some direction to make the trip more enjoyable and effective.

In Chapter 7 we discussed the measurement of quality *in fact* and *in perception*. In Chapter 4 we outlined the improvement techniques necessary to achieve and maintain higher levels of quality. This chapter will discuss how to start developing a quality process in your organization.

The amount of time spent on researching what quality is and how to go about achieving it will influence the time it takes your organization to initiate improvement. It will also have a direct bearing on the level of improvement attained. We have seen the extremes in companies large and small—some diligently research what the quality alternatives are, and then there are those who decide to jump in with what starts out as a quality suggestion program and ends up looking for a way out of an administrative mess.

Sometimes executives take theoretical concepts like "ready, shoot, aim" literally and end up wasting energy and expense. We have seen many debacles referred to after the fact as "stepping stones." Research need not take years for companies to determine what is right and more importantly what is right for the company.

RESEARCH: ASSOCIATIONS

There are several ways for companies to get started through subject or industry specific associations. Several are listed as follows:

Subject—Quality

American Society for Quality Control
230 West Wells Street
Suite 7000
Milwaukee, WI 53203
(414) 272–8575

International Association of Quality Circles
801–B Eighth Street
Cincinnati, OH 45203
(513) 381–1959

Management

American Management Association
135 West 50th Street
New York, NY 10020
(212) 586–8100

Administrative Management Society
Maryland Road
Willow Grove, PA 19090
(215) 659–4300

Industry—Life and Health Insurance

Life Office Management Association
300 Colony Square
Atlanta, GA 30361
(404) 892–7272

Blue Cross and Blue Shield Association
676 North St. Clair Street
Chicago, IL 60611
(312) 440–6000

Insurance—Property and Casualty

National Association of Mutual Insurance Companies
P.O. Box 68700
3707 Woodview Trace
Indianapolis, IN 46268
(317) 875–5250

Banking—Savings

U.S. League of Savings Institutions
111 Wacker Drive
Chicago, IL 60601
(312) 644–3100

National Council of Savings Institutions
1101 15th Street N.W.
Washington, DC 20005
(202) 331–0276

Banking—Commercial

American Bankers Association
1120 Connecticut Avenue N.W.
Washington, DC 20036
(202) 467–4000

Bank Administration Institute
60 Gould Center
2550 Golf Road
Rolling Meadows, IL 60008
(312) 228–6200

Mortgage Bankers

Mortgage Bankers Association of America
1125 15th Street N.W.
Washington, DC 20005
(202) 861–6500

Associations often have seminars on quality or offer sessions within their conventions covering the issue of quality. Although the subjects listed in the conference offering may not be exactly what you need guidance with or more information on, the real value is to talk with other attendees. At industry breakout sessions at the International Association of Quality Circles, attendees often pass around an attendance list where each member notes name, title, company and address, and phone number. The moderator has been know to send a listing after the conference thanking the attendees for their participation and enclosing a list of all who attended. The network developed early in research helps enormously.

The associations often have committees made up of corporate specialists who work to develop informative programs around the topics. When getting started this is a great place to see what has worked in other companies and where the attention must be paid to ensure success.

RESEARCH: BOOKS

There is a wealth of knowledge that can be gained by reading up on the subject of quality. Much of the past information has been developed and targeted to manufacturing. The techniques are transferable if you take time to understand the underlying concepts. We offer a list of books which are varied in use. When developing the list we have inevitably left out some good books. We have also included some from which you may only pick up one or two ideas.

John Guaspari—AMACOM Publishing

- *I Know It When I See It*
- *Theory Why?*

Charles A. Aubrey, III—Hitchcock Publishing Company

- *Quality Management in Financial Services*

Karl Albrecht, Ron Zemke—Dow Jones–Irwin

- *Service America*

Thomas J. Peters, Robert H. Waterman, Jr.—Harper and Row

- *In Search of Excellence*

Thomas J. Peters, Nancy K. Austin—Random House

- *A Passion for Excellence*

Patrick L. Townsend—John Wiley and Sons

- *Commit to Quality*

Phillip B. Crosby—McGraw-Hill

- *Quality Is Free*
- *Quality Without Tears*

Lawrence M. Miller—Warner Books

- *American Spirit*

Mike Robson—John Wiley and Sons

- *The Journey to Excellence*

Craig R. Hickman and Michael A. Silva—New American Library

- *Creating Excellence*

RESEARCH: COMPANIES

There are several ways to go about researching what organizations are doing. As mentioned in Chapter 2, Paul Revere Insurance Companies researched manufacturing organizations in the United States and Japan as well as financial services organizations. Such research will in some cases enlighten, in others inform, but in most cases reinforce. You can read about spirit but you can't feel as confident without talking to people managing within a customer-focused organization.

Why would companies open up and show you how they have achieved some success in quality improvement? Many will not. Some realize, as Paul Johnson, president of Connecticut Savings Bank, alluded, that quality is difficult to achieve and almost impossible to replicate over a short period of time.

Another research tactic is to visit with large companies that you respect and may also be the customer of. Metropolitan Life Insurance used this approach when starting, and it was very informative for John Falzon, senior vice-president of quality, to visit with Xerox and IBM.

In talking about this at our last client's conference we were told that companies like Kelloggs have become much more secretive in recent years due to competition, and we expect, as financial services organizations realize the bottom-line impact of their quality efforts, that only selective information will be shared.

There are risks in visiting companies. Often researchers can become cynical about the efforts of others and may feel that they would have done things better. There is a difference between better and differently. The thrust of quality as a strategic element in financial services organizations is in its infancy. The larger the company, the more difficult it is to shift the organization's focus and orientation. Sometimes it requires sorting out nonbelievers in order to get up a full head of steam. One executive of a large life insurer often cautions impatient middle managers by saying, "It is easier to turn around a dingy than it is to turn an aircraft carrier." But when the ship is turned it will not be as influenced by other noncontrollable forces (weather) as the dingy would.

GETTING ORGANIZED

Where should the leadership come from to initiate the quality process? It must be driven by the company's chief executive officer. Without leadership at the highest level to drive the process it could be viewed as being this year's corporate theme.

In companies committed to quality improvement the message comes across loud and clear that the president must be active to get the attention of every employee. At Metropolitan Life Insurance, Connecticut Savings Bank, Paul Revere Life Insurance, GEICO, Sun Life of Canada, and Carteret the president has kicked off the process and set the expectations. We visited many other companies where quality was left to the managers of each division without corporate leadership. What often results is inconsistency in definition, direction, and certainly the way customers are brought into focus. Often times the customers are never consulted for fear that they may think there is something wrong.

Once the chief executive officer is firmly in front of the process a steering committee should be appointed to shape, guide, and control the overall effort.

QUALITY STEERING COMMITTEE

A quality steering committee is composed of senior executives of the company (or in some cases, the strategic business unit) implementing the process. It is vital that each major business area be represented so that quality and quality improvement will be recognized as being equally important throughout the company. The ideal number of members is between eight and ten, since subcommittees will be needed for the development or purchase of quality measurement systems, promotion, rewards, recognition, and communication. The members have directional responsibility for the process from its inception, and the committee will continue as a way of doing business much in the way that investment committees, asset and liability committees, and audit committees continually contribute to the company's stability and growth.

Early on, the committee will establish what the company's philosophy of quality is to be. There are common concepts being used by many companies, incorporating the following principles:

Do only right things;

Do them right the first time;

Do them on time;

Do them at the right cost; and

Do them with the right attitude.

Further, the concept of improving quality both in fact and in perception will be discussed. Is one more important than the other? Quality in fact is the more tangible measure of timeliness and accuracy that many companies incorporate into their quality control programs. Quality in perception really gets at the heart of quality. The focus is on the customer. How does the customer feel about our products, services, and overall communication today? If a company improves quality in fact but not in perception, will the process be considered effective? How about if the company improves quality in perception, but not in fact? Would this be viewed as a success?

This is the question that a branch manager could easily answer for you. Let's say that a branch office found through analysis and talking with customers that, from the point when the customer entered the branch, on average they were willing to wait no more than five minutes in line before being waited on. The branch manager could then use staffing analysis models to determine when to staff up and when to reduce staff to stay within the customer's expectations. Realizing that excess staff (in quality terms) is gold plating, the manager could reduce the number of tellers at the end of the day when customer arrivals per hour are lower. When this occurs the tellers in many banks remain at their stations to balance their work for the day. This can take from ten to thirty minutes, depending on volumes, problems, and the level of automation at the bank. When this closing and balancing occurs there may be six tellers at their stations but only two waiting on customers. When customers see only two of the six serving customers they could lose patience even though they are being served within the time frames considered good service. Improving quality in fact would require leaving more tellers working, which would eliminate the line. It would also be excessive, and often during the hour several of them would not be working at all. Improving quality in perception could be to move the tellers to a separate balancing room or to construct visual barriers so that the customers would see only the tellers who are open and would not in fact be upset with their short wait.

When you go into a newly constructed branch of a bank examine how they are dealing with this issue. You will find that many organizations are limiting chances of irritating customers in this way.

The steering committee will also set goals for the company and establish the decision criteria for the quality workshops that the middle managers will use as a basis for decision making. Some of the corporate criteria may be the following: improve accuracy with a standard goal as zero defects; improve productivity with a standard of 30 percent; improve timeliness with a standard of what the customer expects; and reduce unit costs with a standard of greater than 25 to 40 percent. These will be used by the quality workshops as a guideline when they establish more specific measures and goals.

The whole concept of establishing goals helps to direct the quality improvement effort so that the middle managers will be consistent with senior management's thinking.

TIME FRAMES

The time frame for getting started will depend on the size, structure, and location of the company. Centralized organizations with a staff size of up to four thousand should be able to plan, improve, and control each unit of the company within a two-year time frame.

Using Paul Revere as an example: planning started in mid 1983; training of quality teams started in the fall of the same year; quality workshops began in December and were completed in the spring of 1985. Other organizational streamlining was completed later in 1985.

Large companies with over four thousand employees are typically decentralized, which changes the coordination and implementation times. Should the process be piloted in one location and "rolled out" to all the others? Rolling out can easily be interpreted as plugging in someone else's ideas. Resistance and lower results can be expected whenever you adopt a roll-out methodology. Remember, it is nearly impossible to roll out enthusiasm and a sense of participation.

It should be remembered that time frames should be relative since there is no end to the journey. The customers' expectations will change due to shifts in disposable income, advancements in technology, competition, new customers influencing the market, and a universal drive for improving over past experiences and, on a macro basis, over prior groups of customers.

Improvement can't begin until a starting point is plotted and a course is charted. When improvement ends your competition takes over.

CONCLUSION

This book is not intended to be a single recipe for quality. It is intended to discuss the various ingredients that are found in most quality processes today and leave the amounts of each portion added to be decided by the companies using the book. Between the time that we finish the book and the point that it is published additional twists will be publicized that we haven't contemplated. If we didn't find one or two we would be greatly disappointed.

To truly master quality improvement, you should know enough to set direction and make substantial gains, but be able to recognize the limitations of managing the value of a process to its customers when the deliverable is intangible, the employee delivering it is often in the job position less than two years, and the customers, although segmented by market type, are each influenced by experiential factors out of the provider's control. Add to this that new customers come into the marketplace daily and you will realize why quality must be a strategic component of the corporate plan in order to be at all successful. It is frightening and exciting at the same time.

CHAPTER SUMMARY

The following are the key points made in this chapter.

1. Quality improvement starts with research. This can take place through associations, through books, or through companies within or outside your specific field. We believe that all research alternatives should be utilized, including consulting specialists.

2. Getting organized most often starts with the chief executive officer. The leadership is then turned over to a steering committee of diverse yet influential executives to develop, direct, and nourish the process as it unfolds and evolves.

3. Time frames are relative. It will often be closely linked to the level of quality and service of direct competitors. It will also be dictated by the company's customers. Time frames should be developed for changing the culture, management information, customer focus, and the improvement approaches. When time frames are developed for completion of the quality process, it should be labeled the end of quality improvement rather than completion.

4. As you read, some competitor is talking to your customers to determine how to deliver services faster and more accurately than you do. Your job will never be finished since service excellence is behavioral.

Bibliography

Albrecht, Karl, and Ron Zemke. *Service America—Doing Business in the New Economy* (Homewood, Ill.: Dow Jones-Irwin, 1985).

Aubrey, Charles A., III. *Quality Management in Financial Services* (Wheaton, Md.: Hitchcock Publishing Company, 1985).

Bain, David. *The Productivity Prescription* (New York: McGraw-Hill, 1982).

Bandrowski, James F. "Techniques for Imaginative Strategic Thinking," *Creative Planning Throughout the Organization*, AMA Management Briefing.

Blanchard, Kenneth, and Spencer Johnson. *The One Minute Manager*, ed. Pat Golbitz (New York: William Morrow, 1982).

Crosby, Philip B. *Quality Is Free: The Art of Making Quality Free* (New York: McGraw-Hill, 1979).

————. *Quality Without Tears: The Art of Hassle-Free Management* (New York: McGraw-Hill, 1984).

Deal, Terrence E., and Allan A. Kennedy. *Corporate Cultures: The Rites and Rituals of Corporate Life* (Reading, Mass.: Addison-Wesley, 1982).

Drucker, Peter F. *Innovation and Entrepreneurship: Practice and Principles* (New York: Harper and Row, 1985).

Geneen, Harold, and Alvin Moscow. *Managing* (New York: Doubleday, 1984).

Gordon, Thomas. *Leader Effectiveness Training* (New York: Wyden Books, 1977).

Guaspari, John. *I Know It When I See It: A Modern Fable about Quality* (New York: AMACOM, 1985).

Heyel, Carl, ed. *Encyclopedia of Management*. 3d ed. (New York: Van Nostrand Reinhold Co., 1982).

Hickman, Craig R., and Michael A. Silva. *Creating Excellence* (New York: New American Library, 1984).

Kanter, Rosabeth Moss. *The Change Masters: Innovation for Productivity in the American Corporation* (New York: Simon and Schuster, 1983).

Kopelman, Richard E. *Managing Productivity in Organizations: A Practical, People-Oriented Approach* (New York: McGraw-Hill, 1986).

Marcus, Stanley. *Quest for the Best* (New York: McGraw-Hill, 1985).

McCormack, Mark H. *What They Don't Teach You at Harvard Business School: Notes from a Street-Smart Executive* (New York: Bantam Books, 1985).

McKay, Edward S. *Marketing Mystique* (New York: AMACOM, 1972).

Miles, Lawrence D. *Techniques of Value Analysis and Value Engineering.* 2d ed. (New York: McGraw-Hill, 1972).

Miller, Lawrence M. *American Spirit: Views of a New Corporate Culture* (New York: Warner Books, 1984).

Mills, D. Quinn. *The New Competitors: A Report on American Managers from the Harvard Business School* (New York: John Wiley and Sons, 1985).

Minnick, Wayne. *The Art of Persuasion* (Boston: Houghton Mifflin Co., 1968).

Mosley, Lloyd W. *Customer Service—The Road to Greater Profits* (New York: Chain Store Publishing Corp., 1972).

Naisbitt, John. *Megatrends: Ten New Directions Transforming Our Lives* (New York: Warner Books, 1982).

Naisbitt, John, and Patricia Aburdene. *Re-Inventing the Corporation* (New York: Warner Books, 1985).

Nolan, Robert E., Ben DiSylvester, and Richard T. Young. *Improving Productivity through Advanced Office Controls* (New York: AMACOM, 1980).

Osborn, Alex F. *Your Creative Power* (New York: Scribner's, 1972).

Peters, Thomas J., and Nancy K. Austin. *A Passion for Excellence: The Leadership Difference* (New York: Random House, 1985).

Peters, Thomas J., and Robert H. Waterman, Jr. *In Search of Excellence: Lessons from America's Best Run Companies* (New York: Harper and Row, 1982).

Porter, Michael E. *Competitive Strategy: Techniques For Analyzing Industries and Competitors* (New York: Macmillan, The Free Press, 1980).

Robson, Mike. *The Journey to Excellence* (New York: John Wiley and Sons, 1986).

Rodgers, Buck, and Robert L. Shook. *The IBM Way: Insights into the World's Most Successful Marketing Organization* (New York: Harper and Row, 1986).

Tewell, Rich. *Quality Circles in the Office: A Practical Guide for Service Industries* (Rolling Meadows, Ill.: Bank Administration Institute, 1983).

Townsend, Patrick L., with Joan E. Gebhardt. *Commit To Quality* (New York: John Wiley and Sons, 1986).

Van Gundy, Arthur B., Jr. *Techniques of Structured Problem Solving* (New York: Van Nostrand Reinhold Co., 1981).

Index

Acceptance, 148

Accountability, 234

Accuracy, 90; attainment process, 125–26; and completeness, 140–41; and control systems, 163; and mortgage banking companies, 131–32; and policy errors, 125–28; and procedural errors, 133–39; and systems errors, 128–33

Accuracy ratios, 139–40

Acquisitions, 1–2. *See also* Merger; Takeover

Advanced Office Controls (AOC), 223, 226

Advantage-Disadvantage evaluation method, 106

Advertising, 13, 16, 19, 68

Albrecht, Karl, 198; *Service America—Doing Business in the New Economy*, 65, 87, 193, 196

Allstate Insurance Company, 216

American Express, 13

American Society for Quality Control, 37

American Spirit (Miller), 194

American Telephone and Telegraph (AT&T), 39

Analogy, in creative methodology, 103

Art of Persuasion, The (Minnick), 195

Attitudes, 30, 90; changing, 192; directions of, 207–8; measurement difficulties, 208; more for less, 226

Automated teller machines (ATMs), 124, 125, 130, 143–44; advantages of, 201

Automation, 105, 129–30, 149; areas of, 224–26; changes in, 164–66; for office retooling, 212–16; problems with, 155–56

Baby boomers, 5

Backlog, 126–27; effects of, 156–57

Bain, David, *The Productivity Prescription*, 63, 88, 90

Bandrowski, James F., *Creative Planning Throughout the Organization*, 100

Banks, 1; and customer retention, 124–25; diversification of, 2; losses by, 9

Belous, Richard S., 6

Birth rate, 7

Blanchard, Kenneth, *The One Minute Manager*, 207

Blue Cross/Blue Shield of Indiana, 68–69

Board of directors, as quality definer, 75

Brand loyalty, 10

Buying binge, 3

Capital spending, 3

Carelessness, as service problem, 150

Carteret Savings Bank, 27–31

Central information file (CIF), 130–31

Chase Manhattan Bank, 125

Chemical Bank, 16

Citibank, 124

Clerical staffs, 220; decrease in, 223–24

CNA Property and Casualty Company, 128

Coldwell Banker, 216

Commit to Quality (Townsend), 109

Community, as quality definer, 75

Community involvement, 68

Competition, 67; and differentiation, 10; foreign, 1, 6, 9, 160, 212

Competitive edge, loss of, 2–9

Completeness, and accuracy, 140–41

Connecticut Savings Bank, 40–44, 101

Consistency, 55, 90; and customer perception/expectation survey, 174–78; and decentralized ownership of results, 188–89; defined, 172; dimensions of, 171; measurement groundwork, 173–74; observations on, 172–73; promotion of, 189; and quality matrix, 182–88

Consultant. *See* Facilitator

Contact points, management of, 87

Control chart, 134, 135(figure), 136, 138

Control systems: benefits of, 162; defined, 160; functioning of, 161; future of, 164; problems in, 162–64

Coordinator, role of, 101

Corporate Cultures (Deal and Kennedy), 197

Corporate mission statement, 39, 41

Corporate philosophy, 84–86

Corporate values, 197–98; and attitudes, 193–94

Cost, 90; of control system, 163

Cost leadership, as competition strategy, 9

Courtesy, toward customer, 199–203

Creative Planning Throughout the Organization (Bandrowski), 100

Creativity, inhibitors to, 101–4

Criticism, 102

Crosby, Phillip, 50–51, 53; *Quality is Free*, 124

Customer: as accuracy ratio determinant, 139–40; alienation of, 125–26; communication with, 38–39; complaints from, 42–43, 60–61; courtesy toward, 199–203; educational level of, 159–60; focus on, 42; identification of, 48, 76–77, 98, 192–93; internal, 179; loss of, 66–67; outside versus inside, 77–78, 180; and perception measurement, 58–61; as quality definer, 75; at quality workshops, 96–97, 98, 100; as silent majority, 203–4; treatment of, 128–29, 199–203, 217

Customer expectations, 84, 145–48, 242–43; changes in, 159; exceeding, 70–71; failure in meeting, 148–58; meeting of, 211

Customer perception/expectation survey: benefits of, 175–77; data usage, 181–82; defined, 174–75; documentation for, 179–80; preliminary activities, 178–79; preparation of, 180–81; problems of, 177–78; tabulation, 181

Customer service representative (CSR), 137, 191–92

D'Albero, Esther, 101

Data massaging, 152–53

Deal, Terrence, *Corporate Cultures*, 197

Debt, 7

Decision making: consensus, 107–8; profit, 126; service, 126; for success, 226–28

Decision matrix approach, 106–7

Delbeseq, Andre, 102

Deming, W. Edwards, 26, 78, 97

Deregulation, 1–2, 28

Differentiation, as competition strategy, 10

Disclosure, types of, 202–3

Diversification, 1, 216–17; and consistency, 172–73

Domings, Bill, 101
Draper, Anthony, 93

E. F. Hutton Life Insurance Company,
149–50
Electronic mail, 213–15
Empathy, lack of, 149
Employees: attitudes toward management, 198–99; and corporate image,
68; education of, 28–29; fears of,
126–27; feedback from, 158; and incentives, 23; motivation of, 24–25;
and ownership, 27; problems with,
81–82; recognition for, 36–37, 48–
49, 55–56; role of, 21, 32; training
for, 33–34, 38, 206; in whole job situation, 205
Employment, growth in, 6
Encyclopedia of Management, 113
Error classification, 122
Error Free Performance program
(EFP), 121–22, 123(figure)
Essential purpose, concept of, 99
Expenses, myopia about, 127–28

Facilitator, role of, 101, 102, 104–5
Factories, aging of, 3
Failure, factors for, 126–27
Falzon, John, interview with, 31–40
F. A. S. T. diagramming, 99–100
Federal Republic of Germany, 3
Feedback, 158, 207
Financial services companies: attributes
of, 66–67; changes in, 4; competition
strategies of, 9–11; decision making
by, 227; fear within, 220; focus on
short-term profit, 219–20; and increased competition, 8–9; past operation of, 220–23; present operation,
223–26; price versus service, 217–
19; products of, 65; retooling of,
212–16; and shifting economy, 216–
17; status of, 1
Financial strength, 67
Fireman's Fund Insurance Company, 93
First Chicago Corporation, 131
First National Bank of Chicago, 13–14,
88

Focus, as competition strategy, 10
Fortune magazine, 105
Freewheeling, 103

GEICO Insurance Company, 58–61
Geneen, Harold, 88, 217, 219–20
General Electric Company, 97
Gilbreth, Frank, 79–80, 221
Gilbreth, Lillian, 79–80, 221
Goals, 86–87, 157–58
Goldome Bank, 124
Gozzo, Frank, 86
Great Britain, 3
Great Western, 28
Gross national product, 2
Growth, and consistency, 173
Guaspari, John, 174; I Know It When I
See It, 204

High technology, and declining pro-
ductivity, 3–4
Hiring, for appropriate attitude, 205–6
Home Federal, 28
Housing, 7
Human resource department, 84

IBM, 26, 39
IBM Way, The (Rodgers and Shook),
85
Ignorance, as service problem, 150
I Know It When I See It (Guaspari),
204
Image, 67–69
Improvement budgeting, for success,
228–30
Improvement pyramid, 94–96
Industry regulators, as quality definer,
74
Industry stagnation, 148, 160
Inflation, 3, 5, 6
Information/processing system, gap in,
130–31
In Search of Excellence: Lessons from
America's Best Run Companies (Pe-
ters and Waterman), 86–87
Interest, lack of, 148–49
Internal politics, and control systems,
163

International Association of Quality
    Circles' (IAQC) State of the Art Sym-
    posium, 109
Investments, 3
Investors, foreign, 219
Issues, avoidance of, 151–55

Japan, 26, 220; image-building in, 79;
    productivity rate, 3; quality circles
    in, 78–79; quality system in, 21, 22–
    24; rebuilding of, 212
Job design, and attitudes, 204–5
Job responsibilities, fragmentation of,
    150–51, 157
Johnson, Paul, interview with, 40–44
Johnson, Spencer, *The One Minute
    Manager*, 207
Juran, J. M., 198

Kennedy, Allan, *Corporate Cultures*,
    197
Korea, 3

Labor force, 5, 6–7
Leadership, 43–44, 52–53, 241–43;
    cost, 9
Lifestyle, changes in, 6–8
Local area networks (LANs), 165
Lovell, Malcolm R., Jr., 5

McCabe, Tom, 116–17
McMurrich, A. R. (Jim), interview with,
    44–49
Mail distribution, 224–25
Maintenance, and control systems,
    163–64
Management Review, 193–94
Management team, as quality definer,
    75
Managers, 29–30, 228–31
Manufacturing: decline in, 1; and for-
    eign competition, 6; and quality, 21;
    and quality assurance, 81; unit labor
    costs of, 3; versus service, 26
Martin Company, 121
Maynard, Harold B., 222
Measurement: of attitudes, 208; of con-
    sistency, 173–74; of productivity,

220–22; for quality, 34–36, 54–55;
    of service, 152; of success, 87–88
Media, 94
Merger, 1–2, 219. *See also* Acquisi-
    tions; Takeover
Mescon, Michael, 171
Mescon, Timothy, 171
Methods Engineering Council, 222
Methods-Time Measurement (MTM),
    222–23
Metropolitan Life Insurance Company,
    13, 31–40
Meyung, Eugene, 58–61
Midvale Steel Company, 220–21
Miles, Larry, 97
Miller, Larry, *American Spirit*, 194
Mills, D. Quinn, *The New Competitors:
    A Report on American Managers*, 84
Minnesota Mutual Fire and Casualty
    Company, 94
Minnick, Wayne, *The Art of Persua-
    sion*, 195
Monitoring, 137–38, 162
Morris, Joe, 9
Mortgage Banking, 158–59
Mortgage services, 8–9
Moscow, Alvin, 88
Motion Time Analysis, 222
MTM Association for Standards and Re-
    search, 222
Mueller, Robert J., interview with, 27–
    31
Mutual of Omaha Company, 68

Naisbitt, John, *Re-Inventing the Corpo-
    ration*, 69–70
*New Competitors, The: A Report on
    American Managers* (Mills), 84
Northwestern Mutual Life Insurance
    Company, 26
Norway, 3

Obsolescence, 212
Oil prices, 3
Organizational analysis, 112–17
Osborn, Alex, 102
Owners, as quality definer, 74–75
Ownership, 27

Parado Principle, 33
Passion for Excellence, A (Peters), 87
Paul Revere Life Insurance Company, 20–27, 93, 101, 108–9, 117, 189, 207
Pay scales, performance-based, 232–34
PBX systems, 212–13
Performance, and pay scales, 232–34
Personal computer, 213
Peters, Thomas, 28; *A Passion for Excellence*, 87; *In Search of Excellence: Lessons from America's Best Run Companies*, 86–87
Piggybacking, of ideas, 103
Policy errors, and accuracy, 125–28
Porter, Michael E., 10
Privacy, 162
Procedural errors, and accuracy, 133–39
Procedures, problems with, 150
Productivity, 2–4, 220–22
Productivity Prescription, The (Bain), 63, 88, 90
Product quality, 63–64
Profit centers, 234
Profitability, 211
Profit sharing, 23

Quality: achievement of, 88, 90; and advertising, 13, 16, 19; associations for, 237–39; company visits for, 240–41; as competitive weapon, 88; definers of, 74; definition of, 63, 69–70, 84, 217; as differentiation strategy, 10–11; fact versus perception, 24, 69; as journey, 31–40; leadership for, 241–43; literature on, 239–40; managers for, 29–30; measurement, 34–36, 54–55; misconceptions about, 78–83; as panacea, 79; as program, 82–83; progress evaluation, 29; research process, 237–41; sampling of perceptions, 71–74; and savings factors, 19; survey of, 19; and systems design, 133; system versus service, 44–49; tenets of, 90; time frames for, 243–44; underlying value of, 64–65; versus quantity, 158–59.
See also Product quality; Service quality
Quality assurance (QA), 81, 94
Quality circles, 79–81; attributes of, 80–81; full participation in, 109; problems with, 110; and quantifying results, 109–10; steps in, 83–88
Quality is Free (Crosby), 124
Quality matrix, 182–88
Quality Performance Chart Book, The, 88
Quality Steering Committee, 54, 56, 241–43; formulation of, 20–27
Quality teams: initiation of, 108–10; problem analysis in, 112; problem identification in, 111; training for, 110–11
Quality workshops: creative phase of, 100–104; creative process rules, 102–3; evaluation methods, 106–8; function of, 96; organization of, 98–108; value analysis basis of, 97–98
Quantity, versus quality, 158–59
Questionnaires, 84

Recordkeeping, 162, 188
Reid, Aubrey, 117
Re-Inventing the Corporation (Naisbitt), 69–70
Reliance Insurance Company, 49–58
Reputation, 67
Rewards, 206; for performance, 230–32; for quality circle members, 109
Rework, 155–56
Roach, Stephen S., 3
Robinson, James D., 105
Rodgers, Buck, *The IBM Way*, 84–86

Schwab, John L., 222
Sears Mortgage Corporation, 216; mission, 194; philosophies, 194–95
Sears Roebuck and Company, 216
Segur, A. G., 222
Service, attributes of, 65–66
Service America—Doing Business in the New Economy (Albrecht and Zemke), 65, 87, 193, 196
Service industry, 3–4, 26

Service organizations, personnel classi-
fication, 193
Service quality, 65–67
Shewhart, W. A., 134
Shook, Robert, *The IBM Way*, 84–85
Simon, Paul, 104
Simplicity, 90; achievement of, 94
Snyder, Paul, interview with, 49–58
Society Bank (Ohio), 195–96
Soule, Charles, 93, 109; interview with,
20–27
Span of control analysis, 114–15
Sponsorship, 68–69
Staff, 220, 223–24; assessment process
for, 115–17; reduction of, 226–28,
242
Standard of living, 5, 6, 23
Statistical quality control, 134–37
Stegmerten, Gustave J., 222
Stonewalling, 102
Stopwatch method, 221
Structural analysis, function of, 113–14
Success: achievement guidelines, 226–
34; defined, 211; factors for, 2; mea-
surement of, 87–88; obstacles to,
212–20
Sun Financial Group, 44–49
Survey, 84; customer perception, 174–
82
Sweden, 3
Systems, complexity of, 149–50. *See
also* Control systems; Information/
processing system; Telephone sys-
tems; Work management systems
Systems analysis, 117–18
Systems errors, and accuracy, 128–33

Takeover, 219. *See also* Acquisitions;
Merger
Taylor, Frederick, 79, 220–21
Technical jargon, 126
Telephone customer service, growth
of, 137
Telephone-oriented departments, 161

Telephone systems, 212–13
Thomas, Richard L., 131
Thrift organizations, 9
Timeliness, 48, 90, 124; and automa-
tion, 165–66; and control systems,
163; defined, 145; implementation,
228; provision degree, 158–60
Time service, 145
Townsend, Pat, 207; *Commit to Qual-
ity*, 109
Training, 33–34, 38, 206. *See also*
Quality workshops
Travelers Insurance Company, 86, 93

Unions, 6
United States, 5, 6; and competitive
edge, 2–9
United States League of Savings Institu-
tions, 9
Universal Life Insurance, 149–50
UNUM Life Insurance Company, 122,
126

Value, perception of, 2
Value analysis, 97–98
Van de Veer, Andrew, 102
Vietnam War, 3

Wages, 5–6; and declining productivity,
3
Waterman, Robert, *In Search of Excel-
lence: Lessons from America's Best
Run Companies*, 86–87
Watson, Thomas, Sr., 85
Westinghouse, 121–22, 124, 222
Women, 8; in labor force, 5, 6–7
Work management systems, 226
Work measurement, 220–22

Zemke, Ron, 198; *Service America—
Doing Business in the New Econ-
omy*, 65, 87, 193, 196
Zero Defects, 121

About the Authors

ROBERT E. GRASING is a Senior Vice President with the Robert E. Nolan Company, a management consulting firm.

MICHAEL H. HESSICK is a Senior Vice President and Director of the Northwest Region of the Robert E. Nolan Company.